THE MOUNTAINS OF CENTRAL SPAIN

Peña Sirio from Canto Cochino car park. (Route 60)

THE MOUNTAINS OF CENTRAL SPAIN

by

Jacqueline Oglesby

Illustrations by Janet Squirrel Walters
Maps and Diagrams by the Author

CICERONE PRESS
MILNTHORPE, CUMBRIA U.K

© Jacqueline Oglesby 1996
ISBN 1 85284 203 2
A catalogue record for this book is available from the British Library

ACKNOWLEDGEMENTS

I have enjoyed the company of many different people in these mountains but I want particularly to thank Hazel Bird who brought so much encouragement and enthusiasm to the earlier walks, and John Phelan, Lynn Foster and Vince Kempsey for sharing the pleasures and pains of Gredos in high summer. I am very grateful to Brian Goodall and Margaret Tiesdall for the information about the flora and to Paloma Gutierrez Jimenez who helped me collect some of the background for the Gredos chapters. My brother, John Porter, gave me a brief but very effective computer course and Maggie Foster provided valuable support services while I was in Gredos. I would also like to thank Domingo Pliego who has generously allowed me to use his excellent map of La Pedriza as a basis for my sketches as well as given freely of his immense knowledge of the Sierra de Guadarrama.

Finally, I must thank my husband, Keith, who also helped a little.

Advice to Readers

Readers are advised that whilst every effort is taken by the author to ensure the accuracy of this guidebook, changes can occur which may affect the contents. A book of this nature with detailed descriptions and detailed maps is more prone to change than a more general guide. New fences and stiles appear, waymarking alters, there may be new buildings or eradication of old buildings. It is advisable to check locally on transport, accommodation, shops etc. but even rights-of-way can be altered, paths can be eradicated by landslip, forest clearances or changes of ownership. The publisher would welcome notes of any such changes.

Front cover: Behind the 'Tail' of El Pajaro. (Route 65)

CONTENTS

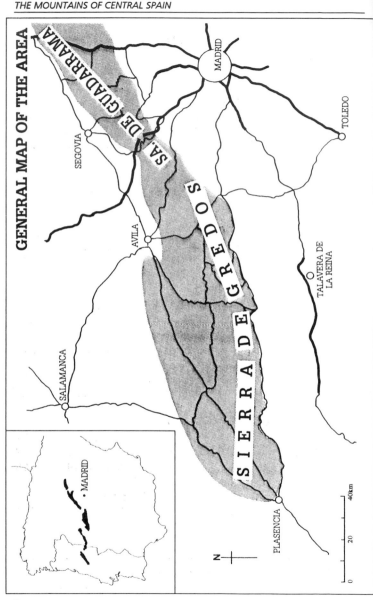

GENERAL MAP OF THE AREA

LIST OF ROUTES

SIERRA DE GREDOS

a. Sierra de Béjar

1. La Plataforma El Travieso - La Ceja - El Torreón - El Calvitero(S) - return
2. Puente de los Avellanares - Arroyo Cuerpo de Hombre - Cueva de Hoya Moros - return
3. El Chorro - Garganta de Trampal - Las Lagunillas - La Ceja - Cuerda de la Ceja - El Chorro
4. El Chorro - Laguna del Duque - Cuerda de los Asperones - El Torreón - Hoyo de Malillo - El Chorro

b. Western Gredos

5. Umbrias/Nava del Barco road (1350m) - Garganta de la Vega - Laguna del Barco - return
6. Nava del Barco - Garganta de Galin Gómez - Laguna de la Nava
7. Navalguijo - Garganta de los Caballeros - Laguna de los Caballeros - Covacha
8. Guijo de Santa Barbara - Portilla de Jaranda - Covacha

c. Central Gredos

North Side

9. Bohoyo - Garganta de Bohoyo - Hoya del Belesar
10. Navalperal - Garganta del Pinar - Circo de las Cinco Lagunas
11. La Plataforma - Los Barrerones - Circo de Gredos - Garganta de Gredos - Navalperal
11a. La Plataforma - Garganta de las Pozas - Puente de Roncesvalles - Garganta de Gredos - Circo de Gredos - Los Barrerones - La Plataforma
12. La Plataforma to the Elola Refuge in the Circo de Gredos
13. La Plataforma - Circo de Gredos - Portilla del Rey - return
13a. La Plataforma - Circo de Gredos - Cabeza Nevada - return
14. Elola Hut - Venteadero - (Gutre Ridge)
15. Elola Hut - Almanzor traverse - Elola Hut
16. Elola Hut - Portilla de los Hermanitos - Cuchillar de Cerraillos - Cuchillar de las Hoyuelas - Morazón - Elola Hut
17. La Plataforma - Morazón - Pozas Valley - La Plataforma
18. La Plataforma - Puerto de Candeleda - La Mira - return
19. 1551m saddle (Plataforma road) - Garganta de la Covacha - La Mira

or Peña del Mediodía - return
20.   C500 (km43.9) - Fuente de Navapalenciana - Puerto de la Cabrilla - Peña del Mediodía - return
20a. Valdehascas Spur - Collado del Charco - Covacha Valley - Peña del Mediodía - Puerto de la Cabrilla - Fuente de Navapalenciana - Valdehascas Spur
21.   Puerto del Pico - La Casa - Riscos de las Morrillas - Arroyo de Garganta Honda - Puerto del Pico

South side
22.   Madrigal de la Vera - Vega de Magazales
23.   (El Raso) - Puente del Pinillo - Garganta de Tejea
24.   (El Raso) - El Jornillo - Peña de Chilla - (Portilla Bermeja)
25.   Virgen de Chilla Sanctuary - Garganta de Chilla - Vega del Enebral - return
26.   (Candeleda) - Albarea Hut - Garganta Blanca - Portilla de los Hermanitos
27.   (Candeleda) - Enebral spur - Puerto de Candeleda - Morazón - return
28.   El Nogal del Barranco - Victory Hut - La Mira - return
29.   El Nogal del Barranco - Cuerda del Amealito - La Mira - La Apretura - El Nogal del Barranco
30.   El Joyuelo - Chorreras de la Lancha - Pico Don Servando - Cobacho col - Chorreras de la Lancha - El Joyuelo
31.   El Nogal del Barranco - Victory Hut - Canal del Gran Galayo - La Portilla - Pico Don Servando - Cobacho col - El Nogal del Barranco
32.   Mingo Fernando - Puerto del Peón - Peña del Mediodía - return
33.   El Arenal - Collado de la Centenera - Puerto del Arenal - Cervunales - Puerto de la Cabrilla - El Arenal

d. Eastern Gredos
34.   Collado de Serranillos - El Torozo Ridge
35.   Collado de Serranillos - Cabezo - return
36.   Puerto de Mijares - Peluca - return
37.   Puerto de Mijares - Gamonosa - La Serradilla - return

SIERRA DE GUADARRAMA
a. Western Guadarrama
38.   *Las Machotas*
38a. El Escorial - Roman road - Las Machotas - Ermita de la Virgen de Gracia - El Escorial
38b. Zarzalejo Station - Las Machotas - Ermita de la Virgen de Gracia - El

Escorial

38c. El Escorial - Ermita de la Virgen de Gracia - Silla de Felipe II - Collado de Entrecabezas - Machota Chica - Collado de E - El Fraile - Ermita de la V de G - El Escorial

38d. Silla de Felipe II - Collado de Entrecabezas - Machota Chica - Collado de E - El Fraile - Fuente de la Reina - Silla de Felipe II

39. Puerto de la Paradilla San Benito - Puerto de la Paradilla - Barranco de la Cabeza - Puerto de Malagon - Hotel Felipe II (El Escorial)

40. *Abantos*

40a. El Escorial - GR10 - Arista - Risco de San Benito - Puerto de Malagon - El Escorial

40b. El Escorial - GR10 - Portichuelo - Abantos - Puerto de Malagon - El Escorial

40c. Hotel Felipe II - Fuente de la Concha - Los Llanillos - Barranco de la Cabeza - Puerto de Malagon - Abantos - ruined hut - El Escorial

40d. Peguerinos - Refugio de la Cueva - Refugio la Naranjera - San Juan - Abantos - Fuente del Cervunal - GR10 - El Escorial

40e. Alto de los Leones - Cuerda de Cuelgamuros - Abantos - Solana muletrack - GR10 - El Escorial

41. Embalse de la Jarosa - Cerro del Cebo de los Lobos - Collado de la Cierva - Refugio de la Salamanca Carrasqueta - Embalse de la Jarosa

42. *Sierra de Malagon*

42a. Collado del Hornillo - Cueva Valiente - Refugio Enmedio Peña Blanca - Collado del Hornillo

42b. Camping Peguerinos - Collado de la Gargantilla - Cueva Valiente - Ref. Enmedio - Peña Blanca - Camping Peguerinos

b. Central Guadarrama (West)

43. *La Peñota*

43a. La Tablada - Peña del Arcipreste - La Peñota - Collado del Rey - Cercedilla

43b. NV1 trunk road (km56) - Collado de la Sevillana - Peña del Arcipreste - La Peñota pista forestal - km56

44. *La Mujer Muerta*

44a. Reservoir in Río Moros valley - Collado de Tirobarra - La Mujer Muerta - Forest roads - reservoir

44b. Reservoir in Río Moros valley - Puerto de Pasapan - Mujer Muerta - Montón de Trigo - Cerro Minguete - Peña Bercial - Collado de Marichiva - reservoir

44c. Chalet de Peñalara - Puerto de la Fuenfría - Cerro Minguete - Collado de Tirobarra - Mujer Muerta - El Espinar Station

44d. Puerta de Navacerrada - Camino Schmid - Puerto de la Fuenfría - Cerro Minguete - Collado de Tirobarra - Mujer Muerta - El Espinar Station

45. *Montón de Trigo*

45a. Reservoir in Río Moros valley - Collado de Tirobarra - Cerro Minguete - Peña Bercial - Collado de Marichiva - reservoir

45b. Chalet de Peñalara - Puerto de la Fuenfría - Roman Road - Casarás - Montón de Trigo - Cerro Minguete - Peña Bercial - Collado de Marichiva - Chalet

45c. Chalet de Peñalara - Puerto de la Fuenfría - Casarás - Fuenfría Meadows - Testeros de los Horcajos - Collado de Tirobarra - Montón de Trigo - Arroyo Minguete - Puerto de la Fuenfría - Mirador de la Reina - Camino Schmid - Chalet

46. Chalet de Peñalara - Puerto de la Fuenfría - Cerro Minguete - Peña Aguila - La Peñota - Forestry road - Collado de Marichiva - Chalet

47. Chalet de Peñalara - Puerto de la Fuenfría - Cerro Ventoso - Collado Ventoso - Segundo Pico - Primer Pico - Mirador de V Alexandre - Chalet

48. Fuenfría Horseshoe

49. *Siete Picos*

49a. Puerto de Navacerrada - Siete Picos - Senda de los Alevines - Collado Ventoso - Camino Schmid - Puerto de Navacerrada

49b. Puerto de Navacerrada - Cerro de Telégrafo - Senda Herreros - Siete Picos - Puerto de Navacerrada

49c. Puerto de Navacerrada - Siete Picos - Navarrulaque - Herrén de Cebrián - Cercedilla

49d. Cercedilla - Camorritas - Siete Picos - Puerto de Navacerrada - El Ventorrillo - Cercedilla

c. Central Guadarrama (East)

50. *Las Cabrillas*

50a. El Ventorrillo - Real Sanatorio - Las Cabrillas - eastern slope - Real Sanatorio - El Ventorrillo

50b. El Ventorrillo - Sanatorio - Las Cabrillas - Puerto de Navacerrada - El Ventorrillo

50c. Puerto de Navacerrada - Las Cabrillas - eastern slope - El Ventorrillo - Cercedilla

50d. La Barranca Hotel - Real Sanatorio - Las Cabrillas - Bola del Mundo - Regajo del Pez - La Barranca

51. *La Maliciosa*

51a.   Puerto de Navacerrada - Bola del Mundo - Collado del Piornal - La Maliciosa - return

51b.   La Barranca Hotel - Cuerda de las Buitreras - La Maliciosa - Arroyo de la Maliciosa - La Barranca Hotel

51c.   La Barranca Hotel - Los Almorchones - El Peñotillo - La Maliciosa - Collado del Piornal - Arroyo del Regajo del Pez - La Barranca Hotel

51d,   Fuente de las Casiruelas - eastern slopes of the Cuerda de los Porrones - Maliciosa Chica - La Maliciosa - Maliciosa Chica - Collado de los Pastores - Fuente de las Casiruelas

52.   *Cuerda Larga* Puerto de la Morcuera to Puerto de Navacerrada

52a.   Puerto de la Morcuera - La Najarra - Los Bailanderos - Asómate de Hoyos - Alto de Matasanos - return

53.   *Cabezas de Hierro*

53a.   Puerto de Navacerrada - Bola del Mundo - Cabezas de Hierro - return

53b.   Puerto de los Cotos - Peña del Aguila - Bola del Mundo - Cerro de Valdemartín - Cabezas - Las Cerradillas - Puerto de los Cotos

53c.   (Puerto de los Cotos) - Valdesqui road - Arroyo de las Guarramillas - NE spur of Cerro de Valdemartín - Cabezas de Hierro - Las Cerradillas - Valdesquí road

54   *Peñalara*

54a.   Puerto de los Cotos - Dos Hermanas - Peñalara - Los Claveles - Laguna de los Pajaros - Laguna Grande - Puerto de los Cotos

54b.   Alternative start via corrie between Dos Hermanas

d. Upper Manzanares Basin

55.   El Tranco -Canto Cochino

La Pedriza Anterior

56.   El Yelmo (normal route)

57.   El Tranco - Collado de la Cueva - Senda Maeso - El Yelmo - Las Cerradillas - La Gran Canada - Mirador del Tranco - El Tranco

57a.   Manzanares el Real - Collado de la Cueva - Route 57 - El Tranco - Manzanares el Real

58.   El Tranco - Gran Cañada - Collado de la Encina - El Yelmo - Hueco de las Hoces - Barranco de los Huertos - El Tranco

59.   Canto Cochino - Refugio Giner - Collado de la Dehesilla - El Yelmo - Hueco de las Hoces - Barranco de los Huertos - Canto Cochino

60.   Canto Cochino - east bank of the Arroyo de la Majadilla - El Yoyo - Jardín de Peña Sirio - Hueco de las Hoces - El Techo - Corral Ciego - Collado de las Vistillas - (El Yelmo) - El Tolmo - Ref. Giner - Autopista - Canto Cochino

Circo de la Pedriza

61. Canto Cochino - Collado de la Dehesilla - Navajuelos - Pared de Santillán - Collado de la Ventana - Arroyo de los Pollos - Autopista - Canto Cochino

61a. Alternative return from 1782m saddle - Collado de las Oseras - El Tolmo - Ref. Giner - Autopista - Canto Cochino

62. Canto Cochino - Autopista - Ao de los Pollos - Los Llanos - Collado de la Carabina - Las Torres - Collado de la Ventana - Ao de la Ventana - Autopista - Canto Cochino

63. Canto Cochino - Autopista - Ao de los Pollos - Collado de la Carabina - Las Milaneras - Collado del Cabrón - Cancho de los Muertos - Canto Cochino

64. Canto Cochino (2nd car park) - Charca Verde bridge - Collado del Cabrón - Las Milaneras (climbers' path) - Arroyo Cuervo - Río Manzanares - Canto Cochino

65. Canto Cochino - West ridge of Cancho de los Muertos - Collado del Cabrón - Senda de ICONA - Puente de los Pollos - Los Llanillos - Arroyo de la Ventana - El Pajaro - El Tolmo - Ref. Giner - Autopista - Canto Cochino

66. Complete ridge walk.

The Western Basin

67. Canto Cochino - Río Manzanares - Collado de los Pastores - Canto Cochino

68. Fuente de las Casiruelas - Peña Blanca - Cuerda de los Porrones - Maliciosa Chica

68a. Collado de los Pastores - Cerro de la Maliciosa - Cerro de las Barreras - Pista Forestal - Fuente de las Casiruelas

e. Eastern Guadarrama

69. *Sierra de Carpetanos*

69a. Puerto de Navafría - Nevero - Puerto de Navafría

69b. Puerto de Navafría - Peña del Cuervo - Hoyos de Pinilla - Nevero (2209m) - Puerto de Navafría

70. *Mondalindo*

70a. Puerto de Canencia - Collado Cerrado - Mondalindo - return

70b. Valdemanco - Peña del Tejo - Puerto del Medio Celemin - Regajo - Mondalindo - Peñas de las Cabras - Valdemanco

71. *Sierra de la Cabrera*

71a. Valdemanco - Peña del Tejo - Collado de Alfrecho - (Cancho Gordo) - Convento de San Antonio - Valdemanco

71b. La Cabrera - Pico de la Miel - Collado de Alfrecho - La Cabrera

PART ONE

Introduction

THE CENTRAL MOUNTAINS

Of the millions of foreigners who visit Spain every year, only a tiny proportion spend time in the very heart of the country. Of these, many are merely en route to the coasts of southern Spain and Portugal while others are visiting Madrid and exploring the medieval splendours of the Meseta* cities - Avila, Segovia, Salamanca, Toledo. For both these groups, speeding by car or coach in the torrid summer heat across the high rolling tableland of Central Spain, the crossing of the mountain chain which splits the Meseta into two must come as a welcome if incidental change. The endless ochres, golds and straw tones broken by the dusty green of scattered oaks, give way to grey granite and the cool shadowy colours of pine forest; arrow-straight roads and distant simple horizons become winding valleys and eruptions of rock.

This line of hills and mountains, known as the Systema Central, lies to the west and north of Madrid, running southwest northeast from the Portuguese border to the Sierra de Pela, north of Guadalajara. With a length of 380km and reaching a height of almost 2600m, it is a barrier of some geographical and historical importance - the main watershed between the great river basins of the Duero (Douro) to the north and the Tajo (Tagus) to the south, as well as the border between the former kingdoms of Old and New Castile.

The system is made up of a number of overlapping or parallel chains of hills. This guide concentrates on the central and highest section: the Sierras of Gredos and Guadarrama. Although they share the same geology and general climate, the two areas offer very different types of walking. The Sierra de Gredos is the highest and most remote part of the system; there are few high roadheads and many long, wild valleys and ridges lead up to the main crest. Day walks are possible without commando fitness but few of them are circuits and it is an area best appreciated by staying overnight in the many glacial corries. Lower in height and more accessible, the Sierra de Guadarrama is a day walking area par excellence. The rich texture of river valley, pine forest, steep rock

* the vast, high tableland of Central Spain.

Devil's Window, Siete Picos

and rolling ridges, as well as a dense network of paths, furnish abundant possibilities for circular walks of various lengths.

The Sierra de Gredos and its extension to the northwest, the Sierra de Béjar, run on a roughly west-east line for some 130km between the towns of Béjar and San Martín de Valdeiglesias which lies 60km due west of Madrid. From there a number of lower parallel ridges connect the big range with the western end of Sierra de Guadarrama at San Lorenzo de El Escorial, where the chain swings northeast, dividing at the Puerto de los Cotos into two branches. The northern branch carries the main watershed across the Puerto de Somosierra into the smaller ranges of the Sierra Pobre and Sierra de Ayllon.

While these mountains are clearly a less impressive barrier than the Pyrenees and lower than the Picos de Europa and Sierra Nevada, they offer many attractions for the adventurous walker: the climate is drier and sunnier than that of the northern ranges and less humid than in the coastal ranges. The scenery is sometimes as dramatic as in the bigger massifs, conditions underfoot are generally dry with few boggy areas and away from the most popular routes, you can be guaranteed almost perfect solitude. For five months of the year there is the choice of walking above or below the snow line and in the spring you can usually enjoy, from the foothills to the ridges, an unbroken carpet of flowers. Added to this is the special, less tangible quality of Spanish walking, in this big country of harsh, grand, empty scenery: the feeling of space as you follow the crest of a long ridge rising out of the infinite tableland, the heat on your back, the tangy resinous smell of cistus, the dry sandy paths and wheeling birds of prey.

CHAPTER ONE

Background

GEOLOGY AND LANDFORMS

The rocks of the two sierras are principally metamorphic, with granite predominating in Gredos and a mixture of granite and gneiss in Guadarrama. They were formed over 300 million years ago in the Hercynian uplift, but the present landscape was largely determined during the alpine upheaval of 25 million years ago when blocks of these old rocks were raised above the sedimentary layers which make up the Meseta on either side. At the same time, following the original Hercynian fault lines, blocks within the mountain zone sank to produce parallel depressions which carry the present main rivers. In Gredos, the area to the south of the range which is now the Tiétar valley settled much lower than the corresponding block to the north. The result today is that the northern depression (the upper Tormes and Alberche valleys today) lies at a height of between 1100 and 800m, while the Tiétar runs between 600 and 200m, well below the average height of the Southern Meseta.

The same tectonic processes were at work in the Sierra de Guadarrama, producing the Lozoya depression between the two eastern branches of the range, and the Peguerinos and Rio Moros valleys between the main range and the Sierra de Malagon and Mujer Muerta Ridge respectively. In Guadarrama, there was no massive downward displacement to the south of the range to correspond with the Tiétar depression. However, in both ranges towards the end of the uplift period, there was a marked tilting to the north, producing an asymmetrical cross-section with steep southern faces, and longer, gentler northern slopes. In addition, big transverse faults produced the principal passes: Tornavacas and Puerto del Pico in Gredos and Navacerrada, Cotos and Somosierra in Guadarrama.

The visible results of these geologically recent movements, which heaved older rocks to the surface, are long ridges with soft profiles but with plenty of exposed rock: this appears both continuously along crests and also in random eruptions on valley sides. In these outcrops, the network of small fractures, caused by the original cooling of the rocks or by the release of pressure when superimposed layers were eroded away (diaclases), are everywhere visible. Often following horizontal and vertical planes, they produce chunky towers of cyclopean blocks. Dramatic in profile, when bunched along a crest, they nevertheless form wide staircases in ascent rather than knife-edges. It is only in parts of Gredos that the predominance of close vertical fracturing, accentuated by periglacial erosion, has resulted in gendarmes and needle-like towers on any scale. Elsewhere, erosion has generally rounded off the angles of the blocks to produce tor-like forms.

A rock landscape different to anything else in the system is found in La Pedriza (and to a lesser extent in La Cabrera) in the Sierra de Guadarrama, where curving networks of faults and the rock's peculiar susceptibility to erosion has resulted in exfoliating domes, alternating narrow corridors and rock spines and improbable sculptural forms. On a smaller scale, circular erosion hollows are found throughout the mountains but are particularly striking in La Pedriza. These pockmark horizontal rock surfaces and at times reach the size of small ponds.

Superimposed on these tectonic and erosional processes are the effects of glaciation. Only the last period of the Ice Age (more than 10,000 years ago) affected the area, and then only partially. In Gredos, full glaciation was widespread with 41 glaciers along the northern slopes in just the section between Puerto de Tornavacas and Puerto del Pico. Many were confined to valley heads, hollowing out a characteristic circular basin, but others extended down the valleys, the largest 10km long and 300m thick. On the southern side, as would be expected, the permanent ice was less extensive and was mainly confined to cirque glaciers, while the Sierra de Béjar with its north-south alignment carried linear glaciers on both slopes. This has produced many instances of valleys with the classic U-shaped cross-section and stepped profile, with a high corrie, corrie lake, polished and striated rock faces and bands of moraine. The spectacular alpine-like rock scenery of the Gredos and Cinco Lagunas cirques is partly the result of the hollowing out of the head walls by the glaciers originating there.

In the Sierra de Guadarrama, full glaciation was confined to a small area along the southeast-facing slopes of the Peñalara-Nevero Ridge where a number of cirque glaciers developed. Some corrie-like features and moraines on the north side of the Cuerda Larga would suggest that permanent ice also rested there for a period.

CLIMATE AND WEATHER

The Madrileños describe their climate as:

> Nueve meses de Invierno
> Y tres meses de Infierno

Nine months of winter and three months of hell. Although this is a slight exaggeration, it does pinpoint the contrast between the intense, dry, hot, but short summers and the more variable conditions of the rest of the year.

Over the whole of Central Spain, the heat clamps down like a shutter somewhere between the middle of June and the beginning of July, then lifts with equally startling suddenness at any time in September. During July and August, there is virtually no rainfall apart from occasional thunderstorms which rarely reach Alpine violence. The heat, while appreciably less in the mountains than the surrounding plains, can still reach +30°C at main valley level in the afternoons. Temperatures in the early mornings and after sunset are generally more comfortable. You can also usually count on two or three brief respites from the baking heat, when cooler northerly winds lower daytime temperatures to the high 20s for a few days at a time.

From the point of view of walking, this is the only season with guaranteed settled weather. With summer humidity of less than 30%, routes along the high ridges, where there is generally a breeze, can be a less sweaty experience than hot days in the Alps. Apart from the obvious precautions of sun cream, sun hat and drinking plenty of water, it is best to avoid long southern and eastern ascents, and to get out of valleys and above 1800m as early as possible. Even so, it has to be said that for many reasons high summer is not the ideal time to visit this area: views are reduced and contours flattened in the persistent heat haze, accommodation and services are stretched, campsites noisy, many streams are no longer running and there is little relief in coming down from a day in the full sun to the dried out, dusty vegetation of the valleys.

Although local walkers can justifiably recommend the other nine months of the year for the frequency of dry sunny days, comfortable temperatures and lack of wind, there is no one period when these conditions are assured. Generally the wettest, most unsettled weather occurs in April-May and October-November. However the statistics show a fairly even distribution of the 40-60 inches of precipitation during the non-summer months. It is just that much of it falls as snow during the winter, lying permanently along the higher ridges and on northern slopes between December and May in Guadarrama and much longer in Gredos.

Nevertheless, the average figures are greatly interfered with in practice by recurring cycles of drought and the general unpredictability of mountain weather. For long stretches, high pressure areas are stationed over or to the west of the Iberian Peninsula, producing weeks of sunny days, light winds, clear skies and cool or frosty nights. This is the time to come to walk: the washed-out skies of summer deepen to an intense blue, the mountains appear magnified as every crack and fissure leaps into sharp focus and the devouring sun once more becomes a comforting ally. Unfortunately for the visitor, the averages are produced by the counterbalance of continuous spells of rain and cloud, occasionally lasting for several weeks.

Bearing all this in mind, I would guardedly say that May and June are the best months to visit. The weather may well be mixed but meadows are still green and streams still running, the carpet of flowers is spectacular, temperatures are comfortable (at least at higher levels) and daylight hours are long. Mid-October and November can be a good time to come as temperatures are generally lower than in May and June, there are the extensive but quieter displays of flowers and fiery pockets of deciduous autumn colours which stand out from the predominant greys and greens of this landscape. However, daylight hours are shorter and periods of rain can also be expected, filling the streams and bringing a new growth of grass. Flash floods are a danger in Gredos at this time.

As for the winter months, December should be avoided for the short days, guaranteed low temperatures and a generally higher probability of cloud, mist and storm. But mid-January to the beginning of April should not be ruled out as this is often the time when the stable periods predominate. The winter climate, at least in Guadarrama, is not severe by mountain standards. The total precipitation is in fact low compared to other European ranges, often falling in showers rather than continuous downpours. Strong winds are relatively uncommon, as are sudden unexpected changes in the weather. Furthermore, on clear days at these latitudes, the heat of the sun is such that even in January you can be walking in shirtsleeves at mid-day after a start in sub-zero temperatures. (This is not to say that severe conditions never occur and walkers arriving during this period should come fully equipped for winter walking.) Although you would be unlucky not to encounter some sunny weather if you visit during these months, should the weather be unstable, good winter walking on the snow and ice of the high ridges can be alternated with exploring spectacular areas like La Pedriza, La Cabrera and Las Machotas which are usually below the snow and cloud line.

Although in Gredos, the lower slopes and valleys on the southern side enjoy a relatively mild and wet winter climate, protected as they are by the mountain wall and subject to moist westerly winds from the Atlantic, these same winds produce a lot of snow on the high ground and most of the interesting walks are above the snow line for nearly six months of the year. Because of the longer distances involved, the more difficult terrain and the frequency of avalanches, especially in early spring, winter walking in Gredos is a more serious undertaking than in Guadarrama. Ice axes may be still needed for hard packed patches in June and even July in the north-facing gullies.

In the summer months, the same Atlantic winds produce, if not rain, a noticeably higher humidity on the southern side of Gredos, making July and August ascents from the Tiétar valley a decidedly masochistic undertaking. Precipitation figures increase as well towards the western end of the range, which gives the Jerte valley and the Béjar area (known as the Oasis of Castile) a lusher, greener appearance, particularly striking in summer. The northern Gredos villages have a cooler and drier climate with between half and two-thirds the rainfall of those to the south and mean monthly temperatures consistently 3-4°C less. As starting off points for walks in the highest parts of the range, they are the best choice for walkers limited to visiting in the summer.

VEGETATION

As would be expected in a mountainous area, altitude is the main determinant of plant and tree distribution and results in successive horizontal bands of the main types of vegetation cover. This simple pattern is then broken up by the effects of aspect, rainfall, drainage, soil type, angle of slope and human activity.

In the foothills and lower valleys, livestock pasture predominates with remnants of the original holm oak cover. This evergreen, so evocative of the drier soils of Central Spain, is an attractive tree which rarely grows to more than 7m here. It has a thick bushy crown and small olive-coloured leaves. Along the courses of rivers and streams and in moister hollows, pockets of other deciduous trees are also found. The exception to this general picture are the more sheltered and wetter southern and western valleys of the Sierra de Gredos which can support more Mediterranean species of trees. Few have survived clearance for agriculture but umbrella pines and cork oaks are found here and there.

Before human interference, the slopes of both the ranges between 1200-1700m were clothed in the deciduous Pyrenean oak. Pasture and pine plantations have taken over much of its natural range and the surviving areas often have a mix of other deciduous trees, particularly ash, poplar, birch and chestnut (the latter once an important cash crop). In Gredos, the pines form a fairly continuous cover along the southern slopes at these heights and, although the upper limit varies substantially, many walks on this side of the range start by climbing through forest. The picture is very different on the north side where the pine plantations are found mainly along the banks of the River Tormes between Hoyos del Espino and Navarredonda, with a few isolated blocks elsewhere. Although there are many attractive remnants of the original oak cover in both the upper Tormes and Alberche valleys, only walks starting from the villages themselves are likely to encounter any trees.

In the Guadarrama range, the pines extend higher because the mid-slope band, where the oaks were replaced, overlaps with the natural range of the indigenous scots pine (*Pinus silvestris*) with the result that the upper tree line on both sides of the range can be as high as 2100m. The north side of the range has an almost continuous cover and, because much of the plantings date from last century, some magnificent stands are to be found, for instance, north of the Puerto de Navacerrada. The southern slopes are steeper and rockier in general and there the tree line loops below scree slopes, crags and ridges. In addition, there are a number of areas which have not been planted, resulting in some walks on the south side of La Maliciosa and La Pedriza which are totally forest-free.

The vast majority of reafforestation in Guadarrama has been with scots pine instead of the black or corsican pine which is used in Gredos and the rest of Central Spain. While both species have been planted for the most part in a loose and random pattern which looks natural and has none of the oppressive darkness of northern spruce plantations, it is the scots pine forest which is particularly attractive. The trees have a russet orange papery bark on their upper trunks and the lopping of their lower branches as they grow creates a long straight trunk topped by a small asymmetrical crown. Towards the upper limit of their range on exposed slopes, their stunted and deformed shapes produce arresting Japanese images as they grasp and curl round rocks.

Pines aren't the only components of this altitude band. Because the upper tree limit is so much higher in Guadarrama, some of the leveller areas within the forest have been left or cleared for summer pasture. These small meadows provide welcome variety and are a mass of flowers in May and June. Then, in dry, sunny, south-facing areas where the trees are thin or absent, there are found extensive thickets of cistus (rock rose or sun rose). It occurs in both ranges but is more characteristic of the south side of Guadarrama, where many paths follow narrow corridors through acres of this straggly, rather scratchy bush, which can grow to a height of one and a half metres. Its sticky buds give out a pungent and evocative resinous scent and in May and June the thickets are a mass of large white papery-looking flowers. There are two species in this area: one has narrow, hairy, grey-green leaves and the other dark green sticky ones (gum cistus). The five petals of the flower surround a mass of bright yellow stamens. Some of the flowers carry a beautiful magenta smudge at the base of each petal.

Another striking plant which can cover extensive areas is the bearberry (*Arctostaphylus uvo-ursi*). Usually found on poor soil within the thinner stretches of forest where there is plenty of light, but also sometimes on open slopes and ridges, it forms a low creeping mat of small, bright green, fleshy leaves. In early summer, it has delicate bell-shaped white flowers tinged with pink and in the autumn, bright red berries which have medicinal uses.

Jara (cistus)

Undergrowth in the forest band varies considerably. In long-established tall stands where the original oak cover has left humus-rich soils, grass and bracken are found, making very easy walking even off the paths. Along stream courses, particularly in wetter Gredos, bramble and buckthorn sometimes form large impenetrable patches. On poorer soils and where the trees are smaller and well spread, various kinds of broom, genista and related shrubs start to appear, including white spanish broom on the southern slopes of Gredos. The moister conditions in the latter range produce more luxurious and sturdier growths of the plant, some of which grow to two metres and form extensive thickets. However, on the edge of the tree line and above, the exposure mostly favours those of lower habit, still tough, springy and densely packed but less difficult to cross. (If you intend to try a route which warns of pathless stretches of dense broom, it is as well to wear trousers as bare legs emerge dripping with blood.)

In the spring when these scrub plants are in flower, whole hillsides are turned a vivid yellow or white and the cloying intensity of the scent can be suffocating. The mats are sometimes mixed with common or prickly juniper and heathers - both the low growing purple-flowered and the taller tree varieties with white flowers. It is common practice, again more often in Gredos, to burn off the vegetation at height to encourage the tough grasses which form summer pasture. The resulting carpet of blackened, spiky branches can make unpleasant and tedious walking.

Beyond this basic permanent pattern, the early spring and summer bring a staggering variety of flowers at all levels, if the winter has been wet enough. For those who are interested in identifying what they see, it is well worth the trouble, at least on day walks, of carrying field guides for Southern European species and/or alpines. What I shall mention here are just the few plants that are so widespread, growing in tens of thousands on whole mountainsides, that you are bound to come across them in the course of one or two walks at the right time of year.

From late March to mid-May, depending on weather and altitude, the ranges are covered in spring crocus and narcissus. These crocus, which are found only in Central Spain and the northern half of Portugal (*C. carpetanus*), vary in colour from white to a medium lilac and grow both in high meadows and on more exposed slopes, nestling under the broom and juniper.

This is not the case with the narcissus, which appears in this area in three quite distinct forms growing in separate habitats. The deep yellow, cone-shaped *Narcissus bulbocodium*, sometimes called hoop petticoat

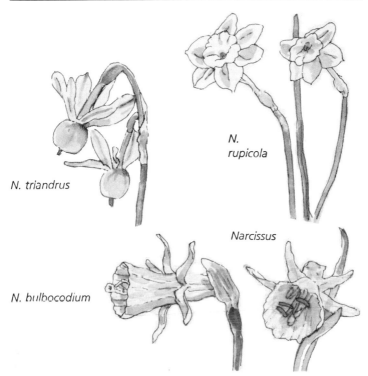

N. rupicola

N. triandrus

Narcissus

N. bulbocodium

narcissus, is found close to streams and in damp grassy areas even along the highest ridges. At lower levels, a creamy yellow version of it sometimes occurs. On dry slopes with poor soils, often among the cistus, you find vast swathes of *Narcissus triandrus*. A delicate cream colour, the flower head is suspended from the end of a drooping stalk with the cup-shaped trumpet hanging down and the surrounding long, narrow petals swept upwards. It is sometimes called Angel's Tears. The third type, *Narcissus rupicola*, is bright yellow with five or six oval petals surrounding a very short wide trumpet. Bunches of these flowers nestle charmingly in broken rocky terrain, presumably needing more shelter than the other two species.

Not as abundant but unlikely to be missed is the early purple orchid which thrives in the shelter of the cistus thickets from April to early June. More open sunny slopes in June and early July become dark purple lakes of French Lavender, with its strong bitter smell and distinctive flower heads. At the same time of year and in the same habitats, you become more aware of other aromatic plants associated with hot, dry summers such as rosemary and various thymes.

By the middle of July, all the flowers except for the alpines on the higher slopes are finished and spectacular grasses take their place, sometimes a knee-high hazy froth, sometimes a jungle of two metre pendulous stems with feathery heads. The first flashes of bright colour return to the landscape at the beginning of September when carpets of *Merendera montana* fill the forest clearings and grassy banks. This is a stalkless flower with six long, narrow petals varying in colour from pale pink to rose-purple but almost white at their base. They appear among the dessicated grass well before autumn rains bring some green back to the landscape. With the return of moisture to the soil, great numbers of an autumn-flowering crocus (*C. asturicus*) appear. Smaller and more delicate than the spring varieties, they have colonised the same areas - open pinewood and broom slopes and crests.

WILDLIFE

According to Jorge Lobo, in his guide to the Sierra de Gredos, the marked difference in climate between the two sides of the range ensure a rich variety of wildlife, with nearly half the Spanish mammal and bird species and a larger percentage of the amphibians and reptiles being found there. Both Gredos and Guadarrama form the northern limit for many Mediterranean species and the southern limit for some Central European ones. Although I have no figures for the Sierra de Guadarrama, I would imagine that the less contrasting climates of the north and south sides, plus more intense "development" than in Gredos, has resulted in a smaller number of species in every category.

In deciding what to describe in this section, I start from the assumption that amateur herpetologists, entomologists etc. have little use for a brief summary, and will turn to detailed field guides, while the interested but non-specialist walker will have neither the time nor experience to search out such native but elusive species as the *Almanzor salamander* or *Graellsiae isabellae* butterfly. So the survey below is empirical, based on what is likely to be seen and easily recognised during a short visit, plus a few of the rarer or shyer species which may be spotted with a little luck.

Surprisingly enough, while walking at height anywhere in central or western Gredos, you can guarantee a sighting of the largest surviving mammal, the Spanish ibex (*Capra hispanica victoriae*). Although nearly

Spanish ibex

hunted to extinction (the fate of the wolf and bear here), the handful of surviving animals were given protection in 1905 through the setting up of the Coto Real (Royal Hunting Reserve), now the Sierra de Gredos National Hunting Reserve. If anything, the policy has been too successful in that the animals are now numbered in thousands and, as their natural range is in the relatively limited area above 2000m, there are now problems of overgrazing and disease.

This small, neat agile animal has a medium brown coat with black markings, and lighter areas on the neck and thighs. The most striking feature are the metre-long curving horns of the adult male. Except during the rut between the end of November and the end of January, males and females stay separate, the latter in herds of up to 30. The males are often seen in small mixed-age groups while the very old are solitary. Like the marmots of the Alps, you are often first aware of the animals by their warning signal - a short, piercing whistle. Nevertheless, they are relatively tame and you can usually approach within a few metres.

The only other mammals you are quite likely to see are red squirrels (larger and darker than the one found in Britain) and possibly weasels.

Wild boar are supposed to be relatively widespread in both ranges and they are still hunted. However, they are shy animals, keeping to the deepest thickets and woods of the lower slopes and I have seen only their tracks and much evidence of rooting round tree boles. In four years' walking here, I have seen roe deer, red deer and even wildcats, but very rarely. Because of recurring cycles of disease, rabbits are less common than would be expected.

Birds, on the other hand, are fairly abundant at all levels. Before even setting foot on a mountain, you will be aware of the white storks, who are mostly summer visitors although some stay all the year round. As in most countries, the Spanish consider them a good omen, and there is barely a village in the sierras and foothills without a nest or two on its church tower or some other tall structure. In Guadarrama, the churches at Manzanares el Real and Soto del Real both host big colonies of seven or eight nests.

At the field and woodland level, you will see many of the small birds commonly found in Britain, but in addition more flamboyant species such as the azure-winged magpie, which survives only in this corner of Europe and is usually spotted in small flocks. Between March and October there are three very exotic visitors to look out for: the hoopoes, smoky brown with gaudy black and white striped wings and tail and a big retractable crest, are fairly common, but you will need more luck to see the gorgeously coloured rollers and bee-eaters. Permanent residents of an equally flamboyant appearance are the woodpeckers, the green in the foothills and the great spotted in the pine forests. Both are easy to spot and seem to be numerous here.

At the other end of the scale of size and habitat, griffon vultures, wheeling in groups above the summit crags, are for me the symbol of these mountains, so frequently are they seen in both ranges. This huge bird, which can have a wing span of nearly three metres, although half that length is more common here, are an impressive sight as they glide down to take a closer look at solitary walkers. The much rarer black vulture is also present in these mountains but unlikely to be spotted. Other common birds of prey at valley level are red and black kites, buzzards, harriers and kestrels. Eagles of various kinds are also found but they are difficult for the layperson to identify.

Of the smaller high mountain birds, the most easily identified are wheatears, crested larks and black redstarts (small black birds with rusty red tails, which follow walkers along summit ridges). In summer, the cuckoo's call is heard all the time in Gredos from the foothills to the main crest and at a higher level it is easy to spot the bird perched on rocks. Among the steeper crags of the highest zones, you find choughs, crow-like birds who move restlessly in large flocks around their nesting sites, while occasionally in the broom, you might disturb red legged partridge, the principal hunting quarry after the wood pigeon.

In the summer, the small mountain lizard is the most commonly seen reptile. It is olive-brown in colour with a darker stripe along its side. Above 2000m and therefore more prevalent in Gredos is a more striking turquoise-green and black mottled species, called verdinegro in Spanish, which is said to have adapted to resemble the siliceous lichens found on the granite. I have also seen a number of times, in La Pedriza and in Gredos, a larger very striking lizard, 30-40cm long with a turquoise head, lime green body and pinkish-grey tail, which may be a variation of the verdinegro. Snakes, including adders, are frequently seen in summer in quieter areas, on the paths, in the broom or by small streams. (I finished my last walk for this guide by stepping on a five foot adder near Navalguijo.) The *Vibora hocicuda* (grumbling or scowling viper) is a local species and it is attracted to the crevices in stone walls.

From the large quantity and variety of insects to be seen, the non-specialist's attention is usually caught either by the more colourful species, such as butterflies and beetles, both of which occur in spectacular variety, or by the ones which cause irritation in the summer. Specialist field guides are needed for the former and insect repellent for the mosquitoes, although they aren't an especially acute problem. Very occasionally, certain combinations of heat and humidity, usually in May or September, result in personal entourages of houseflies which reach horror film proportions. On the open slopes of Western Gredos, grasshoppers occur in such numbers that their constant bombardment can be slightly unnerving.

Scorpions are also supposed to be common in the foothills on the south side of the range, although I have seen only one. Also in Gredos, you will probably be struck by the fearsome appearance of a ubiquitous cricket which lives in the broom - a red thorax, striped wing cases and a long protruding barb. Another interesting phenomenon in both ranges is the concentration of ladybirds among the summit rocks, often so many that it is difficult to move without treading on them.

A very noticeable feature in some areas of pine forest are large balls constructed from layers of web-like material on the end of upper branches. These are the nests of the caterpillars of the damaging pine-shoot moth. You sometimes come across a rope of these hairy brown and black caterpillars moving nose-to-tail along a path. It is wise not to inspect them too closely, as they throw out a dust which produces an irritating rash.

THE HUMAN LANDSCAPE

Evidence of early occupation of this mountain zone is limited to a handful of neolithic wall carvings in natural caves in the Guadarrama range. It is no surprise to find, however, that the first permanent settlements, which were Iron Age, appeared around Béjar, in the Jerte Valley and on the southwestern slopes of Gredos, i.e. in the wettest, most sheltered part of the area with good soils for subsistence agriculture. The best preserved remains are found near El Raso, above Candeleda.

There was little in these mountains of strategic or economic importance to attract the Romans. They mainly developed the existing settlements in the south and west, starting foundries in Arenas de San Pedro and Mombeltran and introducing the cultivation of chestnuts. Their most enduring monuments, as usual, are roads. They put one through each range (over the Puerto del Pico in Gredos and the Puerto de la Fuenfría in Guadarrama) and opened the very important Silver Route which skirted the west side of the Sierra de Béjar. After they left, all three continued to be used until the 18th or 19th century, so stretches are still visible, the best being the restored section just to the south of the Puerto del Pico.

The Visigoths, who superseded the Romans, left some tiny early Christian churches, in various parts of Spain, but there is nothing in these mountains to mark their presence. They were followed at the beginning of the 8th century by the Moors, who held this part of Spain for four to five centuries. However, the whole area between the Duero and Tajo Rivers was a frontier zone for nearly the last two hundred years of their occupation and parts of it changed hands several times. Consequently, the population distribution changed little during that long unsettled period, with little expansion from the established villages and towns to the south and west of the Sierra de Gredos. Even so, in contrast to the rich heritage of the surrounding cities of the Meseta, these humbler agricultural settlements have few examples of Moorish architecture beyond the odd piece of fortification.

In the 9th and 10th centuries, there is some evidence that summer settlements were established for the first time on cleared sites in the dense oak and pine forests of the Tormes valley on the north side of Gredos, and it is possible that something similar occurred in Guadarrama. Toledo fell to the Christian armies for the last time in 1089 and it was the

Reconquest which gave the impetus for the permanent colonisation of these more inhospitable areas, with settlers moving in from Old Castile as the Moors were pushed south. In Guadarrama, the process wasn't a smooth one, as the southern slopes and foothills of the range were claimed by both Segovia and Madrid and in fact the present watershed boundary was only fixed in 1885.

So it was the Middle Ages which saw the establishment of the population pattern, economic base and agricultural landscape which remained virtually unchanged until the middle of the 20th century. The established settlements of the south and west were by now growing a wide variety of crops: vegetables, fruit, nuts, cereals, vines, olives, and after Columbus, cotton and tobacco. The area under cultivation had expanded up the steep slopes as high as 1000m, with terraces carved out of land cleared from the forest, a process started by the Moors. In addition, a rising demand for resin prompted small-scale reafforestation with resin-bearing pines.

Meanwhile, the northern side of Gredos and all of Guadarrama was being developed as sheep runs under the direction of the Mesta, a powerful organisation of landed interests which controlled all of Spain's wool production, distribution and export from the 13th to the 18th centuries. Because of the huge demands for raw wool in Holland, Italy and England, the Mesta constructed roads between the isolated villages and promoted the expansion of the sheep pastures through clearing large tracts of forest. At the same time, the military and economic power of Spain was to reach its zenith, based on the exploitation of its expanding empire. The resulting insatiable demand for both naval and merchant ships eventually used up the remaining oak woods.

Thus, the 12th to 17th centuries were the Golden Age for this area, as they were for Spain itself. All the buildings of note (apart from some 18th-19th century royal hunting lodges) were constructed during this period: churches (including some fine Romanesque Gothic ones), monasteries, castles, palaces, aristocratic houses and arcaded plazas. Nevertheless, it is clear that in spite of the importance and profitability of sheep rearing, the difference in wealth between the south and west of Gredos and north Gredos together with Guadarrama continued throughout the whole period. Not only is there more public and wealthy domestic architecture in the villages of the Tiétar, Jerte and Béjar valleys, but the large three and four storey balconied vernacular village houses there are superior to the low, almost windowless granite-block cottages of Guadarrama and north Gredos, a difference which goes beyond the

29

demands of climate.

The grand exception to this general rule was the enormous palace/ monastery of San Lorenzo de El Escorial, built by Philip II in the 16th century at the southeast end of the Sierra de Guadarrama. The conception of this ambitious scheme was prompted by the King's piety but its positioning by a mixture of pragmatism and pleasure-seeking. It was planned as a summer retreat from the heat of Madrid for the whole court and apparatus of government and therefore needed to be in a mountain range not too distant from the capital. El Escorial was chosen from a number of possible sites because of the quality of the hunting in the vicinity.

The 13th century also saw the start of the transhumance system which shaped the lives of the villagers of Central Spain for generations to come. In this area, the sheep started out for the better winter pastures of Estremadura to the southwest on 29th September (San Miguel) and returned along with the Estrameños and their flocks on 24th June (San Juan) for shearing and the mountain pastures. This way of life, with many of the men away from home for over half the year, started to decline in the 18th century with the collapse of the export market for wool. Some stretches of the vast network of drove roads still exist and are even now used on a small scale. They are best preserved in the foothills of both these ranges but cross, of course, most of the main passes in the ranges. Thus, some of the walks described here follow short surviving mountain sections which are signposted or marked on maps as Vía Pecuaria or Cañada (e.g. Real Segoviana).

The long economic decline of the 18th and 19th century saw, in this area, a fall in population, a return to subsistence agriculture and the start of large-scale reafforestation with pine trees. Both ranges, but particularly Guadarrama, were caught up in the disturbance of the Napoleonic Wars in the early 19th century as well as the Civil War of 1936-39. Indeed, during the latter, virtually the whole of the main watershed in the Sierra de Guadarrama formed the frontline in the struggle, with the Republicans defending the Madrid side of the range. On many of the walks in the area, the remains of trenches, gun emplacements, bunkers and other fortifications from that terrible war are encountered.

For these mountain villages, the immediate post-war period was purely one of survival. Then came the industrial leap forward of the 1950s and 60s, when many of the younger people joined the exodus from rural Spain to take up the better paid jobs being created in the major cities. The result was that the population levels of many villages returned to 18th century levels. Paradoxically, this process did something to stimulate the poverty-stricken agriculture they were leaving behind, as large urban markets for food started to emerge. Livestock-rearing revived in these ranges but this time cattle were to predominate both for milk and meat. Forestry also grew in importance, although the industry's low manpower requirements did little to halt the drift to the cities.

Nevertheless, this farming revival was to be completely overshadowed from the 1970s onwards by the impact of tourism, as growing prosperity in the cities led to increased car ownership and spare capital for second homes. As the weekend crowds poured into the countryside, jobs were created in construction, restaurants, hotels, bars and shops and local families rushed to take them up. Between the mid 1960s and 80s, figures show employment in agriculture in many Guadarrama villages dropping from 60% to 10%. The change to reliance on tourism becomes less marked the further you travel from Madrid, but even so, there is barely a village between Béjar and Somosierra that doesn't have its infills and "suburbs" of new houses and apartments, mostly second homes but also a sign of new prosperity for at least some of the local people.

While these new forms of employment were badly needed, there has been much concern at the haphazard development and obvious environmental damage resulting from the expansion of tourism. Some writers have pointed out the contradiction in the fact that ICONA, the principal agent for conservation in the area, is also the Spanish equivalent of the Forestry Commission and runs the Gredos National Hunting Reserve. Certainly, the extensive new plantings of the last few years using heavy machinery and terracing are interfering with access to the high ground and, more seriously, destroying habitats.

Some critics also argue that hunting interests are too powerful, causing an imbalance in the development of the region. Protection measures only cover the ibex population of Gredos, which is now three times too large for the area of land suitable for the animal. Hunting quotas tend to cull the healthy males rather than the growing number of diseased animals. There has long been a lobby for the setting up of a National Park in Gredos, but even if that were achieved, the situation in existing protected areas, whether National or Regional Parks, suggest that it would not alone solve the problems. Either the legislation restricting inappropriate development and activities in these areas is too weak or there are insufficient funds and manpower to implement it. At the moment, these matters are fairly low on the political agenda.

MOUNTAINEERING

Until the 19th century the high interiors of both ranges were largely ignored except by hunters and shepherds looking for summer pasture. The first documented expedition into the Sierra de Gredos was in 1834 when a group of gentlemen-farmers took five days to cross the range from Candeleda to Hoyos de Espino (a 10 hour walk today) and there were no maps or descriptions until the second half of the same century. In the Sierra de Guadarrama, the first interest in exploring rather than hunting appeared to be after the opening of the railways to El Escorial and Segovia in the early 1860s. A group of naturalists and geologists set up a society for the study of the range at that time.

Although there must have been piecemeal exploration in both ranges from that time on (Collomb mentions the journals of an Englishman, John Ormsby, who may or may not have climbed the highest peak, Almanzor), more widespread interest gathered momentum at the turn of the century. The first properly recorded ascent of Almanzor by two local men was in 1899. By this time the larger game in both ranges, bears and wolves, had been hunted to extinction and steps were taken in 1905 to protect the handful of surviving ibex in Gredos, by setting up the Royal Hunting Reserve.

The first two decades of the 20th century saw the gradual organising of mountaineering interests. In Guadarrama, Los Doce Amigos, the first mountaineering society, was set up. This soon became the Peñalara Society which opened refuges in La Pedriza, the Fuenfría valley and at the Puerto de Navacerrada, while around the same time the Club Alpina de España opened one at the Puerto de los Cotos. Meanwhile, in 1910 a society was formed in northern Gredos which over the next few years improved several of the mountain tracks including the one from Hoyos del Espino to La Plataforma (although it was the 1960s before it was surfaced) and built the Refugio del Rey on the main ridge. The Prado de las Pozas hut, above the Plataforma, was also opened in 1910 and the Arenas-Gredos Society was formed for the development of the south side of the range in 1917. They opened a hut at los Pelaos, below the summit of La Mira, which has not survived.

The remaining years before the Civil War, when of course all recreational activities temporarily ceased, saw different rates of mountaineering development in the two ranges. Gredos, distant from rail lines and with a poorly developed road network, remained largely the preserve of an elite both for hunting and exploring. In 1926, the country's first Parador (one of a chain of nationally-owned luxury hotels) was opened on the north side of Gredos, with the active encouragement of Alfonso XIII, a keen hunter. Even today, it retains the atmosphere of a hunting lodge with its wood panelling, leather furniture and numerous trophies. The early 1930s also saw the first real development of technical rock climbing routes in the area.

By contrast, in 1923, the central and highest part of Guadarrama became accessible to determined but not necessarily rich day-trippers from Madrid when a narrow-gauge mountain railway was opened from Cercedilla (on the Madrid-Segovia line) to the Puerto de los Cotos. There were soon complaints from members of the Peñalara Society about the unsympathetic attitude and behaviour of some of the city-dwellers, suddenly translated to an unfamiliar mountain environment. In 1929, La Pedriza, Peñalara and the Pinar de la Acebeda were declared Sites of National Interest, providing a protection which has had a mixed degree of success over the years.

The post Civil War years were hard and even hungry for the vast majority of Spanish people, both in the cities and countryside. Gredos in particular reverted to the preserve of a hunting elite with Franco coming to shoot there once or twice a year. Still, by the late 1940s, some mountaineering enthusiasts were beginning to organise themselves again. There was much rock climbing activity; for instance the opening of Victory Hut in 1949 led to the first serious development of the Los Galayos crags and it was during the 1950s that virtually all the long, classic Gredos lines were put up. In 1959, the first traverse of the High Level ski route from Puerto del Pico to Bohoyo was recorded. Nevertheless, these specialist activities apart, the real opening up of the high remote areas to more than a handful of enthusiasts came with the prosperity and wider car-ownership of the 1970s as described in the previous section. In 1972, the large, wardened Elola Hut was opened in the Gredos Cirque by the Federacion Española de Montanismo (FEM).

ROCK CLIMBING

There are three principal areas for rock climbing in the area: the Gredos/ Cinco Lagunas Cirques and Los Galayos in Gredos and La Pedriza in Guadarrama. It is all, of course, on granite although the different rock structure in La Pedriza means the most popular routes there are aided face climbs.

The most comprehensive climbing guide for Gredos is *La Sierra de Gredos* by Adrados, Viel and Lopez (Guias de Montaña 1981) which also has useful separate sketch maps of the whole range and the central sector. They list 109 routes in the Cirques, 210 on Los Galayos and 54 scattered through the rest of the range. The climbs around the Cirques rarely exceed 200m and the vast majority are on either side of 100m. Among the tightly-packed towers and buttresses of Los Galayos, 200m+ routes are often constructed by linking two named climbs.

It is said that there are over a thousand named rock climbs in La Pedriza although the main guidebook, *Escaladas en la Pedriza* by D. Rodriguez and J.I. Lujon (Ediciones Desnivel 1992), lists considerably fewer. Much of the climbing is on exposed, featureless slabs which nevertheless have excellent friction when dry. The classic routes, many of them bolted, are found on the domes of Peña Sirio, Cueva de la Mora, El Yelmo, El Pajaro and the Pared de Santillán. In the rest of Guadarrama, there is a scattering of routes on the east side of Peñalara and on the south face of La Maliciosa and its satellite, El Peñotillo.

On the east side of the N1 Madrid-Burgos road near La Cabrera, there is a low range of limestone hills where there is well-developed outcrop climbing, but it hardly compares with the limestone regions of the Picos de Europa or those of the east and south coasts. The guide is called *Patones, Guia de Escalada* (Guias Desnivel No.7).

SKIING

Piste skiing is a fairly marginal activity in Central Spain where snow cover varies dramatically from year to year. The generally reliable north-facing corries of Gredos have thankfully been spared any large-scale development and the only fixed tows in the range are found at La Covatilla in the northwest of the Sierra de Béjar, (reached by a long dirt road from the village of La Hoya) and in the Prao Puerto valley, a 20 minute walk above the Gredos Plataforma. In the Sierra de Guadarrama there are three small ski stations at Puerto de Navacerrada, Puerto de los Cotos and Valdesquí, all within 10 minutes' drive of each other, although unlinked. Dangerously crowded at weekends, they are fine for a mid-week afternoon ski but of little interest to visitors.

The long ridges of the range and variable snow conditions are much more suitable for ski mountaineering. Day excursions are the norm in Guadarrama where continuous snow cover is limited to the Cuerda Larga and the Peñalara-Nevero chain. Gredos/Béjar with its more extensive snow cover offers more opportunity for longer tours, including the classic High Route from the Puerto de Pico to the village of Bohoyo via the Gredos Cirque. The Adrados, Viel, Lopez climbing guide describes other possibilities.

OTHER ACTIVITIES

With hundreds of miles of forestry and farm roads, mountain biking and horse riding/trekking are popular in both ranges and, indeed, in Gredos with the long distances between the villages and the high ground, both sports rival walking as a summer activity. The main centres for riding are Navarredonda and Hoyos del Espino on the north side and Mombeltran on the south. The latter organise, among others, two day trips to the Circo de Gredos. There are numerous stables in the southern foothills of Guadarrama, but the best situated for treks in the mountains is at Manzanares el Real. Mountain bikes can be hired in Hoyos del Espino and, in the summer, from a van in the second car park after Canto Cochino in La Pedriza. There are several guides to mountain bike routes in the area on sale in the Tienda Verde (see Books section).

Parapenting is growing in popularity. The most popular take-off points are the Puerto de Peña Negra above Piedrahita, Torozo near the Puerto del Pico and La Abantera near Pedro Bernardo (all in Gredos); Abantos above El Escorial and Mondalindo above Bustarviejo (Guadarrama).

CHAPTER TWO

Practical Information

ACCESS FROM THE UK

By Air

British Airways and Iberia both have several scheduled flights a day from London and two each from Manchester while Air VK now have a service from Stansted. Aéreolineas Argentina's biweekly Buenos Aires flight to London is via Madrid and there are some regular charter flights as well.

There are plans to build a train link from Barajas Airport, which lies some 12km to the east of Madrid, to the city centre, but for the moment the airport bus which runs every 15mins from outside the Arrivals area is reasonably quick and costs about one-tenth of the taxi fare. Its destination is an underground terminus below the Descubriemento Gardens beside the Plaza de Colón, which is a convenient entry point to the city whether you are spending a night or two there or intending to go straight on to the mountains. For getting to hotels or to the various bus stations, there is a taxi rank at the underground terminal. The more adventurous or impecunious can take the spiral staircase up into the Gardens, where they will find Metro stations either across the Plaza de Colón beyond the column of Christopher Columbus, or at the opposite corner of the Gardens (Colón and Serrano stations respectively).

The most convenient way to go on to two of the main Guadarrama destinations, **Cercedilla** and **El Escorial**, is by train: one block left from the Column corner of the Gardens is the entrance to Recoletos railway station. This is a stop on an underground (but not Metro) line which connects the two mainline stations of Atocha and Chamartín. Go to the Chamartín-direction platform, where direct trains to both Cercedilla and El Escorial run every hour. The journeys take 1hr 20mins and 1hr respectively.

Recoletos station can also be used to go to Atocha for onward trains to **Talavera de la Reina** which is the only viable approach by train to the south side of the Sierra de Gredos. From Talavera, a limited bus service goes to **Arenas San Pedro** (with the odd extension to the Cinco Villas), and **Jarandilla de la Vera** (via **Candeleda**). There is also a service from Atocha to Plasencia for buses to the town of **Béjar**, but in both cases it would be best to start early from Madrid to be sure of connections. For north Gredos, five of the El Escorial trains continue to **Avila** (2hrs from Madrid) from where there are buses either direct to **El Barco de Avila** or an early evening one which calls at all the **Tormes valley villages**.

If preferred, there are direct bus services from Madrid to many of the Gredos villages, taking 3 to 4hrs. In the summer, Doaldi run five buses a day, with more at weekends, from Madrid (Estación del Sur, near Atocha) to **Arenas de San Pedro** with just the 19.00 connecting with one to **Mombeltran** and the other Cinco Villas. There is also one a day to **Jarandilla** via Arenas and **Candeleda**. From the same bus station, Muñoz run two buses a day to **El Barco de Avila** via the Alberche and Tormes valley villages.

Village bases recommended in this guide but not served by public transport are **Candelario** (taxi from Béjar), **Guisando** and **El Arenal** (taxi from Arenas de San Pedro).

Guadarrama destinations are served by the following companies:

Torrelaguna, La Cabrera and **Rascafría**. Continental Autos, Calle Alenza 20 (Metro Rios Rosas).

Miraflores de la Sierra, Bustarviejo and **Manzanares el Real** by Hermanos J Colmenarejo, Calle Mateo I Nurria 11 (Metro Plaza de Castilla).

Cercedilla, Navacerrada (Pueblo and Puerto) and **Puerto de los Cotos** by Larrea and La Sepulvedana, Paseo de la Florida 11 (Metro Norte).

However as timetables, companies and termini are subject to change, it is best to allow a day in Madrid to check the current situation either at the relevant terminus or at the Comunidad de Madrid tourist information centres at Chamartín (315 99 76), Plaza de España (541 23 25) or Calle Duque de Medinaceli (429 4951 or 44 87).

Fly/drive

This is an attractive option if your time is limited and, once away from Madrid, the roads are fairly empty. The disadvantage is that Barajas Airport is on the wrong side of the city for most of the mountain destinations. If you have a choice of flights try to avoid having to set out from Barajas at peak traffic times (8.00-10.00 and 19.00-21.00).

Almost immediately on joining the dual carriageway which borders the airport complex, take the slip road to the right which leads to the anti-clockwise flow of the M40 ring road. For **La Cabrera** and **Rascafría**, take the Burgos Norte exit and for **Manzanares el Real, Navacerrada** and **Cercedilla**, follow the Colmenar Viejo (M607) signs.

Those heading for **El Escorial** or **Gredos** will be able to stay on the M40 when the final section is finished in 1996, as far as the exit to La Coruña (A6) Norte. Meanwhile, follow signs to Villalba leaving at the Colmenar Viejo exit but immediately taking the slip road for Avenida de la Ilustración. This leads onto a dual carriageway/four lane road cutting right across the northern suburbs of Madrid. Leave at the Villalba exit which leads onto the A6 La Coruña motorway. For El Escorial, a fork from the left-hand lane after some 12km leads directly onto the C505 El Escorial road.

For **Gredos**, continue on the A6 motorway, through the Sierra de Guadarrama (tunnel) and on to the tolled section, to leave at Villacastín for the N110 to Avila. Passing below the city's splendid medieval walls, follow signs to Plasencia (still N110) for **Barco de Avila** and **Béjar**.

For the **Tormes valley villages** and **Arenas de San Pedro**, take the C502 turning signposted to the latter town, a few kilometres after Avila. This good mountain road goes over the Puerto de Menga and Puerto del Pico passes. Between the two look out for the unclear turning into the Tormes valley at a hostel called Venta Rasquilla. Signs to Parador de Gredos and El Barco de Avila.

Although on the map this appears a very roundabout route to south Gredos, it is at the moment the quickest and pleasantest route. When the M40 is completed, it may be worth using it to reach the Estremadura (A5) motorway on the west side of Madrid to reach the **Vera villages**.

It is difficult to assess times to the various destinations as it will depend on traffic conditions in Madrid. With a clear run, Guadarrama villages should be reached in between 1hr (Manzanares el Real) and 1³/₄hrs (Rascafría). Allow between 3hrs (Arenas San Pedro) and 4hrs (Béjar) for Gredos. However, if you have the misfortune to be driving out of the city on a Friday night or returning on a Sunday evening, at least 1¹/₂hrs should be added to these totals.

By Car

If a short Channel crossing or the Tunnel is taken, the route across France to the Spanish border at Irún can be all on motorway (most of it tolled) or dual carriageway. However, this involves more driving than by taking the 6hr Portsmouth/Poole to Caen/Cherbourg/San Malo crossings. From the latter ports, there is a 4hr-plus drive on N roads through pretty Normandy countryside until the motorway system can be joined at e.g. Tours or Poitiers.

It is also worth considering the expensive but most relaxing way to travel to Northern Spain which is by the Plymouth-Santander (Brittany Ferries) or Portsmouth-Bilbao (P&O) ferries. In fact, unless you are doing the overland route on the cheap (camping and N roads), the overall costs are comparable.

For destinations in both ranges, there is a common route from Irún on the French border to Burgos, all on motorway. For Béjar, El Barco de Avila, the Jerte valley and the La Vera villages, it's a matter of choice then whether you go via Valladolid and Salamanca or take the N1 Madrid road and turn off on the N110 through Segovia and Avila. The latter is the best route for the Tormes valley villages and south Gredos, turning off a few kilometres after Avila on the N502.

Guadarrama destinations are also reached by the N1, which is now all dual carriageway. Having crossed the range at the Puerto de Somosierra (tunnel), the Rascafría turn-off (M604) is well signposted. Further on the exit to the M608, (follow Guadalix signs) is used to reach all other Guadarrama villages. The M608 runs along the south side of the range, through Manzanares el Real. It meets M607 at an island at Cerceda - turn right for Navacerrada Pueblo and Cercedilla.

For El Escorial, leave the M607 after only a few hundred metres to the left at the next island, for the M610 to Villalba, a town lying next to the A6 motorway. Cross the bridge over the motorway and go right at a roundabout onto a link road to the NVI trunk road. Follow the latter north for a few kilometres looking for a left turn to Galapagar. This cuts across to the M505 El Escorial road.

By Coach
Buses leave from Victoria Coach Station in London and arrive at the Estación Sur de Autobuses, just to the south of Atocha Railway Station.

By Train
This is not a fashionable or cheap option, except with students on Interrail tickets. At the moment the London Madrid journey involves changing stations in Paris. The Paris trains come into Chamartín Station on the north side of the city.

ACCOMMODATION
Hotels and Guesthouses
Tourist accommodation in Spain is officially categorised as follows:
Hotels - one to five stars
Hostels (hostales) - one to three stars
Guesthouses (pensiones) - one to three star.

This classification is complicated by some hotels and hostels being called Residencial. All establishments display their class and grade outside e.g. HR***. Below luxury hotels, however, the system doesn't really work as a clear guide to prices or standards. Because of the impossibility of distinguishing between the better "hostales" and the more basic hotels, as well as the confusion it would cause by using "hostal", with its connotations of dormitories in English, I refer to all accommodation in those categories as hotels. Very basic accommodation, often just rooms in private houses, can be found in Fondas and where you see the sign Camas (beds).

You will find everything from camas to four-star hotels in these mountains, but as most of tourists here are day-trippers or own second homes in the area, there is little choice in any one area and it is advisable to book ahead during holiday periods. The official *Guía de Hoteles - España*, available from tourist offices and the larger book shops, covers most of the classified accommodation available in Guadarrama and Gredos.

Camping
There are about 20 commercial campsites scattered through the two ranges. One or two are open all the year round but most have an Easter to the end of September season. With the exceptions of the one at Candelario (Béjar), they cater almost totally for Spaniards, many of whom move onto the sites for the whole summer. Few people are there to walk in the mountains and the rhythm of life is similar to that of Madrid, with the most animated period between 23.00 and 03.00 or 04.00hrs. This is a problem if you are hoping for an early start. In general the prices are higher and sites less well run and equipped than those in France or the Alps. Again there is an official *Guía de Camping*.

Wild Camping
Prohibido Acampar signs appear in many places in both ranges and especially in the ICONA-managed areas and protected sites like Peñalara and La Pedriza. However, my impression is that there don't appear to be enough resources to enforce the restrictions everywhere.

Refuges
There are only three "walk-in" refuges in the area which offer food and accommodation at holidays and weekends - Prado de las Pozas, above the Gredos Plataforma, the Elola in the Circo de Gredos and the Giner in La Pedriza. A number of refuges and "Albergues" at roadheads or road passes offer a similar service, some open all the year round. Unwardened

shelters are fairly widespread in both ranges and vary from locked buildings with bunks and some equipment, to more often, open huts often in some state of disrepair. More details are given at the beginning of each chapter of routes.

Anyone hoping to get an uninterrupted night's sleep should avoid the more accessible open shelters, (which means all those in Guadarrama), at weekends and holidays when they are often taken over by big groups intent on marathon parties. The rubbish heaps around these buildings can be appalling.

FOOD

As the majority of the visitors from the surrounding cities see lunch as the central activity of their day out, there is no shortage of restaurants or bars with dining rooms (comedores) in both ranges and all the hotels and hostales are open to non-residents for meals as well. Most restaurants offer a Menu del Día at lunchtime, a good value all-in price for three or four courses, bread and wine, with often a choice within each course.

Lunch is usually served between 13.30 and 16.30 and dinner between 21.00 and 24.00. The lateness of the evening meal can be a problem when you come off the hills ravenous, but many bars serve selections of tapas or raciones (larger portions) right through the day. Another possibility are platos combinados of the ham, egg and chips variety.

CHANGING MONEY

Even in the late 1980s there were problems with changing travellers' cheques in some banks in the area. Now things have improved a lot although you still often have to queue, commissions are high and cash machines are found only at the larger branches. If you are staying in the Tormes valley villages, you will have to go down to El Barco de Avila to change money or pay high rates at the hotels. Banking hours vary between banks and from summer to winter. Usually they are open only in the morning with sometimes one evening opening a week.

BUSINESS HOURS

Shops open, with some variation, between 10.00-14.00 and 17.00-20.00. This changes in June to September to 11.00-14.00 and 18.00-21.00 or 21.30. Large department stores and public galleries and museums in Madrid stay open all day, although most of the latter close on Mondays.

POST

All the larger villages have post offices (Correos) and are usually open mornings only, until 13.30 or 14.00. Mail from Madrid takes about six days to the UK and two to four days longer from the mountains. Stamps can also be bought from tobacconists (Estancos) which have a yellow and brown sign.

MAPS

For access and large-scale planning, I have found the Michelin 1:400,000 Northern Spain sheet (442) to be adequate. It covers central northern Spain from Madrid to the north coast. Firestone's 1:75,000 Madrid and Outlying Areas is useful but not essential for the Sierra de Guadarrama, and it has a large map of central Madrid on the reverse.

For walkers used to the accuracy and clarity of the OS and Alpine walking maps, the Spanish ones are disappointing. The 1:50,000 military maps from Servicio Geografico del Ejercito (SGE), which cover the whole country, have many inaccuracies and are tonally rather uniform which make them difficult to read. Some haven't been updated in 50 years. Nevertheless, relief, drainage and the position of settlements and surfaced roads are shown accurately enough and the following sheets are essential to fill in the gaps missed by more readable commercial maps:

West Gredos

599	Jaraíz de la Vera

East Gredos

555	Navatalgordo	578	Arenas de San Pedro
556	Navaluenga	579	Sotillo de la Adrada

West Guadarrama

507	El Espinar	532	Las Navas
533	El Escorial		

The Instituto Geográfico Nacional (IGN) has produced very usefully a 1:50,000 tourist map, called Sierra de Guadarrama. This covers the rest of the range except for the northern branch between Reajo Capón and the Puerto de Somosierra. (This guide doesn't include any walks in that section, but if you intend to go there you will need SGE sheet 458 - Pradena.) The tourist map is essential, but its main drawbacks are again the tonal range and also that the unsurfaced forestry roads (many of them closed to cars) cannot be distinguished from minor roads.

Editorial Alpina have three maps for the area:

1. Sierra de Gredos which covers the central area from Cinco Lagunas

to Puerto del Pico. 1:40,000.
2. Guadarrama - from the upper Rio Moros valley to Cabezas de Hierro. 1:25,000.
3. La Pedriza which has a slight overlap with the last to cover the upper Manzanares basin, most of the Cuerda Larga and Peñalara. 1:25,000.

These are clear to read and it is helpful to have the larger scale but much of the details, including contours, are Inaccurate. At the time of writing, a new corrected edition of the Guadarrama maps is in preparation.

Cayetano Enriquez de Salamanca has produced two 1:50,000 Gredos sheets:

1. Macizo Occidental covering the Sierra de Béjar and Covacha
2. Macizo Central which includes much the same area as the Alpina map.

These are easier to read than the SGE sheets but are based on them, so preserve most of the inaccuracies. Their great advantage is that they cover in two maps two-thirds of the range, where six SGE sheets would be needed.

If you intend to walk only in the Central area or across El Torozo, the Federación Española de Montañismo 1991 1:50,000 map of the area is the best choice. Not many paths are marked and it has not been able to keep up with changes in the forestry tracks, but it is very well designed and readable.

All the walking maps can be bought at La Tienda Verde, Calle Maudes 38, 28003 Madrid. They are also available in London at Stanford's Map Centre, 12-14 Long Acre, London WC2E 9LP and also The Map Shop, 15 High Street, Upton-upon-Severn, Worcs WR8 0HJ.

BOOKS

There has been very little written in English about this area. Two guides produced in the 1980s have something on the Sierra de Gredos and both are useful if you are thinking of combining a visit here with another mountain area of Spain: *Gredos Mountains and Sierra Nevada* by Robin Collomb (West Col 1987) includes a short section on walks mainly in the Cirques and Los Galayos areas. Recent forestry work on the south side of the range has altered the start to some routes described there. For serious scramblers, the Gredos Cirque skyline is dealt with in some detail. *Trekking in Spain* by Marc Dubin (Lonely Planet 1990) covers most of the main mountain areas of Spain, giving a small section to Gredos, and inexplicably dismissing Guadarrama in one sentence. It is, however, a useful book for the practicalities of backpacking in remote areas of Spain.

The warden of the Elola Refuge has recently published a book called *Gredos - A Guide of(sic) the Dangers* (Miguel A. Vidal and Jose L. Rodriguez. Fondo Natural S.L. 1994). It isn't a walk-by-walk guide but appears to be aimed at the many ill-equipped and inexperienced people who wander into these wild mountains at all seasons. Nevertheless, with an English translation running alongside the text, it has some useful information on the nature of the terrain on specific walks, the spots most prone to avalanche etc. as well as having the best photographs I have seen of the range.

MOUNTAIN RESCUE
In both ranges there are specially-trained units of both the (Cruz Roja) Red Cross and the Guardia Civil (Police) who have helicopters. In the severer conditions and terrain of Gredos, the El Barco de Avila rescue team have dogs trained for avalanche rescue and the Elola, Prado de las Pozas and Victory huts have two-way radios. Otherwise you will have to phone direct to the rescue teams from a village:

GREIM (Barco de Avila) 34 00 10
EREIM (Arenas de San Pedro) 37 00 10
Unidad Alpina Cruz Roja (Avila) 22 48 48

In Guadarrama, the general switchboards are phoned:
Cruz Roja 522 22 22
Guardia Civil 062 533 11 00

THE ROUTES
A substantially larger number of routes have been selected in the Sierra de Guadarrama, the smaller and lower range of the two. This is a reflection of the very different character of the terrain and the walking in the two sierras as well as the greater accessibility of Guadarrama with its better developed roads and public transport. This is discussed more fully in the introduction to each range.

There is rarely an access problem in these mountains even though large areas are privately owned. There are one or two Prohibido el Paso signs found on established and well-documented routes, and it can only be supposed that, as these are often jeep tracks, they apply to cars rather than walkers. Coto Privado de Caza (Private Hunting) signs are everywhere, often just a metal rectangle divided diagonally into black and white halves. However, these are warnings to freelance hunters and not intended to exclude walkers. Painted markings on routes are relatively scarce in Gredos but are more common in Guadarrama where red and white stripes indicate long-distance footpaths and yellow/white ones mark some principal local routes. Others are mentioned as they occur. Generally there are too many cairns on the many multi-stranded lines in Guadarrama and too few in Gredos.

The route descriptions have had to be constantly revised even while the guide has been in preparation: an identifying sculpture disappears from a summit, a farmer fences across a well-established path, ICONA restricts car access to the head of a popular valley. In the nature of things, some changes will be missed. Added to this, the continuing extension of forestry work in both ranges, but particularly on the south side of Gredos, means there is a strong likelihood that some routes will alter in the future. Meanwhile in Guadarrama there is a long-term programme to mark out a comprehensive network of routes as Pequeña Recorridas (PR), so walkers will undoubtedly come across yellow and white stripes where I haven't mentioned them. Any corrections or additional information from guide-users would be welcomed.

Conventions used in the route descriptions

Each description is in two parts: 1. an introduction (in bold type) giving a general picture of the walk plus a mention of any interesting features. 2. route instructions. The highest point on a route is indicated in the title by its spot height. Heights given here and in the descriptions are often only accurate to within 20m, either because the spot heights vary from map to map, or because they are estimated from the contour lines.

The time printed after the title is an estimation which allows for rest/ food stops, while those in italic type in the text are walking times between salient features, rounded up to the nearest 5mins. Both, of course, are only a broad guide.

Where a number of metres "of ascent" is given, this indicates that the route has a continuous rise to a high point followed by a continuous descent to its finish. Other routes with a "Total ascent" figure can have a number of ups and downs e.g. over a string of tops on a ridge walk. In both cases the figure may be approximate because of the unreliability of the spot heights. No allowance is made for the many small gains and losses of height when scrambling along the typical Guadarrama/Gredos ridge, punctuated by a succession of relatively small outcrops.

Where "left" and "right" banks of a water course are described, I prefer and use the apparent left or right, according to the direction of travel rather than the true one. The words "stream" and "streambed"

*Typical fuente
(mountain spring)*

should be treated interchangeably as their use depends upon the season in which the route was walked. Most of the smaller streams dry up for longer or shorter periods in late summer and autumn.

Natural springs are found all over these mountains and local people are justifiably proud of the quality of water they produce. At roadside fountains, people queue to fill plastic containers to take back home. In summer when walkers will need 2 or 3 litres of water to avoid dehydration, the position of these springs can be an important consideration on a route. I mention the ones I know for certain run all the year round, but for many I have no way of checking. The springs themselves can be anything from a muddy trickle to elaborate dressed granite constructions, engraved with poems and dedicated to various of the pioneers in the area. For brevity I refer to them all by the Spanish word fuente.

The routes have not been graded for difficulty. I hope that the combination of the estimated overall time and metres of ascent given after each title, and the mention of any difficulties (e.g. steep scrambling, pathless sections, dense vegetation) in the route introduction will be enough to give a picture of the severity or otherwise of each walk.

Names

Map reading is greatly speeded up if there is a quick reference for the Spanish words for natural and man-made features which regularly appear on the maps and occasionally in the text. These are listed alphabetically in the first part of the glossary at the end of the book. In addition, visitors who know no Spanish often seem to find difficulty and confusion with the polysyllabic place names. The second part of the glossary is an alphabetical list of the place names occurring in the guide, which can be translated more or less directly into English (e.g. the Collado de *Quebrantaherraduras* is *Break-Horseshoes* Pass and Peñacabra is *Goat* Crag). I hope these two quick references will make map reading slightly less laborious as well as giving a richer understanding of the area.

You may also notice on the maps, especially in Gredos, the same name occurring at two different points in the same area - this is hardly surprising where adjoining valleys were (and still are) isolated from each other and many names are straightforward descriptions e.g. Risco Negro (Black Cliff). Watch for this when matching text and map. Another characteristic of these mountains is that many features have several names: some very ancient, some attached by the early explorers and newer ones assigned by post-Civil War walkers and climbers. I have tried to find out the currently accepted one in each case.

Diagrams and maps

The sketch maps are intended primarily to show the relationship between the routes in an area for planning purposes, rather than a precise guide to each walk. At the few points in Guadarrama where there is a particularly complicated knot of routes, a three-dimensional diagram is included as well.

THE MOUNTAINS OF CENTRAL SPAIN

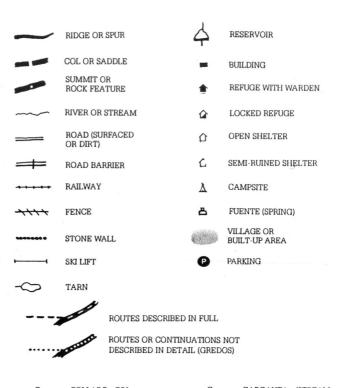

RIDGE OR SPUR		RESERVOIR	
COL OR SADDLE		BUILDING	
SUMMIT OR ROCK FEATURE		REFUGE WITH WARDEN	
RIVER OR STREAM		LOCKED REFUGE	
ROAD (SURFACED OR DIRT)		OPEN SHELTER	
ROAD BARRIER		SEMI-RUINED SHELTER	
RAILWAY		CAMPSITE	
FENCE		FUENTE (SPRING)	
STONE WALL		VILLAGE OR BUILT-UP AREA	
SKI LIFT		PARKING	
TARN			

ROUTES DESCRIBED IN FULL

ROUTES OR CONTINUATIONS NOT DESCRIBED IN DETAIL (GREDOS)

C - COLLADO COL
P - PORTILLA
Po - PUERTO (ROAD PASS)
R - RIO (RIVER)

G - GARGANTA (STREAM
Ao - ARROYO
Ca - CUERDA (RIDGE)

48

PART TWO
The Sierra de Gredos

INTRODUCTION

As a physical barrier, the Systema Central is at its most impressive in the Sierra de Gredos. The highest point in the whole chain, Almanzor (2592m), is found in its central sector and in the 100km between the town of Béjar and the Mijares Pass, there are few summits below 2000m while only three roads cross the divide. At the same time, the system broadens out into three parallel ranges and while they all reach a respectable height, it is the most southerly sierras of Gredos and Béjar which have the most interesting walking.

As already described in the main introduction, geography and climate have combined in Gredos to provide a dramatic contrast between the north and south sides of the range. (This is less marked in the Sierra de Béjar with its different alignment.) Although it is a comparison which is difficult to sustain in the heat of August, the landscape to the north of the divide has echoes of Scotland. A drive along the high valleys of the Tormes or Alberche, which bound the range to the north, reveals treeless, rounded slopes, odd patches of pine plantation, and glimpses into long, winding valleys and of the distant main crest, sometimes enticingly serrated.

The scenery softens in the main valley bottoms, with extensive areas of deciduous trees between the clusters of drystone-walled fields. At the lower western end of the Tormes valley, the villages are surrounded by acres of orchards but higher up these give way to hay pasture with a few vegetable patches near villages. Further east again, it is a surprise to find, in the fairly exposed upper Alberche valley, a rolling patchwork of vineyards. Most of the north Gredos villages nestle into south-facing folds some way above the main rivers. The original houses are rough, low agglomerations of random granite cobbles, topped by broad waves of terracotta pantiles, and seem to hunch, croft-like, against the weather.

Meanwhile, a few kilometres to the south, the heavily forested southern slopes plunge steeply to the low trough of the Tiétar valley. On ledges and along steep streambeds, photogenic villages form the centrepieces to terrace systems carrying fruit, almond, hazel and chestnut trees, vines, olives, figs and vegetables, all framed by dark green swathes

SIERRA DE GREDOS
Road system and villages mentioned in the text

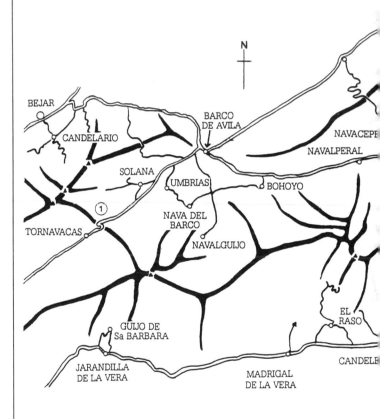

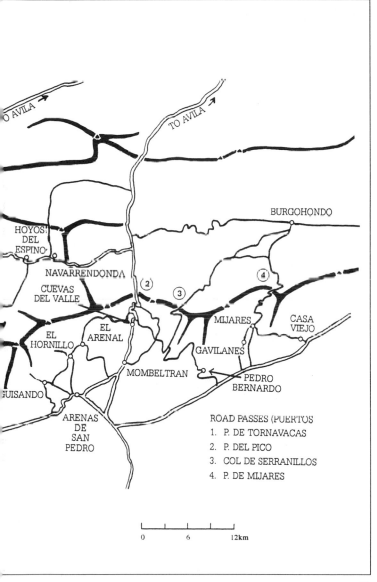

ROAD PASSES (PUERTOS
1. P. DE TORNAVACAS
2. P. DEL PICO
3. COL DE SERRANILLOS
4. P. DE MIJARES

0   6   12km

of pine forest. Within the villages, steep, narrow alleyways meander between tall, half-timbered houses with overhanging eaves and wooden balconies - an atmosphere both more claustrophobic and more Mediterranean than in the villages across the watershed.

Another sharp contrast with the north side, where cattle and horse are taken right up to the main crest for summer pasture, is the feeling that the southern landscape is quite divorced from the mountain wall above. Apart from herds of goats at middle height in wild valleys which cut back towards the divide, human activity seems to cease at the upper forest line - people in the villages speak of "going to Gredos" as entirely another place and possibly mean the north side of the range.

In the summer, the whole range becomes a slightly cooler retreat for Madrid and the other Meseta cities and is a popular weekend destination in spring and autumn. This puts considerable pressure on the facilities of the villages on both sides of the range. Some inappropriate second home developments have been tacked on to nearly all of them, but so far it is only at the eastern end, easily accessible from Madrid, where blocks of flats have completely altered the character of the old settlements. Everywhere else, agriculture still appears to be the main activity and the traditions of rural Spain persist with more donkeys than tractors and the occasional sight of bullocks circling on threshing platforms. Hayfields are still raked and stacked by hand, Sunday horse sales take place in the plaza, widows still wear black and unemployed men pass time on the street.

The Gredos range and its extension to the northwest, the Sierra de Béjar, cover 130km between the towns of Béjar and San Martín de Valdeiglesias. Lying due west of Madrid and aligned on a WNW-ESE axis, the main range has a simple linear form throwing out long ridges to north and south and one fully fledged subsidiary system, the Sierra de Tormantos, at the western end. Parallel to the latter, on the opposite side of the great fault line of the Tornavacas Pass and Jerte valley, the Sierra de Béjar extends some 30km, between the El Barco de Avila-Béjar road and the village of Hervás. It has a more complicated structure than the main range, with a short central spine fanning out at either end into a number of long but lower ridges.

ROUTES

In spite of its large size, the Sierra de Gredos has a relatively small number of well-constructed footpaths. These are concentrated in the 10km or so between the Gredos Cirque and the Los Galayos spur, where the best access combines with the most glamorous scenery and the major climbing crags. Although only a tiny proportion of the visitors to these mountains are interested in reaching the high ground, they are enough to overwhelm this small area at peak times when the crowds, noise and litter can detract from the mountain experience. Some environmental damage has been inevitable and although this larger issue remains to be addressed, it is generally easy to avoid the crowds by arriving at less popular times or by exploring the many parts of the range that are hardly visited at all.

The scarcity of walkers in all but the central area means that the footpath system is barely developed once above the tracks leading to the highest summer farmsteads. It is often a matter of struggling up steep broken ground or through unyielding expanses of chest-high broom with discontinuous runs of cairns along the way. Furthermore, because of the linear nature of the range and the distance between roadheads and the main crest, few circular daywalks are possible and I think most people would agree that the most satisfying routes here start and finish in different places. Given the limited bus services, and the complete lack of them above the main valleys, only a few of these lines can be accomplished by visitors unless they are prepared to camp high and/or endure over 10km road walks at each end. (Apart from La Plataforma and El Nogal del Barranco at peak times, hitching to and from the routes cannot be relied on as traffic is negligible.) It should also be borne in mind that if a car is left on one side of the range, the problems of linking bus services to return to it from the other are formidable.

Balancing the limitations faced by visitors with the need to give as full a picture as possible of the walking possibilities, all the well-known (but not necessarily well-used) routes in the range are at least mentioned and shown on the sketch maps. Those of them that make satisfactory daywalks, usually out and back to the same point, are described more fully. Then for those walkers keen on camping in high remote areas and undeterred by the long walk-ins and transport difficulties, the possible extensions to each daywalk are set out in the introduction to each route. These usually cross the main divide or descend to a different point on the same side. The best multi-day, cross-range lines, from the point of view of both the logistics and the quality of the walking, are included in the Gredos Traverse in Part Four.

Finally, while I have walked all the routes in the Sierra de Guadarrama, it has not been possible to do the same here. All the starts have been checked, as particularly at village level many of them are complicated. Where I have had to rely on distant observation and local guidebooks and information to complete the description of a route, they are shown as a dotted rather than dashed line on the sketch maps, intermediate times are omitted from the instructions and the overall time estimate is prefixed with "Approx".

I have divided the walking into four zones:

a. **Sierra de Béjar**
b. **Western Gredos** between the Puerto de Tornavacas and the Puerto de Peones.
c. **Central Gredos** between the Puerto de Peones and the Puerto del Pico.
d. **Eastern Gredos** between the Puerto del Pico and the Portacho de las Serradillas.

South Gredos village

CHAPTER THREE

Sierra de Béjar

TOPOGRAPHY

This small range at the western extremity of Gredos is a wedge-shaped piece of country between the roads from Avila and Salamanca, just north of where they converge on Plasencia. While its northern limit is clearly defined by the El Barco de Avila to Béjar road, the southern end falls away gradually towards Plasencia in a long low ridge. Although the general axis is NE-SW, the main watershed zigzags from the Puerto de Tornavacas through the central part of the range, almost due north to the Puerto de Solano.

The central section from Canchal Negro (2369m) in the north to La Nijarra (2214m) in the south is a simple high spine with long spurs to both sides enclosing valleys which have undergone varying amounts of glaciation. From Canchal Negro southwards as far as La Ceja (2423m), the highest point in the range, the crest is a wide bare stony upland with one undistinguished top, called El Calvitero (2405m). Just south of La Ceja, the glaciers have cut back on both sides to produce a narrower crest poised above the backwalls of corries.

The two principal tops on this section are El Torreón (2374m) and El Calvitero (2401m), after which the ridge drops away to La Nijarra. There is some disagreement in the naming of the first two summits on the various maps, which adds to the confusion of having two Calviteros on the same ridge. The disagreement is discussed in more detail in Route 1 and the Calviteros are distinguished in the descriptions by their position (N or S).

Although the Béjar slopes are cut by numerous small valleys below the tree line (about 1600m), only two have been substantially enlarged and lengthened by glaciation: the valleys of the Arroyo del Oso, below Canchal Negro, and the Arroyo Cuerpo de Hombre at the foot of El Torreón/Calvitero(S). On the east side of the range, two adjacent valleys, the Trampal below La Ceja and the Malillo below El Torreón, are classic glaciated valleys carrying tarns. South of the latter lies the circular glacial hollow of Hoyo Talamanca. The three depressions are divided by two well-defined ridges: the Cuerda de la Ceja and the narrow, serrated Cuerda de los Asperones respectively.

Height falls away rapidly both north and south of this central section

Chapel in Candelario

and the single spine subdivides into a number of long but less interesting ridges.

VILLAGE BASES

While the best walking is concentrated in a relatively small area of the range, there is no one base which is ideal for the three starting points involved. On the west side, the village of **Candelario** is the best choice. Apart from it being well placed for both walks on that side, it is outstandingly picturesque, and considering its popularity with Salamancans, relatively unspoilt. It has several hotels, restaurants, food shops and a well-run campsite. Petrol, banks and other supplies are to be found in the attractive town of **Béjar**, just 2km away in the valley bottom. This also has a large range of accommodation, being situated on a main route to Portugal. Another possibility is the very reasonable Hostal-Refuge on the road to the Plataforma El Travieso, above Candelario, a peaceful spot with good views west and, at 1640m, usually benefiting from a cooling breeze in the summer.

For the eastern approaches, **El Barco de Avila** is really the only choice. Perched above the River Tormes, next to its 15th century castle,

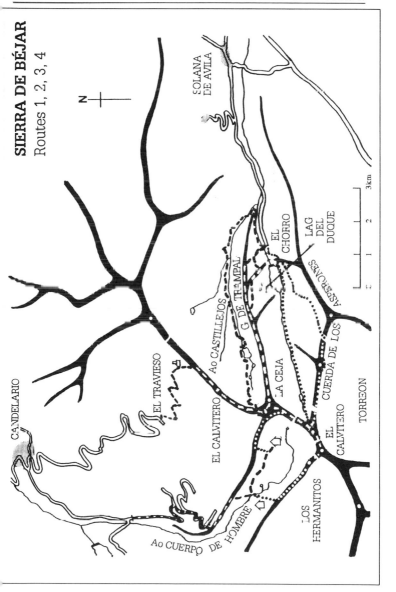

SIERRA DE BÉJAR
Routes 1, 2, 3, 4

it is an attractive town with all services and a modest hotel in the town and a more upmarket one on the Puerto de Tornavacas road. There is a campsite a few kilometres to the east, down towards the river from the C500 Tormes valley road (sign to Los Llanos).

REFUGES
There are no serviced refuges in the range but there are two shelters, used mainly by climbers, in the Cuerpo de Hombre valley on the eastern side: the **Hoya Cuevas**, a stone hut about 2^1/$_2$hrs from the roadhead and the **Cueva de Hoya Moros**, a walled-in cave under a boulder, 1^1/$_4$hrs further up the valley. The **Covatilla** hut at the north end of the range is associated with the piste skiing in the area and is probably just a bar.

ROUTES
The best walking in this range is concentrated in the central zone which has the highest summits, the most interesting ridges and the best examples of glaciated valleys. Four routes cover this easily, but if you want to spend more time in the range, other possibilities include exploring the north end of the range from the Peñalaiz roadhead, above the village of La Hoya, or the climb to Calvitero(S) from the village of Hervás, along the Pinajarro spur.

1. LA PLATAFORMA EL TRAVIESO - EL CALVITERO(N) - LA CEJA (2423m) - EL TORREON - EL CALVITERO(S) - RETURN.

Time: 6-6^1/$_2$hrs
Total ascent: 890m

This is a walk along the highest part of the ridge and back, starting at La Plataforma El Travieso (or El Quemal as it is called on the maps), the highest access point in the range. The first hour is an uninspiring slog up the wide, convex, open slopes to the crest, but the reward is icy water from a tiny fuente at the surprising height of 2300m. The springs in the range are noted for their clear cold water and there is a local saying that the waters of the Sierra de Béjar are better than the wines of Salamanca.

At first, most of the interest in walking the wide bare crest lies in the outstanding views to the east, with the deep trough of the Trampal valley cradling its string of tarns below, and the main

Gredos range spreading out beyond. After the plateau-like top of La Ceja, the ridge narrows considerably above the Malillo valley to the east and the spacious hollow of the upper Cuerpo de Hombre valley, contained by the crags of Los Hermanitos, to the west. A rocky staircase then leads up to the climax of the walk, two summits connected by a steep cleft, called "the Devil's Step" (which has a short length of fixed rope).

There is some confusion in the naming of these tops so for the purposes of this guide, El Torreón is the rocky point to the north of the cleft, where three provincial borders meet, and the other summit with the survey point is El Calvitero(S).

A good surfaced road leads from Candelario to the El Travieso Plataforma (1900m), which is a large rough terrace bulldozed out of the hillside with ample parking space. Walk back along the road a few metres and cross the fence to the right, where it has been flattened, onto a path which meanders uphill. At first it trends slightly left towards a wire fence, from where it makes a long diagonal right, partly through broom, to arrive at the **Fuente del Travieso** (*25mins*), a dribble of water and a boggy patch.

Go right on the horizontal path above it then immediately left at a fork. This path is the original one and is wide, well-graded and cairned but there are numerous shortcuts heading directly up the convex open slopes. From any of these, you should make for a tall, well-constructed cairn (called Pepeillo) standing on a small outcrop, when it comes into view higher up. The main path meanwhile finishes at the **Fuente de la Goterita** (2300m, *45mins*), which is 100m to the left of the cairn.

Take the horizontal track from the spring, which passes behind Pepeillo then ascends the last few metres to the top of the wide crest. It continues south, bypassing to the left the jumbled rocks which make up the summit of El Calvitero (N) and giving the first views into the Trampal valley. Dropping to the saddle at the head of that valley, where there are the remains of a stone shelter, the good path crossing the col is joined. Following it to the right, it winds up the northwest slopes of La Ceja. After momentarily rejoining the crest, it traverses right, some way below the summit. A well-marked branch on this section leads up to the wide plateau of La Ceja's unmarked summit (2423m, *50mins*).

Follow cairns south across the plateau to rejoin the main track as it heads for the lip of the headwall of the Malillo valley. Then a diagonal descent across slopes to the right leads onto the now much narrower crest at the point where the dramatic Agujas gully plunges to the Cuerpo de Hombre corrie. A descent to a saddle is followed by a climb up a steep rocky shoulder to a headland overlooking the same cirque. Immediately behind it is a small col which is the true head of the Malillo valley and just beyond that, the path leading to the Cuerda de los Asperones leaves to the left. Instead continue up the rocks of El Torreón until the deep cleft of the Devil's Step is reached. Descend to the gap by a steep gully to the left of the summit rocks. Although not difficult, the latter can be avoided by following cairns into the next gully but one to the left of it, then working back up to the col. A few minutes above is the summit of **El Calvitero**(S) (2401m, *45mins*) with its survey point.

2. PUENTE DE LOS AVELLANARES - FORESTRY ROAD - CUERPO DE HOMBRE VALLEY - CUEVA DE HOYA MOROS REFUGE (2100m) - BARRERA DEL CANTERON - FORESTRY ROAD - PUENTE DE LOS AVELLANARES.

Time: 8-8¹/₂hrs
Total ascent: 900m

This walk explores the isolated upper valley of the Cuerpo de Hombre River which glaciation has carved into three pronounced steps as well as producing a succession of moraines, tarns and crags. The route ends in a big corrie, a tranquil place ringed by the cliffs of Las Agujas, El Torreón, El Calvitero(S) and dominated by the spectacular pyramidal mass of Los Hermanitos, which has the best rock climbing in the area.

The walk can be extended by climbing the easy slopes to the crest of the broad spur to the north to start a traverse of the skyline above the corrie. After Los Hermanitos, continue on the crest until above the the Hoya Cuevas Refuge. This is really a two day walk with a night in one of the two shelters in the valley. The route can be shortened on some weekends when the forestry road, which is drivable as far as the T-junction, is open to cars.

The Puente de los Avellanares is on the road from Candelario to the village of La Garganta. Where the road turns sharply right to cross the bridge, go straight on (sign to Azud), to an ample space for parking in front of metal gates. Follow the forestry road, which starts at the gates, through a mixture of oak forest and meadow as far as a T-junction (*40mins*). Go right and a few minutes later, take a branch road at the outside of a left bend. After crossing a small stream the oaks give way to pine plantation and on the steeper zigzags which follow there is a last fuente. At a left-hand hairpin, climb to the open crest of a ridge, just above and parallel to the road (*50mins*).

Ascend the moderately steep and cairned crest, with the first views into the Cuerpo de Hombre valley to the right. After crossing a stile, the ridge levels off but becomes rockier and Los Hermanitos comes into view. When the ground steepens again, after passing a small meadow on the left, the cairns leave the crest to contour across a wide slope of broom into the valley on the right. In the mixture of rock and grass beyond the broom, there is a choice of cairn lines: one heading straight over the rock step barring the valley ahead, while the other continues to the stream where it pours down a large area of fractured slabs (1800m, *1hr*).

The bowl beyond is filled with wet meadows and small tarns dotted around the winding course of the river and is backed by another rock barrier. The Hoya Cuevas Refuge can be seen on a ledge up to the right. The cairns disappear, but by taking a line along the left edge of the meadows then over a small spur which cuts into the bowl from the left, the worst of the bogs are avoided. Continue across the flat meadows behind (if dry enough) and start up into the rocks using sloping ledges to the left of the course of the stream. Once the angle eases, follow the streambed along a narrow strip of meadow blocked at the top by a big moraine belt. Cairns appear leading up to the left into a long grassy corridor, divided from the main valley floor by a huge lateral moraine. At the far end, the markers descend slightly through a jumble of blocks into the wide corrie at the head of the valley and lead directly to **Cueva de Hoya Moros Refuge** (2100m, *1hr 15mins*) below a gigantic block of rock.

A trackless variation is possible on the return route by working across the slopes of the Loma de la Culebrilla to reach the broad Barrera del Canterón spur which can be followed down to rejoin the ascent route (*55mins*).

3. EL CHORRO HEP STATION - TRAMPAL VALLEY - LA CEJA (2423m) - CUERDA DE LA CEJA - EL CHORRO.

      Time: **9-9$^{1}/_{2}$hrs**
      Total ascent: **1043m**

Two long, wild, glaciated valleys cut into the eastern side of the range below the high central section of the main ridge. The Trampal valley is the more northerly and rises in a succession of chaotic rock steps, with the upper ones caught between the towering cliffs of the Cuerda de la Ceja on one side and a less steep but vast band of slabby polished rock on the other. Three tarns are cradled in successive hollows towards the head of the valley. The lowest has been dammed but the other two are perfect places to camp. Most if not all the campers reach these Lagunillas, as they are called, from the El Travieso Plataforma on the other side of the main ridge in a little over 2hrs. For this reason, there is a very good path from the tarns up to the crest, while the 3hr climb up the valley to them is virtually trackless except for sporadic cairns. Apart from the distance and the difficulty of route-finding, ascents of these two valleys are not particularly popular because a permit from the electricity company is required to park at the HEP station at El Chorro (details given below) and both valleys face east and are therefore in full sun from 08.00 in the summer.

The Cuerda de la Ceja, followed in descent from the summit plateau of La Ceja, has an asymmetrical cross-section, so there are fine views from the crest, of the Lagunillas at the foot of the steep northern crags, but the gentler, convex, slabby southern slopes deny any glimpse of the Malillo valley bottom until the Laguna del Duque appears towards the end of the walk. Nevertheless, there is a continuously fine panorama of the jagged Cuerda de los Asperones on the opposite side of the valley as well as more distant views of the Covacha group.

Permits to park at El Chorro cost at the time of writing 200pts per car per day, 500pts to stay overnight, and are on sale in the nearby village of Solana de Avila: coming from El Barco de Avila, a notice at the start of the village announces that permits are available from the Centro Cultural. This may be so, but they are more easily obtained from one of the last houses on the left of the main street. A small faded wooden sign advertising the "permisos" is attached to it. If in doubt, ask for Maruja. The fine for not having a permit is only 100% of the fee and it appears that policing is not zealous, at least during the week.

A surfaced road up the Solana valley leads to a parking area in front of the gates of the small El Chorro HEP station (1380m), positioned dramatically at the foot of a 100m rock step. Cross the streambed and

One of the Lagunillas in the Trampal Valley

follow a path on the right side of the deep channel carrying the diverted water round into the Trampal valley. Where it joins the Trampal stream, cross the small dam, then a sluice gate in the continuation of the channel, to gain the right bank (*20mins*).

A hint of a track heads upstream across often boggy ground. (It is nevertheless a better option than the good track on the opposite bank which soon disappears.) Where the stream issues from a gorge at the foot of the first small rock band, climb to the right to pick up cairns leading through the rock section into a leveller area of boggy meadow with a barn. Follow the top edge of the meadow then look for a fairly clear track through the broom behind the barn, which winds up into the next rock passage. Vestiges of paving appear briefly, but soon all traces of path are lost, replaced by occasional stone markers. As these are difficult to follow in the complicated terrain, take care in the next half hour not to be side-tracked up the Castillejos tributary, which is in a more prominent valley than the main stream. Once beyond the junction, however, the markers are clearer up a straight but narrower section of valley. Higher up the stream is crossed and shortly after the dam below the **Laguna El Trampal** (2020m, *2hrs 30mins*) is reached.

Cross the dam and follow the right bank, over slabs and screes, to a delta at the head of the lake. The streambed above leads to the next tarn but cairns which appear to the right of the bed go directly to the third and highest lake (2120m, *30mins*). Here a good path climbs into the last, meadow-filled hollow before zigzagging up the screes at the valley head to a nameless saddle on the main ridge (2325m, *30mins*). The good path continues across the col but turns left immediately to climb the northwest slopes of La Ceja. At a well-cairned fork on the upper slopes, take the left branch to go directly to the summit plateau of the mountain, continuing across the slightly rising ground to the unmarked highest point (2423m, *20mins*).

This is also the start of the Cuerda de la Ceja, which can be followed either along the crest itself with dramatic views down into the Trampal valley, or slightly to the right across the slabs and broom of the southern slopes. After a pronounced saddle (*45mins*), it is probably simpler to stay with the crest than follow a complicated line lower down on the right-hand slopes. Either way, the various alternatives converge on a grassy hollow with a barn, high above the power station. At the eastern end of the lip of the hollow, pick up a line of big cairns which descend through rock and broom, passing to the right of a plantation lower down, to reach the car park (*2hrs 30mins*).

4. EL CHORRO HEP STATION - CUERDA DE LOS ASPERONES - EL TORREON (2374m) - HOYO DE MALILLO - LAGUNA DEL DUQUE - EL CHORRO.

Time: approx. 10-11hrs
Total ascent: 994m

Above the cliffs behind the power station is the substantial reservoir of the Laguna del Duque with the Malillo valley rising in steps above it. The valley is bounded to the south by the Cuerda de los Asperones which in its upper section has a narrow, airy crest with a steep scramble from the Portilla de Talamanca to the main ridge behind Torreón. The descent of the Malillo valley appears to be trackless until the Laguna del Duque is reached.

Park in front of the power station at El Chorro (1380m) and take the track to the left of the boundary fence. This follows the main water pipe towards the cliff face then moves left to climb steep slopes to a shoulder above the reservoir. The path continues down to the lake shore, but from

Upper Vega Valley with Covacha

Laguna de Gredos in winter

Los Galayos and El Torreón

Looking down the Pelayo Valley to the Refugio A. Victory, from the main crest

Cuerda de los Asperones

the shoulder a narrower track traverses left, high on the steep slopes to end in a grassy streambed falling to the top end of the Laguna. Climb the bed to arrive in a huge expanse of sloping meadow and follow its top edge to a wide saddle (1910m) on the crest of the Cuerda de los Asperones.

The crest narrows after the Canchal del Turmal (2339m) and the succession of towers is avoided on the left side of the ridge. When the angle eases on reaching the main crest, work slightly left for the summit of Torreón (see Route 1). The true head of the Malillo valley is the small sandy col, just to the right of where the main crest was joined, and a rough descent starts there.

CHAPTER FOUR

Western Gredos

TOPOGRAPHY

The main ridge in this section stretches west to east from the Puerto de Tornavacas (1277m), which carries the Avila-Plasencia road, to the Puerto de Peones (2190m), almost due south of the village of Bohoyo. As the crow flies, the two passes are 20km apart but the ridge describes an arc to the south between the two points, making the distance on foot more than 29km.

At about a third of the way along from the western end is the highest point, Covacha (2399m), which stands at the centre of a knot of high ridges radiating both to north and south. The block of highland to the north is cut by three long glaciated valleys, each carrying a large tarn at its head: from west to east the valleys contain the Gargantas de Vega (and the Laguna del Barco), Galin Gómez (Laguna de Nava) and Caballeros (Laguna de los Caballeros).

Glaciation has produced steep crags above the three interlocking valley heads, and some narrow sections of crest, although continuous knife-edges like those of the Circo de Gredos have not developed. The principal rock features west-to-east along the highest section of the ridge are Castifrío (2307m), Las Azagayas (2343m), La Angostura (2370m), Covacha itself and La Solanilla (2365m), although they are not all named on the maps. East of Covacha on the main crest is a long series of crags called Riscos Morenos (2110m), the last rock interest until Cancho (2275m), 6km further east again. Thereafter, miles of broom is enlivened with rock only near the Puerto de Lucia (2098m) and the Casquero de Peones (2271m). Beyond them, the already broad crest spreads into a plateau at the Puerto de Peones (2190m) where the El Tormal spur leaves to the northwest, maintaining its height for nearly 5km.

To the south of the watershed, where glaciation was less pronounced, the long ridge of the Sierra de Tormantos runs southwest from a point to the west of Covacha in a slow descent to the Tiétar valley for a distance of some 30km. About a kilometre after leaving the main ridge, the huge Losar spur splits off to run due south, so enclosing the Jaranda valley above the village of Jarandilla de la Vera. This carries the only recognised route to Covacha from the south side of the Sierra de Tormantos. On the north side of the latter range, another long spur leaving westward from the Gredos watershed at Castifrío curves southwest to run parallel to the Jerte valley and thus encloses a well-hidden valley system containing a maze of multi-named streams. East of the Losar spur, several long, steep, enclosed valleys run back into the range above the La Vera villages. With so little of interest on the crest here to justify the huge vertical ascents, this must be the least known or visited area in Gredos.

VILLAGE BASES

All except one of the routes described in this sector can be reached easily from **El Barco de Avila**, which is the only village with accommodation on the north side of the area, apart from Bohoyo with its one fonda. By contrast most of the Vera villages have at least one hotel and the obvious choice to stay for the one route on the south side is **Jarandilla de la Vera** which has two hotels and a Parador. There is also a hotel above **Tornavacas**, at the head of the pretty Jerte valley. Campsites are found in Jarandilla and Aldeanueva on the south side, in the Jerte valley near the village of the same name, and near El Barco de Avila, as mentioned in the Béjar section.

Chozo (shepherd's shelter) in Gredos

REFUGES

The only documented refuge in this sector is the **Nuestra Señora de las Nieves**, which is found at the top of the Jaranda valley, 3hrs walk from Guijo de Santa Barbara from where the key can be obtained. In addition, an old shepherd's hut with an unlocked door, at the end of the made-up path in the Caballeros valley, is used as refuge (3 ^{1}/2hrs from Navalguijo).

ROUTES

The great attractions of this area are its fine glaciated scenery, its remoteness and its knot-like structure, so different from the ridge-with-lateral spurs found everywhere else in the range. The main objective is Covacha, the highest point and at the centre of the knot, but it is really out of range for a comfortable day walk if you have to return to a car. The best approaches are up the Jaranda or Caballeros valleys with an overnight camp or stay in the huts mentioned above. The other two northern valleys are not as convenient for approaching the summit but make good day walks as far as the lakes. The three western approaches, mentioned in local guidebooks, have been omitted. Two start at Puerto de Castillos and the bleak Puerto de Tornavacas respectively but both are interminable struggles up dreary slopes of dense broom and it is unlikely that they are used except in descent as part of a traverse of the area. The third is theoretically the shortest approach to Covacha but an off-road vehicle is needed to negotiate the farm tracks in the San Martín valley above the village of Tornavacas. From the highest drivable point, it is then a steep and trackless slog to the Canchal de la Angostura, a short distance west of Castifrio on the main crest.

The Jerte valley and the Vera villages are very attractive areas to visit, particularly the former in April, when its thousands of cherry trees are in blossom, but the walking possibilities on the south and west sides of the range are limited. The rambling ridges and valleys of the Sierra de Tormantos are rather too low and lack the kind of interesting summits which would bring them within the scope of this book, although one guidebook recommends a walk across the hidden valley system between Tornavacas and Jarandilla, over the Puerto de las Yeguas.

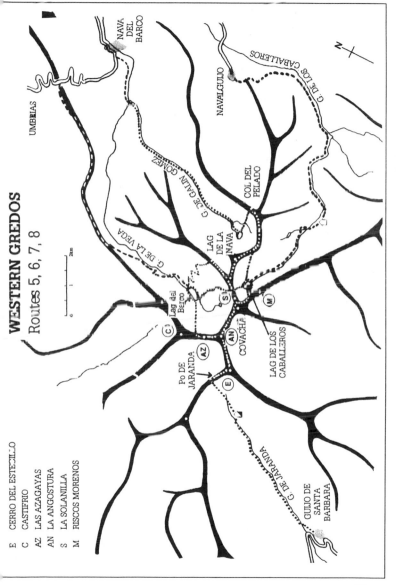

WESTERN GREDOS
Routes 5, 6, 7, 8

E   CERRO DEL ESTECILLO
C   CASTIFRIO
AZ LAS AZAGAYAS
AN LA ANGOSTURA
S   LA SOLANILLA
M   RISCOS MORENOS

5. FUENTE DE LOS HORCOS ARRIBA - CARDIEL - GARGANTA DE LA VEGA - LAGUNA DEL BARCO (1790m) - RETURN.

Time: 6½-7hrs
Total ascent: 540m

Of the three long glacial valleys on the north side of Covacha, this walk into the westernmost is the easiest, as it takes advantage of the height gained by the road linking the villages of Umbrias and Nava del Barco to start out along the continuation of the Risco del Aguila spur. However, to reach Covacha from the lake involves a steep trackless climb up the backwall of the cirque, then a ridge scramble, taking probably about 6hrs in total. There is little possibility of spreading the walk over two days as the Laguna del Barco is a reservoir and camping is not allowed anywhere in the valley. Nevertheless, the walk as far as the lake and back makes a good day out, as it is a mixture of open ridge walking and splendid rock scenery in the Vega's upper valley - all on an excellent path.

Coming from Nava del Barco, park at the highest point (1350m) on the Umbrias-Nava del Barco road at the beginning of a jeep track which leaves to the left. Follow the track round the right flank of Cabeza Redonda and along the wide level ridge beyond. The track winds through the meadows on the crest, contouring round small rises and passing through three gates to arrive at a fourth set with a Finca Privada sign (*1hr 30mins*).

Pass through the smaller gate to the left, and continue along the narrower crest then on a switchback line into the valley bottom, reaching the streambed just beyond a barn (*30mins*). The track stays on the right bank until a ford at the beginning of the upper corrie is reached (1750m, *35mins*). If the water is too high, continue along the right bank with no difficulties, apart from a few boggy areas, to the dam at the bottom end of the **Laguna del Barco** (1790m, *20mins*).

There appear to be three onward routes: a path begins behind a ruined shepherd's shelter just downstream from the dam and makes wide zigzags up the Barrera de Cuesta Mala onto the wide sloping plateau above. The second climbs the steep trackless streambed which falls from the left at the top end of the lake to reach the Portilla Honda. From there, there is a direct descent to the Laguna de los Caballeros. The third is also up a trackless streambed at the head of the lake to arrive at the main ridge

Laguna del Barco with Covacha on the left

between Castifrío and Las Azagayas The ridge can then be followed east to Covacha.

6. NAVA DEL BARCO - GARGANTA DE GALIN GOMEZ - LAGUNA DE LA NAVA (1970m) - RETURN.

Time:	approx. 8hrs
Total ascent:	820m

With substantially more ascent, the climb to the middle of the three lakes is a much harder day out than Route 5 and the Laguna de la Nava is not well placed for going on to Covacha. Nevertheless, the lake is in a fine lonely situation at the head of a stepped valley. As it is used as a reservoir, there may be restrictions on camping.

From Nava del Barco, take the Umbrias road for a short distance out of the village. Just after a stone cross on the left, a dirt road leaves on the same side. Park there, and take the rising right branch at the immediate fork, across slabby ground scattered with small oaks. After a few minutes, at a triple fork, take the middle branch leading between fincas on the

71

slopes to the right of the Galín Gómez stream. Passing a branch to the left leading down to a ford, continue to a bridge just above the junction of the streams from Lagunas del Barco and de la Nava. On the far side take the left-hand track which leads into the Nava valley, keeping to the right of the stream, through more fincas at first. In the open valley above the farms, there appears to be a continuous track through the alternations of rock bands and grassy hollows. The stream is forded about two-thirds of the way up the valley and there is a fuente in the hollow above the next step.

The easiest way to the skyline from the lake is directly to the left to reach the Collado del Pelado. From there, the crest can be followed to the right as far as the Portilla Honda, after which the cliffs of La Solanilla bar the way to Covacha but there is a rough descent right to the Laguna del Barco. If, however, you want to reach the Laguna de los Caballeros, it is quicker to leave the crest before the ascent to point 2348m for a descending traverse past the Fuente de la Hoyuela.

7. NAVALGUIJO - GARGANTA DE LOS CABALLEROS - LAGUNA DE LOS CABALLEROS - COVACHA (2399m).

Time: 5-5¹/₂hrs to the lake.
Approx. 1¹/₂hrs more to Covacha
Total ascent: 1199m

Although this is the longest of the three valleys it is the most popular walk in the area, at least as far as the lake. But popular is a relative term in this little visited area and if you decide to camp at the very beautiful and isolated Laguna de los Caballeros, you should, even in high summer, have the place to yourself as long as you go midweek. Surprisingly, the valley has much less savage rock scenery than those of Nava, Barco or the Béjar area. Apart from the Chorrera (or Chorreo) cliff, a short gorge section and the crags of Riscos Morenos, Covacha and La Solanilla at the top of the valley, it is mostly long rising passages of meadow, and with smooth skylines to either side. The path is good as far as the old shepherds' hut/refuge.

(The Caballeros (Gentlemen) were supposedly medieval knights, who were rewarded for their reconquest exploits with big tracts of "meadow and mountain country" in the area.)

As there is little space in the two or three narrow streets which make up the very rural hamlet of Navalguijo (1200m), it is best to park at the entrance to the village, where the road forks. Walk along the main street and go left at the only fork to a fuente where the houses end. A dirt road continues through fields and an oak wood (where there is rough camping) then across a stream. Just after passing a branch on the left, the track divides with the left branch cutting below a block of pines. This is the Caballeros valley track and it works across a mixture of open and wooded slopes to turn right into the entrance of a narrower, long, straight section of the valley (*30mins*).

Keep to the horizontal strand where it entangles with an old irrigation channel and ignore a branch down to the stream which is some way below. Passing above an oak wood the long meadows of Majaltero are reached and the profile of the La Chorrera cliff can be seen at the far end. However, its big main face, split by a waterfall, is not in view until the track rounds its base (*45mins*). At the junction with the Covachas stream soon after, the track works to the right with the main valley into a twisting gorge with some big scree slopes. The valley then opens up on the right-hand slopes and the path crosses more meadows before becoming temporarily lost on a slope up to a small rock band. A choice of cairn lines leads to its reappearance just below the big outcrop on the skyline. Rounding the latter to the left (*1hr 10mins*), the valley changes direction once more, now to run due west, and the peaks at its head come into view for the first time.

In this long, wide, straight section, the path soon crosses the stream to take advantage of the easier grassy terrain on the left bank, then finishes at the old shepherds' hut, now used as a refuge (*20mins*). Cairns continue in the meadows beyond as far as the base of a rock step. There is a line of cairns through the complicated ground by the stream but it is difficult to find. On better ground, and probably as quick, is a detour half right into a shallow tributary valley. You can work left from the bed on rising meadows behind the first outcrops of the step, to rejoin the main stream. Cairns then lead through the rest of the rock bar into the final long run of meadows (*35mins*).

Continue on the right bank, but if the ground is boggy enough to be a problem, look for a cairned path running across the broom slopes up to the right. At the top of the meadows a rising band of scrub and rock leads to the Laguna de los Caballeros (2080m, *40mins*) which doesn't come into view until you are a few metres from its banks.

The onward route to Covacha is up the steep slopes of loose stones to the left of the lake and there appears to be a faint zigzagging path to a wide saddle on the main ridge. The only route description I have doesn't work directly up the crest line to Covacha from there, but heads for the narrow gap between the latter and La Solanilla to the north, then climbs diagonally left up rocks to the summit.

8. GUIJO DE SANTA BARBARA - JARANDA VALLEY - PORTILLA DE JARANDA - COVACHA (2399m).

Time: approx. 6¹/₂-7hrs
Total ascent: 1499m

Although a couple of kilometres shorter than Route 7, this walk involves considerably more ascent and is partly trackless so I would be surprised if it took much less time. It can be spread over two days by using the Refugio de Nuestra Señora de las Nieves at 1700m near the head of the long Jaranda valley.

Leave the village on the dirt road at the end of the Calle del Llano, which descends to the stream and crosses to the left bank. Higher up, the road is left for a narrower track but always on the left bank. The climb to the Portilla de Jaranda, above the hut, is pathless. The ascent from there to the Cerro de Estecillo has some airy passages but the continuation north along the Cuerda Mala to La Angostura, although rocky, is not exposed.

CHAPTER FIVE

Central Gredos

TOPOGRAPHY

Central Gredos covers 38km of the main ridge between the Puerto de Peones (2190m) in the west and the Puerto del Pico road pass (1352m) in the east. The general axis is WSW-ENE, but the crest has more local changes of direction than in other parts of the range and also makes a shallow arc to the south in its western half. That half also contains the highest and most heavily glaciated area in Gredos, centred on the ridges circling the big, steep-walled corries of Cinco Lagunas and Gredos, which drain from their tarns north along the Pinar and Gredos valleys respectively. Almanzor (2592m), the highest point in Central Spain, is situated at the back of the Gredos Cirque. (The principal features of the Cirques area are shown in map and profiles on pages 85 and 89.)

To the south of the Cirques, much less intense glaciation produced a little modelling near the main crest, but the general pattern is of long spurs running south, divided by deep V shaped valleys. In the northwest, however, the normal fish spine pattern is varied where the Callejon de los Lobos/Barquillo spur, which forms the western wall of the Pinar valley, throws out two subsidiary but very long ridges to the west. These enclose the Bohoyo and Navamediano valleys, which initially run parallel to the main ridge before curving north to join the main Tormes valley.

On the east side of the Cirques area, beyond the Morazón-Los Barrerones spur, which bounds that side of the Circo de Gredos, the relief returns to the characteristic pattern for the rest of its length. The generally broad crest is interrupted by a series of outcrops, all of which present their steeper faces to the south. Of these, the most important is La Mira (2343m), a bulky headland from which the long spur of the Cuerda del Amealito, serrated in its upper section, descends south. Just to the east, across the Pelayo valley, the Galayos spur runs south from the Pelaos plateau. The western side of its upper section is a 2km wall of pinnacles, towers, buttresses and gullies, culminating in the rock bastion of Gran Galayo (2235m). Nothing on the remaining section of the main ridge rivals the scenery of the Cirques or Los Galayos, although there is a succession of rock summits, the highest of which is the elongated plateau of Peña del Mediodía (2224m). One further point of interest is that the main Duero-Tajo watershed leaves the Gredos spine at a featureless area

Hoyos del Espino

west of the Puerto de la Cabrilla and runs between the headwaters of the Tormes and Alberche to continue along the crest of the parallel ranges to the north.

VILLAGE BASES

Bearing in mind the concentration of routes starting from the high Plataforma roadhead, the obvious base on the north side is the village of **Hoyos del Espino**, at the beginning of the branch road to it. This small settlement of typical granite farmhouses has, however, only one hotel, a fonda and limited services, although there are several bars and restaurants and a tourist information office in summer. There is more choice of accommodation (two hotels and the Parador) in and around **Navarredonda**, a much more dispersed village a few kilometres to the east which also has a petrol station. (Incidentally, the Parador usually has some good value half-board, mid-week offers outside the summer season.) Further east again, at the C500's junction with the Puerto del Pico road, the Venta Rasquilla offers basic rooms and meals. Meanwhile, to the west, **Navacepeda** has one hotel and **Bohoyo** a fonda.

On the south side of the range, **Arenas de San Pedro** and **Candeleda** have the largest range of hotels and services, as would be expected from their size. They are both, however, rather functional-looking towns by Gredos standards, in spite of the restored castle and old bridge in Arenas. The only alternatives to Candeleda at the western end of the zone are Madrigal de la Vera and a hotel/restaurant on the Candeleda-El Raso road. There are three picturesque mountain villages above Arenas but, of these, only Guisando and El Arenal have accommodation (2 hotels, and 1 hotel plus 2 fondas respectively). Both are well-placed for a number of roadheads and have food shops, bars and restaurants. El Arenal has in addition a taxi service and a bank.

Without doubt, though, the best place to stay, if you want a single base from which to try routes on both sides of the range, is **Mombeltran** in the Cinco Villas (Five Towns) valley leading up to the Puerto del Pico. Its position on the good road which leads over that pass means that you can reach the furthest of the main roadheads in this sector, except those above El Raso, within not much more than an hour. As the "capital" of the valley, it has a faded elegance with a large elongated plaza, a medieval castle with an esplanade served by several bars and a restaurant, a fine gothic church and the usual warren of narrow streets. There are two hotels: a basic one on the castle esplanade and a modern, comfortable and friendly one set back from the main road at the southern edge of the village. **Cuevas del Valle**, the village just below the Puerto del Pico, is equally well-placed and picturesque but has only one small (but recommended) fonda.

The two big campsites in the Tormes valley are very urban and noisy in high season. Both are in attractive spots by the river, surrounded by pinewoods: one on the Plataforma road and the other south of Navarredonda. In addition there is a small one in San Martín del Pimpollar. On the south side of the range, another big site, Prados Abiertos (which also has a guesthouse), is found on the main road a few kilometres south of Mombeltran. The one on the loop road above Guisando is well-placed for the Nogal del Barranco roadhead, but west from there, there isn't another commercial operation until you reach Madrigal de la Vera (at the junction of the main road and the Alardos River).

REFUGES
North Side
Three shelters with unlocked or no doors and no equipment serve the long walk-ins at the western side of the zone: the **Seca** shelter near the

fuente of the same name in the Bohoyo valley is very small and at only 1300m (Route 9). The **Barranca** in the Pinar valley on the way up to Cinco Lagunas is better placed at around 1700m (Route 10). The **Novillera** hut is found in a hollow high on the slopes on the north side of Cabeza Nevada and is reached from the Garganta de Gredos above the Roncesvalles bridge.

At the head of the Laguna de Gredos is the **Refugio José Antonio Elola** (1970m, Route 11 and 12). It is advertised as open daily from June to October and weekends and holidays during the rest of the year, except 25-26th December. There are 59 places and a simple meal service operates. At other times there is access to one dormitory with blankets and cooking facilities. Its position makes it extremely popular and it is necessary to book in advance or at least ring to check if there are places prior to setting out: 920 348158 (hut) or 920 228393 (Avila office).

On the meadowy crest (1950m), to the west and just above the Plataforma, are two ICONA buildings. One is open from July to September and has dormitories and a simple bar/restaurant, the other is a permanently open shelter with water outside. These are known as **Reguero Llano** or **Prado de las Pozas** and there is a total of 120 sleeping places. A steep scrambling ascent to them up the right-hand slopes at the head of the Plataforma car park is possible, but Route 11a is a better approach with a pack. Camping is allowed, and indeed encouraged, near these last two huts.

South Side

The little visited valleys at the western end of this zone have no 'official' huts although there is a scattering of goatherds' shelters in varying degrees of ruin, which might serve in an emergency. The most westerly of the mountain refuges is the **Albarea** (950m) by the bridge across the Blanca stream, some 10km above Candeleda along a very poor unsurfaced forestry road (Route 26). Keys have to be collected from the ICONA staff in Candeleda.

At the **Nogal del Barranco** roadhead (1160m) above Guisando, there is a refuge with 14 places but no facilities. The key can be obtained from the forestry warden in Guisando. Just beside it is a bar/cafe which serves simple meals in the summer. 2^1/2hrs' walk up the same valley is the **Antonio Victory** refuge on a small platform opposite the Galayos crags. For a long time it was in a semi-ruinous state, but has now been repaired and has a warden in the summer. Even so it has only 14 places and no facilities except water piped from a nearby stream (which can dry up in late summer). It is very popular with climbers with the huge weekend overflow camping or sleeping out on the small platform around it, on tiny pockets of grass or in stone enclosures in the area round about.

ICONA have another locked hut at the Mingo Fernando roadhead (1160m, Route 32) above El Hornillo, also without any services. Next to it is a simple cafe, open in the summer holidays. A few minutes up the track, on the right, is a tiny doorless stone shelter. Yet another ICONA building, maybe locked as well and not really relevant to any walks in this area, is the **Barranca** hut (1300m). This is found in the pretty valley below the Peña del Mediodía and is reached by taking the Cebedilla fork below Mingo Fernando, then a right fork higher up. The unsurfaced road is rough in parts.

ROUTES
North Side
The walks chosen on this side fall into three categories: the first three are old-established approach routes to the Gredos Cirque/Cinco Lagunas area using long tributary valleys of the Tormes. Because of their length, they have fallen into relative disuse since the Plataforma road was surfaced. The next eight routes (11 to 17) cover the best possibilities for walkers in the area of the two big cirques, although some of them involve sustained scrambles on steep, loose terrain and along the airy crests. Within that group, the three which start from the Elola Refuge are viable as hard day walks from La Plataforma if conditions are good and you don't wish to stay in the Cirque. All of the remaining routes make for particular tops at the eastern end of the sector and are longer or shorter rambles over open moorland and crest.

9. BOHOYO - GARGANTA DE BOHOYO - HOYA DEL BELESAR (FUENTE DE SERRANOS 2220m).

Time:	**approx. 6-6$^{1}/_{2}$hrs**
Total ascent:	**1085m**

At 14km, this is the longest of the valleys leading up to the Circo/ Cinco Lagunas area and makes a long curve south then east to its head. It was well used at the beginning of the century, before the Plataforma track was constructed and the Seca shelter dates from that period. The lower part of the valley is an irrigated patchwork

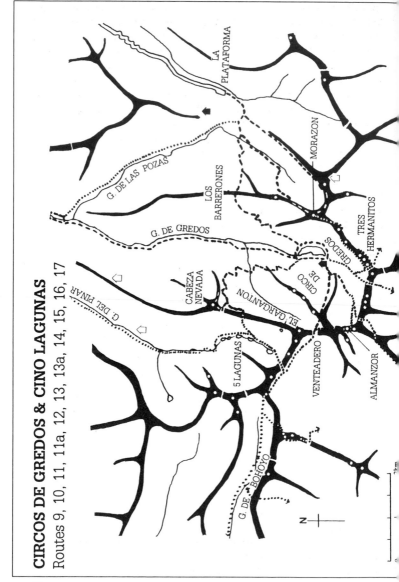

CIRCOS DE GREDOS & CINO LAGUNAS
Routes 9, 10, 11, 11a, 12, 13, 13a, 14, 15, 16, 17

LA PLATAFORMA

MORAZON

G. DE LAS POZAS

LOS BARRERONES

G. DE GREDOS

TRES HERMANITOS

CABEZA NEVADA

G. DEL PINAR

CIRCO DE GREDOS

EL GARGANTON

5 LAGUNAS

VENTEADERO

ALMANZOR

G. DE BOHOYO

N

of fields and woodland with a complicated access from the village. While there is supposed to be a clear path, or at least cairns, right into the Hoya del Belesar (the corrie at the head of the valley and a good place to camp), it is quite likely that some route-finding will be necessary through the moraine piles and rock steps of the wild upper half of the walk.

The onward journey to the Circo de Gredos is southwest to the main ridge then along the south side of the Gutre Ridge to Venteadero (reverse Route 14). In poor visibility, route-finding may be a problem in the rather featureless area before the Portilla de Cinco Lagunas is reached. Old routes down wild ravines to southern villages leave the upper part of this valley over the main watershed to the south (following the Tejea stream to El Raso and the Sauce stream or Cantaelgallo spur to Madrigal de la Vera (Routes 22 and 23). They are difficult to locate in this direction. For instance, the headwaters of the Tejea is a maze of gullies some of which lead down to vertical cliffs. All these descents involve at least 6hrs' more walking.

The most straightforward way into the valley leaves from the Bohoyo-Navamediana road, just beyond the Bohoyo stream, but it crosses a finca which displays a Prohibido la Entrada notice. The alternative is to leave the village (1140m) on the other side of the stream and cross to the better path higher up the valley: driving into Bohoyo from the C500, bear left at the small triangular Plaza de Campillo and park anywhere in the street beyond.

Continue out of the village where the surfaced road changes to a wide shady track between fields, then passes through gates to rise across open slopes. (Ignore two narrower left branches on the way.) About 50m before it reaches two stone barns, turn left on to a narrow and initially wet track between stone walls (*25mins*). This improves and widens as it progresses between fields and woodland. After about 10mins, reaching the end of a small stonewalled field to the left, the view opens out and the good farm track on the opposite slopes can be seen. Follow the field wall down to a slab across an irrigation ditch then cross rough ground, ditches, streamlets and bog to reach the bank of the main stream (*20mins*), which is at this point full of boulders and generally easy to cross. Join the wide track rising gently across the opposite slopes, leading into woods. The route stays on that side of the stream right to the head of the valley. Several fuentes are passed on the way.

10. NAVALPERAL DE TORMES - GARGANTA DEL PINAR - CIRCO DE LAS CINCO LAGUNAS (2120m).

>   Time: approx. 5hrs
>   Total ascent: 890m

The route from the main roadhead at La Plataforma to the Cinco Lagunas Cirque crosses three valleys and intervening spurs, so the small number of walkers and climbers wanting to camp by the five tarns usually prefer to carry in heavy sacks straight from the Tormes valley using this route. The obvious continuation is to the Gredos Cirque, most easily accomplished by a steep climb, on loose stones with some grass, from the left side of the second highest lake to the Portilla del Rey. From there, Route 13a can be reversed to the Laguna Grande (1^{3}/$_{4}$hrs from 2nd lake). A longer and harder way round is to climb to the Portilla de las Cinco Lagunas then reverse Route 14 over Venteadero then down to the Elola Hut.

At the western end of Navalperal, turn off the C500 into the narrow main street and follow it right through the village and down to a bridge across the Tormes. There is parking on both sides. Cross the bridge and follow the farm track rising to the right which rounds a low shoulder then forks, with the right branch leading down to the bridge across the Garganta de Gredos. On the far bank, working through fincas and woodland, the track leads upstream to the entrance to the Pinar valley where there is a bridge across the stream. Beyond it, leave the path continuing up the Gredos valley to branch right, following the left side of the Pinar stream.

11. LA PLATAFORMA - LOS BARRERONES (2160m) - LAGUNA GRANDE - GARGANTA DE GREDOS - NAVALPERAL DE TORMES.

>   Time: 7^{1}/$_{2}$-8hrs
>   Total ascent: 390m

In spite of the constantly changing terrain and fine mountain scenery in the higher part, it is unlikely that anyone would choose to do the 5-6hr walk up the Gredos valley from Navalperal to the Circo de Gredos, when the latter is only an easy 2hrs from La Plataforma. Instead, this route descends the valley and is feasible

for the visitor, in spite of different start and finishing points (taxi from Hoyos del Espino and afternoon bus (about 15.00) back to Hoyos from Navalperal). The route starts on the most popular track in Gredos, leading into the Gredos Cirque (more details in Route 12), then crosses the Garganta de Gredos at its outlet from the Laguna Grande to start the descent of the valley. When the vast accumulations of snow in the Cirque are melting in May and June, the water level at the outlet can be too high to cross and it may be necessary to walk right round the lake, adding 35mins to the time.

The Plataforma roadhead (1770m) is a long narrow car park squeezed alongside the Prao Puerto stream between steep rocky slopes. In summer, there is a kiosk selling cold drinks. At the top end, a wide cobbled track winds up the narrow valley to the right of the stream. Where the stone surface finishes, leave on an eroded multi-stranded path to the right which shortcuts across a big loop in the original track. It then continues across an almost level area of grass, bearing slightly left, to reach a cement bridge across the **Pozas stream** (_30mins_).

Multiple tracks lead over the Barrerones spur (good fuente to left just before the path reaches the crest, but buried under snowbanks to the end of June), to descend diagonally left on the well-constructed path into the Cirque. On the slopes just above the northern end of the **Laguna Grande** (1960m, _1hr 30mins_) a wide track leaves to the right which leads to a ford across the Garganta de Gredos just below where it issues from the lake. Cross and continue to a grassy area, just before a well-marked junction of routes and leave to the right, connecting up grassy terraces between the outcrops but maintaining height for a while although to the right the stream drops away steeply. Reaching a shallow subsidiary streambed, follow its alternating grass and boulder-strewn course down to the main stream where there is a trace of a path, then cairns, descending through outcrops, always to the left of the main channel.

After this initial drop, level boggy sections alternate with rocky passages, marked by sporadic cairns until the features of glaciation end above the junction with the Pozas stream. Just below that point, the **Roncesvalles Bridge** (1490m, _2hrs 30mins_) is reached. Paths continue on both sides of the river, neither of them very clear and often through thick vegetation, until the field systems of the lower valley are reached. The track on the right bank is said to be the better of the two and for its last couple of kilometres, widens into a farm lane which leads over a small shoulder to descend right, to the bridge across the Tormes (1220m, _1hr_

Circo de Gredos from Los Barrerones

40mins), just below Navalperal.

11a. LA PLATAFORMA - GARGANTA DE LAS POZAS - RONCESVALLES BRIDGE - GARGANTA DE GREDOS - LAGUNA GRANDE - LOS BARRERONES - LA PLATAFORMA.

> Time: approx. 8hrs
> Total ascent: 900m

Although not everyone relishes starting a walk with a 460m loss of height, this route is one of the few circulars possible in the area and has the merit of passing through continuously spectacular glaciated scenery.

Follow Route 11 as far as the returning loop of the main path which to the right crosses meadows to the Prado de las Pozas Refuge (1950m). Before reaching the latter, leave the path diagonally left to drop into the Pozas valley following the right bank of the stream down to its junction with the Garganta de Gredos and the **Roncesvalles Bridge** (1490m, *2hrs*).

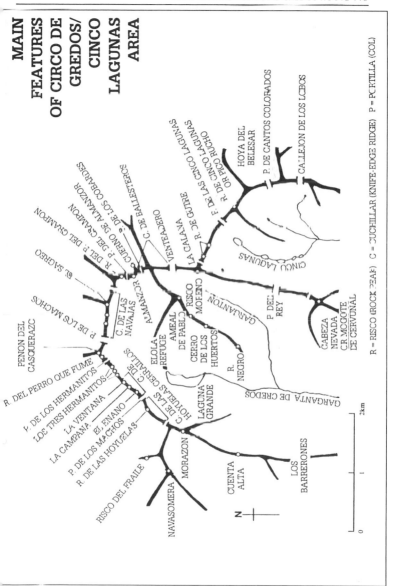

MAIN FEATURES OF CIRCO DE GREDOS/ CINCO LAGUNAS AREA

R = RISCO (ROCK PEAK) C = CUCHILLAR (KNIFE-EDGE RIDGE) P = PORTILLA (COL)

P. DE CANTOS COLORADOS
HOYA DEL BELESAR
CALLEJON DE LOS LOBOS
F. DE LAS CINCO LAGUNAS
R. OR PICO RUCHO
LA CALAVA
R. DE GUTRE
C. DE BALLESTEROS
VENTEADERO
CUERNO DE LOS COBARDES
R. DEL P. DEL CRAMPON
R. DEL P. DEL CRAMPON
EL SACREO
C. DE LAS NAVAJAS
ALMANZOR
RISCO MOFENO
GARGANTON
P. DEL REY
CINCO LAGUNAS
CABEZA NEVADA
CR MOGOTE DE CERVUNAL
PENON DEL CASQUERAZO
P. DE LOS MACHOS
AMEAL DE PABLO
CERRO DE LOS HUERTOS
R. NEGRO
ELOLA REFUGE
R. DEL PERRO QUE FUME
P. DE LOS HERMANITOS
LOS TRES HERMANITOS
LA VENTANA
LA CAMPANA
P. DE LOS MACHOS
R. DE LAS HOYUELAS
C. DE HOYUELAS CERRALLOS
C. DE LAS CERRALLOS
EL ENANO
LAGUNA GRANDE
GARGANTA DE GREDOS
RISCO DEL FRAILE
NAVASOMERA
MORAZON
CUENTA ALTA
LOS BARRERONES

N

2km

1

0

Cross the bridge and climb a small boggy bank to pick up a bit of a track leading upvalley. This becomes lost in an old field system higher up then re-emerges in a passage of broom before finally disappearing for good. Occasional runs of cairns lead through rock passages alternating with flat boggy meadows. When a good track is joined just below the **Laguna Grande** (1960m, *approx. 3hrs*) reverse the beginning of Route 11 to the **Plataforma** (*1hr 50mins*).

12. LA PLATAFORMA - LOS BARRERONES - LAGUNA GRANDE - ELOLA REFUGE (1970m) - RETURN.

Time: 5¹/₂-6hrs
Total ascent: 600m

This is by far the most popular walk in the whole of the sierra and it is probably true to say that this path, together with the one from El Nogal del Barranco to the Victory Refuge, carry more people than all the rest of the routes in the range put together. Not only is it the direct way to most of the good walking and climbing around the Cirque but its length is often littered with picnicking families. Needless to say this pressure has led to path erosion, the worst of which has been well repaired on the slopes down to the lake. The route crosses a low spur which divides the Plataforma from the Pozas valley, then a much larger one, called Los Barrerones, from where a spectacular view of the west wall of the Cirque suddenly appears.

In spite of the track being such a motorway, it needs to be treated with respect outside the summer months: crampons are often needed to cross Los Barrerones in winter and the east side of the lake is in the path of avalanches from the spectacular Morazón gullies above. Likewise in the spring/early summer thaw, parts of the path flood as the lake rises and a fixed rope leads across ledges above the water level. In the same season, both the Gredos stream and the one draining into the top of the lake, just to the east of the refuge, can be difficult to cross. Although the majority of people go no further than the hut, it is the start for Routes 14, 15 and 16 as well as more technical scrambles/easy rock climbs to Peñon del Casquerazo, Cuchillar de Las Navajas, Ameal de Pablo and La Galana.

From the Plataforma car park, follow Route 11 to the junction above the **Laguna Grande** (*2hrs*). Go left through the rocks along the left bank, then across the meadows and a stream at the head of the lake to the **Elola Refuge** (1970m, *20mins*). The return route can be varied by taking the path along the other bank of the lake, turning right at a T-junction (big cairns) at its northern end, to cross the outfall stream and rejoin the Los Barrerones path (*20mins*).

13. LA PLATAFORMA - LOS BARRERONES - LAGUNA DE GREDOS - GARGANTON - PORTILLA DEL REY (2374m) - RETURN.

Time: 8¹/₂-9hrs
Total ascent: 1464m

The Portilla del Rey is a col in the Galana-Cabeza Nevada ridge which divides the steep rocky Gargantón valley, just to the west of the Gredos Cirque, from the Circo de Cinco Lagunas. While obviously not arriving at a summit, it is quite a popular day walk because of the good path and views from the col, although the five tarns themselves cannot be seen from that point. The route partly follows the remains of the Trocha Real, a stone-surfaced path built at the beginning of the century for royal hunting parties, which starts above Candeleda on the south side of the range (see Route 27).

As can be seen from the time and total ascent, this is quite a hard day out. Apart from the sub-500m climb from the Gargantón stream to the Portilla, it involves the crossing in both directions of two intervening valleys and substantial spurs. If you arrange to be dropped at La Plataforma and picked up in Navalperal, you can follow a quite popular option, which is to scramble steeply down from the Portilla to the lakes then reverse Route 10 down the Pinar valley.

From La Plataforma car park, follow Route 11 as far as the junction at the northern end of the **Laguna Grande** (1960m, *2hrs*). Go right to ford the Gredos stream just below the lake and to meet the west bank path from the Elola Refuge at a T-junction. Follow the cairns right, at first rising gently then in zigzags on steeper ground, to cross a spur coming down from Risco Negro, from where they descend to the **Gargantón stream**

(1880m, *55mins*).

The path zigzags up the opposite slopes on the southeast side of Cabeza Nevada but eventually straightens out below the lowest crags of that summit and heads left across a small hollow some way below a double col. The latter presents an alternative way over to Cinco Lagunas, but the Trocha Real continues on a wide terrace rising through broken rock to round the base of a crag and climb steeply to the **Portilla del Rey** (2374m, *50mins*).

13a. LA PLATAFORMA - LOS BARRERONES - LAGUNA DE GREDOS - GARGANTON VALLEY - CABEZA NEVADA (2433m) - RETURN.

Time: 9-9¹/₂hrs
Total ascent: 1543m

This route is virtually identical to the preceding one except that the objective in this case is the bulky summit of Cabeza Nevada, on the same ridge and to the north of the Portilla del Rey. The fine viewpoint it affords of the whole area is worth the extra metres of ascent.

Follow Route 13a all the way to the end of the zigzags up the southeast slopes of Cabeza Nevada where the base of the summit outcrops are met. Work right below these up on to the broad east shoulder of the mountain. Climb it on easy ground to the wide summit (*1hr 10mins* from Garganton stream). An alternative return to the Trocha Real is to scramble down the rocky south ridge, keeping to the right side to avoid difficulties, until the double col, noted in Route 13a, is reached. The second, more southerly of them has the easier descent to rejoin the Trocha Real, although both are steep (*30mins*).

14. ELOLA HUT - VENTEADERO (2518m) - (FOR THE GUTRE RIDGE).

Time: 2-2¹/₂hrs
Total ascent: 548m

The wide saddle of Venteadero is a lower section of the main crest to the north of Almanzor, between the spiky towers of the Cuchillar

THE CIRCO DE GREDOS SKYLINE

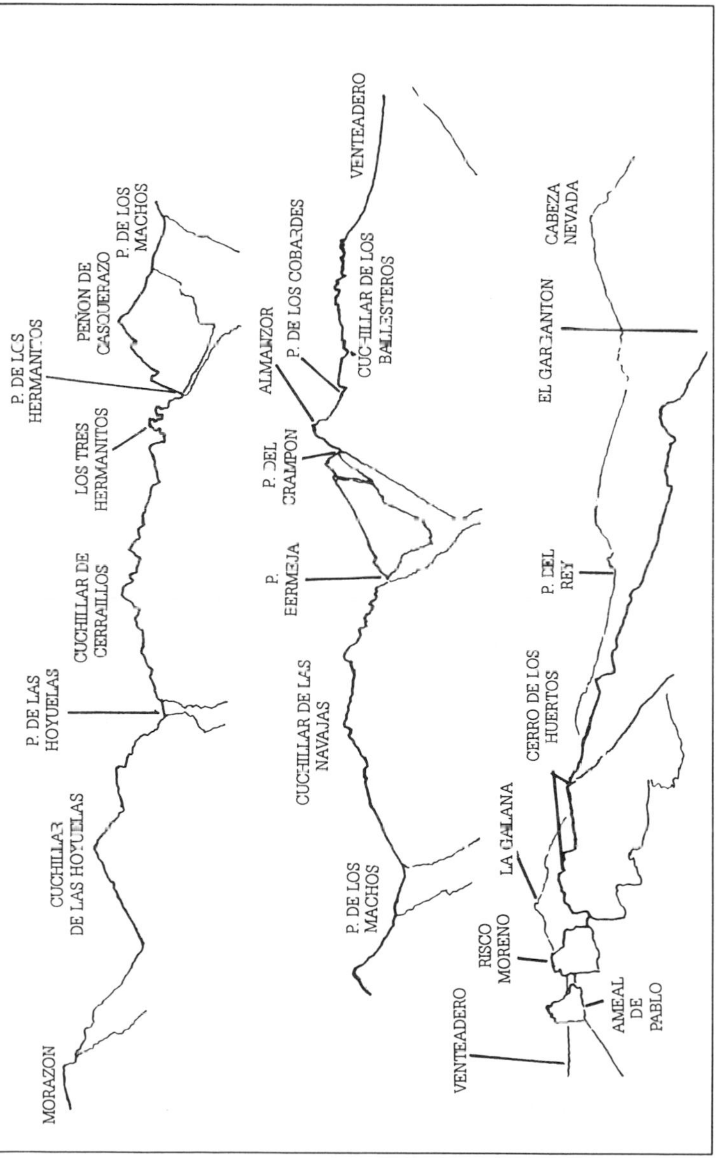

MORAZON

CUCHILLAR DE LAS HOYUELAS

P. DE LAS HOYUELAS

CUCHILLAR DE CERRAILLOS

LOS TRES HERMANITOS

P. DE LOS HERMANITOS

PEÑON DE CASQUERAZO

P. DE LOS MACHOS

VENTEADERO

ALMANZOR

P. DE LOS COBARDES

CUCHILLAR DE LOS BALLESTEROS

CABEZA NEVADA

P. DEL CRAMPON

P. BERMEJA

EL GARGANTON

CUCHILLAR DE LAS NAVAJAS

P. DEL REY

CERRO DE LOS HUERTOS

P. DE LOS MACHOS

LA GALANA

RISCO MORENO

AMEAL DE PABLO

VENTEADERO

de los Ballesteros and the pyramid of La Galana. The direct route from the Elola hut, after an initially messy start in the slab banks behind it, follows a well-marked line on firm ground up the steep valley below the Risco Moreno towers and across the spur thrown out into the Cirque by Ameal de Pablo. (If preferred, a trackless but less steep line climbs the spur on its other flank by linking up terraces.) The corridor below the south side of the Ameal de Pablo tower still had substantial sloping slabs of hard packed snow in mid-July.

The Gutre Ridge forms the back wall of the Cinco Lagunas Cirque and presents an impressive line of cliffs on its northeast face above the corrie. However, the three tops which make up the ridge can be reached with less difficulty from the gentler-angled southwest slopes. From Venteadero, a track traverses out on that side of the ridge then continues beyond it to descend west into the Hoya del Belesar at the head of the Bohoyo valley (Route 9) which is the line taken by the High Level Ski Traverse from the Gredos Cirque.

Alternatively, a loose steep descent to the Cinco Lagunas from the Portilla of the same name at the northwest end of the Gutre Ridge links in with Route 10 which can be reversed to Navalperal. If, however, you are staying in the Gredos Cirque, a 7hr round is possible by scrambling up to the Portilla del Rey from the right bank of the second highest lake and reversing Route 13a to the Laguna Grande.

Just above the hut terrace (1970m) is a signpost to Venteadero vaguely pointing left into a complicated terrain of rising slabs and terraces, made worse by competing strings of cairns threading through them. Connect these up to make a line which climbs the slope but works diagonally left into a big area of meadow at the foot of a valley enclosed by the Risco Moreno towers to the right and the long rocky spur from Ameal de Pablo to the left. Make for the back of the meadow where the stream issues from a small ravine (*20mins*).

Cairns lead straight into its bed then climb out to the right onto a rising mixture of rock and grass on the wide valley floor. At the top, follow cairns left across the streambed and up the debris on the left side of a long steep grass gully. Higher up, after a short section up the grass itself, look for cairns leaving left which lead to a short scramble then a grassy rake rising right to rejoin the main gully near the top. The gully line continues as a corridor at a considerably easier angle, with cliffs to the right and less continuous outcrops to the left. Climbing over debris from the cliffs, a small col is reached (*1hr*).

The cairn line continues in the same direction below Ameal de Pablo then crosses the hollow at the head of the Garganton valley. Stone slopes lead up to the level section of skyline which is **Venteadero** (2518m, *10mins*).

15. ELOLA HUT - PORTILLA DEL CRAMPON - ALMANZOR (2592m) - PORTILLA DE LOS COBARDES - ELOLA HUT.

Time:	approx. 4¹/₂-5hrs
Total ascent:	622m

Almanzor is the highest point in the Sierra de Gredos and indeed in Central Spain and this is the normal traverse. The 500m scramble up to the Portilla del Crampon is very steep in its upper part (50-55°) and snow can linger in the gully until late July. Earlier in the season, the slabs above the gap may still be ice-covered. The descent via the Cobardes col is less steep but also holds snow. In other words, before high summer this can be a serious climb needing full equipment.

From the Elola hut (1970m) various cairn lines lead through the slabs and grass at various distances to the right of the main streambed. Whichever you take, the object is to reach the end of the big rocky spur descending left from Ameal de Pablo. After rounding it to enter the deep hollow called Hoya Anton, the cairns take to the wide bouldery streambed for a while then move onto the left bank, working round to the left and the foot of the long stony gully leading up to the Portilla Bermeja (*30mins*). Ascend the channel on bits of track to reach a debris slope rising steeply right towards Almanzor. At the top go left into the gully above and where it splits stay left for the final very steep climb to the **Portilla del Crampon** (2550m, *1hr 30mins*). Climb round on the left to the upper gap then work left over slabs, rising slightly to reach the steep summit rocks. Link up gullies with good holds to reach the iron cross (2592m, *25mins*).

Returning to the slabs below the steep summit, work down and round to the right until the crest is regained at the top of the Portilla de Cobardes. Descend the loose 20m gully then rubble slopes below, working left to contour below the Ballesteros ridge on rough slopes and round to the saddle below Ameal de Pablo, where Route 14 is joined and reversed to the Elola Refuge (approx. 2hrs).

16. ELOLA HUT - PORTILLA DE LOS HERMANITOS - LOS TRES HERMANITOS - CUCHILLAR DE CERRAILLOS - CUCHILLAR DE LAS HOYUELAS - MORAZON (2393m) - LOS BARRERONES - ELOLA HUT.

>
> Time: approx. 6-7hrs
> Total ascent: 443m

This scramble takes to the Cirque crest next to the three rock towers of Los Tres Hermanitos (three little brothers), then follows airy terraces on either side of a succession of towers to reach the bulky headland and wonderful viewpoint of Morazón, the last summit on the east side of the Cirque before the crest drops away north along the Los Barrerones spur. As this spur can be followed down to join the main Plataforma-Cirque track, a longer circle can be made starting and finishing at the roadhead. As with all the other routes around the backwall of the Cirque, snow lies late in the gullies and on the terraces.

Cross the stream immediately to the east of the hut and follow its left bank up into some slabs. Just above this section, climb grassy slopes to the left which lead to the foot of the wide stony gully below the Portilla de los Machos. Ascend on loose stones on the left-hand side and to the left of a big outcrop in the centre of the channel. Halfway up beside this, a small track leads up a rising terrace to the left then up a gully to the col (2306m, *1hr 15mins*).

Los Tres Hermanitos can be bypassed on steep rough terraces on either side of the ridge, while the subsequent and much longer run of towers, the Cuchillar de Cerraillos, is avoided on the Cirque side. From the Portilla de las Hoyuelas, an airy scramble can be taken along the crest of the Cuchillar de las Hoyuelas (or it can be avoided on the right this time), to a small saddle below the broken slopes leading up to **Morazón** (2393m, *approx. 1hr 30mins*).

Continue in the same direction, down the summit ridge following cairns which, at a steeper section, drop from the crest to run down a parallel corridor just to the right. They return to the crest at a small col (*25mins*) where a track leaves down rough slopes on the left side to join

Los Tres Hermanitos, Circo de Gredos

Route 11 above the Laguna Grande. It is easier, however, to continue down the crest to meet that route at Los Barrerones.

17. LA PLATAFORMA - NAVASOMERA - MORAZON (2393m) - POZAS VALLEY - LA PLATAFORMA.

     Time: **5-5½hrs**
     Total ascent: 613m

Morazón's sensational views along the crenelated ridge backing the Cirque, sweeping round to Almanzor and the Ameal de Pablo-Risco Moreno spur, can be enjoyed without the exposed ridge scramble of Route 16, as the direct approach from La Plataforma is the easiest and shortest walk in the area to a main summit. The mostly trackless return route down the beautiful upper Pozas valley makes this a very varied and, for once, circular walk.

Follow Route 11 as far as the level area of grass, just before the Pozas bridge, then head to the left up the broad spur, initially trackless. As the first top is approached, a cairned path emerges which contours below and to the right of the rocks. Where the grass gives way to low, dense broom, take the left branch at a fork which leads straight to the main ridge path (*1hr 10mins*). Go right on it towards the broad bulk of Navasomera. (Water can be found at the nearby ruined Refugio del Rey.) Then take the left fork where the cairns split, to cross Navasomera just to the north of its summit. Dropping to a wide, flat saddle (2279m, *20mins*), head towards the Morazón ridge which lies beyond, with its axis at right-angles to the saddle and the summit at the left-hand end of the sloping skyline. There are a couple of cairned routes up to the ridge although it is difficult to identify where they start in the chaos of broken rock on these eastern slopes. Both lines run along grassy channels in their upper section, one almost directly ahead and the other well to the right (thereby reaching the ridge at a much lower point). Once on the ridge, continue to the left over a series of rock outcrops to the summit of **Morazón** (2393m, *45mins*).

From the summit, follow Route 16 as far as the col (*25mins*) where a track leaves left down to the Cirque. Instead, take a track to the right which descends into another rake and stay in it when it crosses another clear path (Trocha Real) coming from the crest to the left and heading into the upper corrie of the Pozas valley. When the corridor becomes a streambed which turns sharply right downhill, leave it to continue straight on, over a few rocks, into the next depression. Follow this steeply down to reach the Pozas stream just below a huge rock step (*30mins*). There is no track down the valley but the terrain is a pleasant mixture of meadow, outcrops and pools. Join Route 11 near the cement bridge and reverse it to **La Plataforma** (*1hr 5mins*).

18. LA PLATAFORMA - PUERTO DE CANDELEDA - LOS CAMPANARIOS - RISCO PELUCA - MOLEDERAS - LA MIRA (2343m) - LOS CAMPANARIOS - UMBRAZO SPUR - LA PLATAFORMA.

Time:	7$^{1}/_{2}$-8hrs
Total ascent:	693m

Following a fine section of the main crest, this is one of the best day walks in the range. It is, however, high and exposed and the two traverses across northern slopes plus the final climb to La Mira can still be snow-covered into June. Approached from the pretty

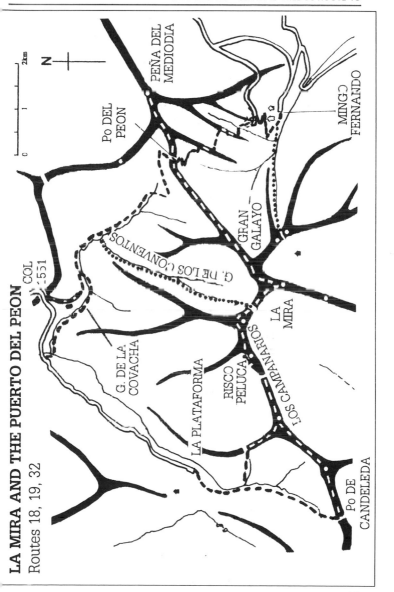

LA MIRA AND THE PUERTO DEL PEON
Routes 18, 19, 32

N 2km

PEÑA DEL MEDIODIA

MING FERNANDO

Po DEL PEON

GRAN GALAYO

G. DE LOS CONVENTOS

COL 551

LA MIRA

G. DE LA COVACHA

LA PLATAFORMA

RISCO PELUCA

LOS CAMPANARIOS

Po DE CANDELEDA

meadows of the upper Prao Puerto valley, the ridge itself is full of variety and has constantly striking views both of distant peaks and plains as well as into deep ravines to the south. La Mira is a striking headland poised above the Pelayo valley, although only the upper part of the Galayos towers can be seen from the summit which carries the circular stone base of an old observatory. The return route is varied slightly by leaving the ridge after Los Campanarios for a more direct line to La Plataforma. Using this variation would obviously save time on the way out, but it means exchanging some spectacular ridge walking for a long tramp up broom slopes.

As for Route 11, follow the cobbled path from the head of the Plataforma car park (1770m), but leave it to stay with the river bank at a signpost for the Puerto de Candeleda. First dipping across a small tributary stream then climbing through a rocky zone, the path continues into the long, gently rising, grassy upper valley of the Prao Puerto. Keep to the right of the stream which is boggy in parts and has several lines of cairns. In the shallow, bowl-shaped head of the valley, make directly up the back slope to a large marker cairn which is at the **Puerto de Candeleda** (2018m, *1hr 10mins*).

The ridge to the east starts as a broom-covered switchback but there is a cairned path which much of the time follows the steep drop above ravines running down to the Garganta Lóbrega. From the 2022m col (*35mins*), wider broom slopes leading up the Prado de Barbellido to the beginning of Los Campanarios have several lines of cairns but those nearest the crest are the least vegetated. From the start of Los Campanarios, there is more rock and less broom with a very clear path which keeps to the crest except for two well-constructed traverses round the north side of the towers of Risco Peluca and Molederas. Arriving at the 2209m col (*1hr 40mins*) at the foot of the triangular north slope of La Mira, cairns go off in various directions. Take the ones heading straight up the right-hand side of the slope which pass over a minor top just before reaching the stone observatory base and survey point on the summit (2343m, *25mins*).

Return along the ridge as far as the westernmost high point of **Los Campanarios** (2166m, *1hr 30mins*). Beyond it, the main ridge turns abruptly to the left down the Prado de Barbellido. Instead, move slightly right, away from the crest, onto a path with occasional cairns and red and white paint marks. These lead down the long, wide Umbrazo spur which is covered in dense but short broom. Reaching a saddle just below

Looking east from the summit of San Benito

Looking west from the summit of La Machota Chica

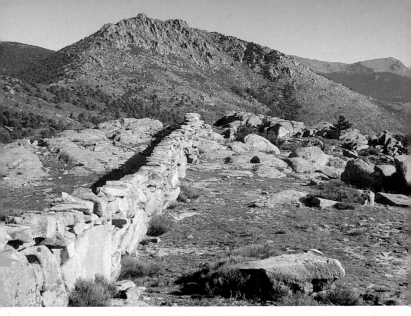

South face of la Peñota
Séptimo Pico in winter

Summit of La Mira

2000m, the cairns lead left into a shallow valley. When they finish at the lower edge of the broom, continue down grass slopes, keeping well to the right of the stream to avoid the worst of the bogs. When the Prao Puerto stream is reached (*40mins*), cross where you can to rejoin the cairns coming up from the **Plataforma** (*30mins*).

19. LA PLATAFORMA ROAD (COL 1551m) - GARGANTA DE LA COVACHA - PUERTO DEL PEON - PEÑA DEL MEDIODIA (2224m) OR LA MIRA (2343m) - RETURN.

Time: 6-6¹/₂hrs or 7-7¹/₂hrs
Total ascent: 744m or 863m respectively

The wedge of land between the Plataforma and Puerto del Pico road offers some of the easiest approaches to the main ridge, but also some of the least interesting with an alternation of broad spurs and open treeless valleys (although the the main valley between Hoyos del Espino and the Parador is completely forested with pines). This is a straightforward and relatively short walk up

97

one of the valleys, joining the main ridge at the Puerto del Peón, from where two summits are within range: Peña del Mediodía is nearer but La Mira the more interesting. If the latter is chosen, a trackless alternative approach is to climb the Conventos tributary valley, joining Route 18 at the shallow 2209m saddle at the foot of La Mira's north slope.

Although all maps and guidebooks show this well-established route starting at the 1551m col on the Plataforma road, the first part crosses a finca with a Prohibido el Paso sign. There is no obvious alternative path from the bridge at the confluence of the Covacha and Prao Puerto streams, 1500m further on, but any attempt to start there would have to cross the Prao Puerto and follow the right bank of the Covacha to begin with.

Park in a layby where the road crosses the col and go through the metal gates on the left on to the surfaced finca road. This crosses a slope, past farm buildings, and drops to the Covacha streambed. Follow the stream up on its left bank passing the junction with the Conventos stream and, higher up, another with an unnamed tributary. Above there, the bed is crossed and a big swing to the left, then right, up the steep broom slopes, leads to the **Puerto del Peón** (2035m, *2hrs*). Follow the ridge left for **Peña del Mediodía** (2224m, *45mins*) or right for **La Mira** (2343m, *1hr 15mins*).

20. km43.9 ON THE C500 (JUST EAST OF THE PARADOR DE GREDOS) - PUERTO DE LA CABRILLA - PEÑA DEL MEDIODIA (2224m) - RETURN.

Time: 7¹/₂-8hrs
Total ascent: 859m

This is an open moorland tramp and an easy way to reach the main ridge, but again has no particular merit except its open views and gentle gradients for most of the way. The first short section is on an old drove road, then the Alberche/Tagus - Tormes/Douro watershed is followed for much of the way to the Peña del Mediodía. See Route 33 for onward details to the village of El Arenal from the Puerto de la Cabrilla and Route 20a for its incorporation in a circuit from the River Tormes.

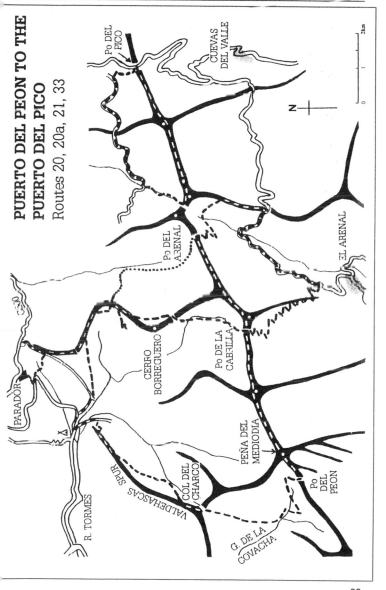

PUERTO DEL PEON TO THE
PUERTO DEL PICO
Routes 20, 20a, 21, 33

Travelling east from the Parador, park on the bare patch of land above a rubble tip (1570m), which is on the right, just before the km44 sign. A dirt road curves below and to the left of the tip then passes between two blocks of plantation. Take the right branch at a triple fork, to follow the edge of the right-hand block, then go left at the next fork, across a cattle grid.

(Walkers starting at the Parador can reach this point by cutting through the woods below the hotel - a path begins below the terraced garden and descends to a well-made forestry road. Follow the latter left but leave it at the outside of a wide bend to the right. Tyre tracks, then later a good wide track, lead across a meadow and a stream to climb the opposite slopes, arriving at a gate leading out of the plantation and opposite the cattle grid.)

After descending briefly through a young plantation, the wide track keeps to the broad open crest of the low watershed until it reaches the lip of a wide grassy hollow which contains the Fuente de Navapalenciana, the source of the River Tormes (1597m, *30mins*). Circling the back of the depression and passing through a makeshift gate with a Prohibido el Paso sign, the track turns left to reach a T-junction. Straight ahead is the path to the Puerto de Arenal. Instead take the one to the right which starts to climb a slope and, after a left fork, continues gently up and across the eastern side of the Cerro de Borreguero.

While crossing a small saddle (1819m, *50mins*), the track drops slightly then turns left up the spur again. Leave it there to follow tyre tracks from the outside of the bend, which head across boggy meadow then move left through broom to reach the left bank of the Cabrilla stream. A little higher up, cross the stream with the tracks but where they turn away continue following the right bank. The stream makes a long curve to the right and when the source is reached, the partly broom-choked dry bed is followed the short distance to the **Puerto de la Cabrilla** (1950m, *50mins*). To the right, occasional cairns in the broom mark the rough path along the ridge to the survey point on **Peña del Mediodía** (2224m, *1hr 20mins*).

20a. RIVER TORMES - COLLADO DEL CHARCO - GARGANTA DE COVACHA - PUERTO DEL PEON - PEÑA DEL MEDIODIA (2224m) - PUERTO DE LA CABRILLA - RIVER TORMES.

Time:	8^1/$_2$-9hrs
Total ascent:	846m

This is a long circle which makes use of the surfaced lane running down to the River Tormes from Navarredonda to reach a starting point at the end of the Valdehascas spur. All maps show a clear track running up the crest of this ridge to the Collado del Charco but the lower third has been given over to forestry for some years, so the most viable line is now on its southeast slopes, following the existing forestry roads. Above the tree line, the way is trackless but for once in Gredos there is no real struggle with the vegetation and the gradient is always easy. A vague track works round from the Collado del Charco to the Covacha valley bed, crossing meadows which are boggy for much of the year. The rest of the route is cairned or has good tracks except for one short section below the Tormes source.

Coming from the Parador, turn left at a Camping sign just before the petrol station in Navarredonda, into a narrow surfaced lane which heads south towards the Tormes. After passing the big campsite, turn left at a T-junction in the wooded valley bottom, then right at a fork to cross two bridges. Park anywhere beside the road in open woodland about 100m after the second bridge (1480m).

Take the wide forestry track which climbs into the trees to the right of the surfaced road (white 7 on a tree). In a couple of minutes take a left fork and some time later another one, just after climbing a wall where the road is fenced across. This leads to a T-junction below a field. Go left again, later passing a branch to the right, to where the track ends in the upper part of the **Garganta de la Cañada de los Pastores** (*45mins*). With meadows to the left and plantation to the right, continue alongside a stone wall then cross a barbed wire fence and continue through scattered broom to the spur crest, keeping more or less parallel with the stream on the left. Once on the broad crest, work slightly right for the easiest ground. At the head of the stream, cross a fence at a pile of stones to join a farm track running parallel is joined, which to the right leads to the **Collado del Charco** (1782m, *55mins*).

In the shallow grassy valley, just beyond the Reserva Nacional sign, is a stone-built but often dry fuente. A little further down, an indistinct path emerges which moves to the left of the stream and picks its way along the upper edge of large boggy meadows. Working round to the left it arrives at the Covacha streambed just at the confluence of the stream and its upper tributary descending from the right (1700m, *45mins*). From there, follow Route 19 to the **Peña del Mediodia** (2224m, *1hr 30mins*), then reverse Route 20 to Point 1597m to the north of the hollow containing the Tormes' source (*2hrs 30mins*). Instead of turning north with the track, continue west over a slight rise with no path, heading for the point where the plantation on the right-hand slopes meets the river bed. From there, the partially flooded continuation of a drove road follows the right bank of the river, merging with a better grade forestry road then meeting the surfaced lane from Navarredonda. Turn left to cross the bridges and reach the parking spot (*40mins*).

21. PUERTO DEL PICO - LA CASA - RISCOS DEL BIEZO - LOS RISCOS DE LAS MORRILLAS (1998m) - ARROYO DE GARGANTA HONDA - FORESTRY ROAD - PUERTO DEL PICO.

Time: 6¹/₂-7hrs
Total ascent: 551m

This walk starts at the road crossing the Puerto del Pico and follows the main crest west, but as the return route is along the gentler northern slopes, it is included in this North Side section. The ridge itself is well worth doing with good rock scenery and extensive views north and south and it is something of a mystery, given the relatively high starting point, why it isn't more popular. The climb from the road pass to La Casa is trackless and involves a little easy scrambling, as does the crossing of the Riscos del Biezo/Fría. All maps show a path traversing the southern slopes from the Puerto del Arenal track back to the Pico Pass. This would make an interesting alternative route but there is now no trace of it at either end. The maps also disagree in differentiating between the summits called Fría and the Riscos del Biezo and show the forestry road incorrectly.

The N502 over the Puerto del Pico (1352m) is a good modern road. Coming from the south, park at the top of the pass on the right. Cross the road and the boggy meadows beyond to pass behind a large stone war memorial to start the climb of steep slopes covered in outcrops, debris and scrub. Discontinuous bits of path can be linked up to reach a conspicuous flat-topped tower, from where a good stretch of track can be found, above to the left. Once the angle eases, at the top of the wide crest (*1hr 15mins*), a rough track appears and there is an occasional run

Resin-collecting on the southern slopes of Gredos

of cairns. For just over a kilometre there are only minor changes in height then the gradient steepens to climb the rock summit of **Risco del Biezo/Fría** (1986m, *1hr10m*). The easiest way off is to the left, down to a small saddle beyond which a series of large outcrops, the Riscos de las Morrillas, present a continuous set of cliffs to the south, but are easily traversed on their gentler northern slopes.

After descending to the wide 1918m saddle beyond (*40mins*), start down terraces to the right at the head of the the Garganta Honda valley and follow the stream down (no track) to where it is crossed by a dirt road (*40mins*). This winds to the right around a couple of spurs then passes through a stretch of open pinewood. Immediately before it is crossed by a wire fence (*1hr 10mins*), leave to the right on a rough track which heads round a small spur and drops to meet a wider track. Follow it to the right, back to the Puerto del Pico (*30mins*).

103

South Side

Although visitors often prefer the south side of the range because of the richer, more "Spanish" scenery of the lower slopes and the picturesqueness of the villages, it is difficult to be wholeheartedly enthusiastic about the routes which start there. Those which head for the higher ground are usually former hunting roads or old tracks which were used to connect the north and south side villages. Making for the various saddles or clefts in the main ridge by either valley floor or the crest of spurs, they are long, monotonous and often have steep, rough, trackless upper sections. West of Guisando, all approaches take between 5 and 7hrs to the divide, and involve 1100-1700m of ascent, even if they are started from roadheads well above the villages. In addition most of these roadheads are at the end of extremely poor forestry or farm tracks, better suited to off-road vehicles. Although the scenery is spectacular with wild, deep valleys cutting back into the immense rock wall of the main ridge, it has to be asked if the effort is worth it, even to arrive at an exciting point on the backwall of the Gredos Cirque. Not surprisingly, therefore, all but the Apretura route to La Mira are used most often in descent, if they are used at all.

Nevertheless, walkers wanting to enjoy the ambience of the southern villages can make some worthwhile day excursions into the valleys at the western end, as well as reaching some of the summits in the more accessible eastern half. To give the fullest picture therefore, the least accessible of these cross-range routes are merely listed here with some details about their starting points. The rest, which either take less than 4hrs to the main crest, or have better approach roads and/or a lower section which would make a satisfactory day walk in its own right, are described more fully.

22. (MADRIGAL DE LA VERA) - GARGANTA DE ALARDOS.

Routes up the Alardos valley behind the village of Madrigal de la Vera were at one time used to connect the village with Bohoyo and Navalperal in the Tormes valley: one track avoided the steep headwaters of the stream and took to the Cantaelgallo spur, joining the main ridge at Casquero de Peones. Others followed the Encinoso tributary to the Puerto de Peones or the Garganta del Sauce to cross the main divide into the upper corrie of the Bohoyo valley. For the last two, local guidebooks give the starting point as

WESTERN END OF SOUTH SIDE, CENTRAL GREDOS

Routes 22, 23, 24, 25, 26, 27

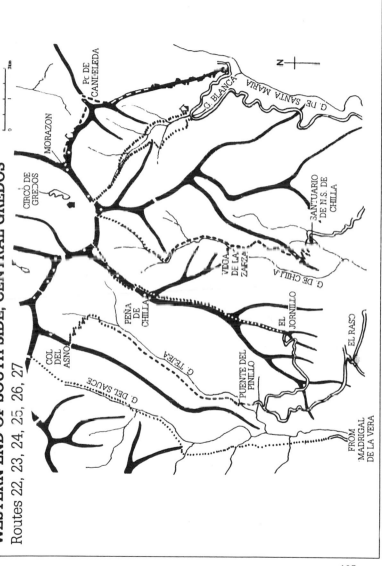

the Vega de Magazales, at the junction of the two tributaries and reached by a dirt road. While a farm track does run along the west bank of the Alardos, it is debatable whether some sections are drivable and many branches and forks to the various fincas make it less than straightforward. As the surface deteriorates badly about 3km out of Madrigal, a day walk could be started from there, continuing up the valley between the farms to explore at least the lower part of one of the tributaries.

Driving into Madrigal from the Candeleda direction, turn right into the side street next to the Café Bar Marcos. Bearing slightly right, this leads up through the houses and out onto a narrow farm track between fincas. Keep right at two forks to pass a ruined mill and arrive at the banks of the Alardos.

23. (EL RASO) - PUENTE DEL PINILLO - GARGANTA DE TEJEA.

An often poor but just about drivable dirt road heads up the eastern side of the Alardos from the hamlet of El Raso, to reach a roadhead at the lower end of the Tejea stream. The latter's steep-sided narrow valley, trapped between the ridges of the Hermanitos de Tejea and the Peña de Chilla drops from the tremendous rock wall on the south side of Almanzor and the Gutre ridge. The track up the valley is another old connection with the north side of the range, called the Camino de los Hortigales, which crosses into the upper Bohoyo valley. It is apparently still recognisable even on the steep climb up the western slopes to the Collado del Asno (which, with 1270m ascent, would probably take 5hrs from the roadhead). For a day walk, it is enough to explore the valley bed although there is no particular point to aim for. The track leaves the streambed for the climb to the col at about 1700m, some 3 1/2-4hrs from the road.

The stream itself, which has a succession of inviting pools and cascades, is the water supply for El Raso and bathing is banned in the whole valley. On the drive up to the roadhead, the site of a Celtic hill village is passed. The excavated foundations date from the Roman Occupation, although there is apparently evidence of much earlier settlement.

Approaching El Raso from Candeleda, take the first turning on the right as you enter the village, to cut up to the Calle Rosa, which, when followed to the right, soon leaves the houses again. When the cement surface finishes, turn left at the junction and follow the road for about 5km to the Pinillo bridge (700m) where there is space enough on either side for parking. Start the walk on the narrower continuation of the road which crosses cistus slopes and, by keeping left at two forks, descends to the stream and a cement bridge (*15mins*). A poorer track continues on the opposite bank, taking a gently rising line some way above the bed, across steep bracken slopes dotted with oak and juniper. The path deteriorates even more once past some old stone enclosures, crossing steep and crumbling slopes, but is well-marked with cairns.

After about 2hrs, the Chozos del Tio Domingo (shelters) are reached, but the path stays on the left bank until the next ruined huts are reached (Vaera del Zapato), near the confluence with the stream descending from the Canales Oscuras below Almanzor. The path starts the climb up the western slopes to the Collado del Asno 20mins higher up the valley at yet more ruins.

24. (EL RASO) - EL JORNILLO - PEÑA DE CHILLA - PORTILLA BERMEJA (2405m).

Time: approx. 5-6hrs
Total ascent: 1265m

This old north-south connection, called the Camino del Tio Domingo, follows a spur rather than valley line and crosses into the Circo de Gredos at the Portilla Bermeja, just to the southwest of Almanzor. The walk from the El Jornillo roadhead to the Elola hut in the Cirque would take 6½-7hrs, while a return to the roadhead from the col would mean a hard 10hr day. The bulky twin-headed rock tower of Peña de Chilla dominates the spur and would make a possible objective in itself for a more manageable day walk (850m ascent and a scramble to the summit) although the track is apparently quite difficult to follow. Furthermore, the dirt road between the Puente del Pinillo and the El Jornillo platform is narrow, rutted, steep in parts and occasionally boulder-strewn.

From El Raso, follow Route 26 to just before the Pinillo bridge and continue along a narrow, and at first steep, branch road leaving to the right. This winds round the southern end of the Chilla spur, across cistus slopes scattered with deciduous oak, to finish at the El Jornillo platform on an open grassy shoulder (1140m). The onward path is marked by tyre tracks swinging uphill. The trail climbs the spur, then after passing a right branch keeps to the right side of the crest until it reaches the saddle after the Peña de Chilla. Avoiding Risco Redondo on the left, it recrosses the spur at a saddle and makes a rising traverse across rock slopes to the stony gully below the Bermeja col.

25. SANTUARIO DE NUESTRA SEÑORA DE CHILLA - GARGANTA DE CHILLA - VEGA DEL ENEBRAL (1390m) - RETURN.

>   Time: 6-6½hrs
>   Total ascent: 720m

The lower reaches of this attractive, hidden valley are well worth doing as a day walk. The Chilla valley, although steep-sided, is more open than the Tejea, especially in its upper part, and swimming appears to be allowed in the stream's many pools. Another advantage over the Tejea walk is a surfaced road to the pretty starting point at a chapel 5km above Candeleda. The Sanctuary has an idyllic setting in a sheltered valley surrounded by deciduous woods and fincas, although nearby restaurants, bars and a gift shop suggest it may be very busy at times. The Virgen de Chilla is the patron saint of Gredos and on the second and third Sundays in September there is a romería (procession/picnic/party) to the chapel.

The onward route to the Gredos Cirque over the Portilla de los Machos is, as usual, trackless, rough and steep, requiring another 990m of ascent from the Vega del Enebral. From the Vega de la Zarza, another path is described as leaving up the shallow depression behind it to connect with the Tio Domingo trail (Route 24).

Driving out of Candeleda on the Madrigal de la Vera road, the lane leading to the chapel is signposted on the right, just after the bridge over the Santa Maria stream. Once in the car park at the end of the road (680m), three wide tracks leave from the opposite end to the sanctuary. Take the middle one which passes a row of cottages then crosses the stream at an amphitheatre for outdoor services. It then climbs the western slopes downstream, to leave the oak wood and to continue almost horizontally for a while. At a fork above a finca, take the uphill branch, which in long zigzags up bracken slopes leads to the **Collado de Chilla** (801m, *25mins*) and the first views of the towering rock walls of the main ridge.

The track doesn't cross the spur but starts to climb it. Almost immediately a narrow path leaves diagonally right through a stone wall with small cairns. This cuts off a bend in the original track, crossing it higher up to continue up the spur with more cairns. The path then moves onto the steep eastern slopes of the Chilla valley, high above the stream. Taking a slightly rising line through the bracken and scattered oak trees, it winds in and out of a succession of tributary streambeds. After some abandoned summer shelters on a small spur, there is a short descent to the main stream at the **Vega de la Zarza** (900m, *50mins*) with its terraces, copse of deciduous trees and rickety wooden bridge.

Continue on a less good but cairned path, still on the right bank of the stream, now called El Chorro. The valley widens and the path wanders up the bouldery bed, passing a subsidiary valley to the right which leads up to the Portilla de la Vaca. It is a matter of choice how far to continue up the main valley, but the stream junction at the Vega del Enebral is about an hour above the Vega de la Zarza. The right-hand valley there leads to the Portilla de los Machos.

26. (CANDELEDA) - REFUGIO DE LA ALBAREA - GARGANTA BLANCA - PORTILLA DE LOS HERMANITOS (2306m).

Total ascent:	**1406m**

There is little to recommend this route. The 11km approach road from Candeleda is almost continuously pitted with deep ruts and channels and from the Albarea hut, it is a rough 5^{1}/₂hrs of ascent to the col. From the Portilla de los Hermanitos, there is a steep loose descent into the Gredos Cirque (Route 16).

Drive out of Candeleda on the Madrigal road and turn right just before the bridge across the Santa Maria stream, to cross instead a narrow stone bridge parallel to it. At a roundabout just beyond, turn right on to a cement lane which leads through scattered houses and on to the ICONA forestry road, signposted for the Garganta Blanca. Follow it for some 11km, through fincas, then forest, until the bridge across the Garganta Blanca is reached in an open valley with two goat farms.

There is a path starting up the right side of the stream, from the Albarea hut. However, one starting above the higher set of farm buildings, on the opposite slopes upstream, is supposed to continue further up the valley. It rises across open slopes into the streambed of the Garganta de la Casqueruela, then crosses the spur opposite to traverse back into the Blanca valley.

27. COLLADO DEL ENEBRAL - PUERTO DE CANDELEDA - NAVASOMERA - MORAZON (2393m) - RETURN.

Time: 8¹/₂-9hrs
Total ascent: 1493m

It hardly seems likely that many people would choose this long, rather dull approach to Morazón instead of the easy ascent from the Plataforma. However, I have met Spanish parties who have made it into a two-day expedition, overnighting at the ruined Refugio del Rey then continuing to the Elola Refuge and, if you are prepared to drive up the very poor track to the Enebral spur from Candeleda, this is probably the easiest way from the south side to get a glimpse into the Circo de Gredos. The refuge and the path, which is called the Trocha Real, were built in the early part of this century to give hunting access to the Cirques of Gredos and Cinco Lagunas, although it is believed that the track was paved as early as the beginning of the 16th century for transhumance traffic. None of the surface remains today. While it would be difficult to lose the track up to the Puerto de Candeleda, care should be taken in mist on the continuation to Morazón, because of the meandering line of the crest.

If cross-range routes are being considered, Morazón could be missed and the Trocha Real followed across the head of the Pozas valley, all the way into the Gredos Cirque. From Morazón itself, Route 16, gives various ways of reaching the Elola hut or La Plataforma. The obvious onward route from the Puerto de Candeleda is straight down the Prao Puerto valley to La Plataforma, although this walk is almost always followed in reverse. (In which case, the

continuation of the Trocha Real down to Candeleda, from where this route starts, is some 300m east along the forestry road.)

Drive along the forestry road running north from Candeleda, as described in Route 26. The road continues beyond the Garganta Blanca bridge downstream. After about 1¹/₂km, the Garganta de Santa Maria, descending to Candeleda, comes into view on the right as the road starts to round the southern end of the Enebral spur (not named on any of the maps). It is just possible to park on the verges where the Trocha Real starts, after a left bend (900m).

The track, as wide as a forestry road at first, winds up through mixed pine and oaks, with occasional glimpses of the Garganta Blanca and the back of the Tres Hermanitos. Emerging from the trees (*45mins*), the now narrower and cairned path climbs the broad spur, sometimes along the crest but more often to left or right, with many multi-tracked sections. A dribble of water across the path around 1760m indicates a fuente. The spur is left, some way below the main crest and a rising line to the right taken, across bouldery slopes, to a prominent cairn at the **Puerto de Candeleda** (2018m, *2hrs 15mins*).

From the Pass, follow cairns to the left initially on the crest but soon moving right across a shallow grassy depression to make straight for the ruined **Refugio del Rey** (2160m, *25mins*). Continue on Route 17 to **Morazón** (2393m, *45mins*).

28. EL NOGAL DEL BARRANCO - LA APRETURA - LA MIRA (2343m) - RETURN.

Time:	7-7¹/₂hrs
Total ascent:	1183m

This is by far the most popular walk from the south side of the range and deservedly so, as it is a climb through constantly spectacular scenery up the ravine-like higher part of the Pelayo valley, passing below the magnificent towers and buttresses of Los Galayos. The route emerges from this enclosed situation very abruptly at the point where the Galayos spur leaves the main ridge and it is only a short and easy walk then above the headwall of the valley to the stone observatory base on the summit of La Mira.

Wild as the scenery is, at weekends and holidays the crowds

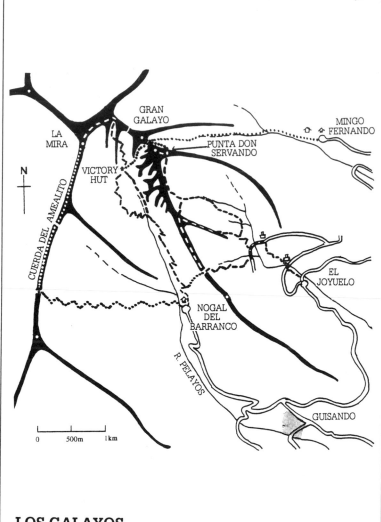

LOS GALAYOS

Routes 28, 29, 30, 31

rival those found on the Plataforma-Gredos Cirque path. On one June weekend, I counted about a hundred climbers camping in the area around the Victory Refuge and many people who would probably not regularly walk in the mountains are tempted along the initially well signposted path to the hut.

In spite of the scenery, returning to the roadhead by the same route is slightly tedious, as long sections are steep and loose. If you can arrange matters, continuing west from La Mira to La Plataforma on Route 18, or east to the Puerto del Peon then on Route 32 to Mingo Fernando make much better days out. In the winter and spring, the path through the narrow Apretura section of the valley, at the base of the main Galayos towers, is regularly subject to avalanches.

Coming from Arenas de San Pedro, follow the camping signs on reaching Guisando. These lead along a narrow steeply rising street on the east side of the village, avoiding the centre. Once above the houses, follow signs to El Nogal de Barranco (1160m). This is a large turning circle, in the valley bottom and almost at the tree line. There is a fuente, picnic tables, the usually locked ICONA refuge and a cafe and toilets

The path starts at the back of the circle, passing to the right of the hut and cafe, and is wide, well-made and waymarked with yellow and white. Signposts with times to the Victory hut and La Mira are found at the beginning and at the two fuentes passed on the way. Following the right side of the stream but some way above it, with several sets of zigzags, the track finally meets the bed at the foot of a pronounced narrowing of the valley, called **the Apretura** (1600m, *2hrs*) where there is another fuente. The most direct and popular way to the hut is to continue on the right of the stream on a rough, steep path. This climbs the narrows, right along the foot of the Galayos crags, crossing debris from the various gullies above, to reach the **Victory Refuge** (1950m, *30mins*), which stands on a platform to the left of the bed.

(Alternatively, from the foot of the Apretura, the waymarked path can be followed across the streambed. Although longer, this is the more interesting route with better views of the Galayos towers: after tight zigzags up a steep wall, the clear path finishes and cairns and paint are followed up a steep, loose rib then across a succession of plunging gullies to come out just below the hut platform (*40mins*).)

From the back of the hut, a paint mark can just be made out on the left-hand edge of the wide channel of debris falling from the head of the valley. Cairns and marks zigzag up this slope, generally keeping to the left side of the scree. Not far below the crest, they move steeply left to climb round into a shallow valley with a choice of two exits to the Galayos ridge line, just at the point where it joins the southeast corner of the Pelaos plateau (2162m, *35mins*). Two lines of cairns leave to the left: the right-hand one leads to the ruins of a refuge on the plateau and the one to the left heads across easy ground directly to the summit of **La Mira** (2343m, *20mins*).

29. EL NOGAL DEL BARRANCO - EL PORTILLO - CUERDA DEL AMEALITO - LA MIRA (2343m) - LA APRETURA - EL NOGAL DEL BARRANCO.

Time:	approx. 9-10hrs
Total ascent:	1183m

This very long tough scramble along the Amealito ridge, on the other side of the valley from Los Galayos, is sometimes taken to reach La Mira: from El Nogal del Barranco, the steep trackless slopes to the east are climbed to join the Cuerda del Amealito spur at the Portillo saddle, immediately to the west. The crest is then followed to La Mira, avoiding the succession of rock pinnacles, where necessary, on the less steep left side of the ridge. The round is completed by returning to the roadhead via the Apretura (Route 28).

30. EL JOYUELO - CHORRERAS DE LA LANCHA - PUNTA DON SERVANDO (2180m) - COBACHO COL - CHORRERAS DE LA LANCHA - EL JOYUELO.

Time:	8½-9hrs
Total ascent:	1080m

The eastern slopes of the Galayos spur, known as the Espaldar, are less steep than those above the Pelayos stream and this route heads up them to join a climbers' path running just below the crest on that side. The highest point on the spur is Gran Galayo (2200m), a massive rock tower at the top of the ridge beyond a deep cleft called La Portilla. All routes to its summit from the south require a rope, so the objective for this walk is Punta Don Servando which is the preceding highest point and on the other side of the gap. It is an equally good viewpoint and easily reached from the path.

Although the traditional line, straight up the slabby slopes below the highest towers, is an easier way to reach the Galayos crest than any of the gullies on the western side, it is a long trackless slog and is in full sun from early morning. The huge slabs help progress but are steep enough to cause difficulties in wet weather and, worst of all, the higher part is covered with dense tall broom through which it is difficult to force a way. A ten-year-old route description talks of a clear path but a widespread fire and new plantations seem to have obliterated it. Two other approaches to points lower down the spur now appear to be more popular and are described here instead, but forestry work is continuing and it is possible that these lines may also change again in the future. The return route follows the ridge south to the col north of Cobacho, from where a tedious but relatively short pathless descent links into a forestry track.

There is one other recognised route up this eastern flank of Los Galayos, which starts at the Mingo Fernando roadhead and follows the Cantos stream into the enormous Reseca Gully below the Portilla Gap. Like so many ascents in this area, it is trackless, rough, steep and loose.

To reach the El Joyuelo roadhead (1100m), take the steeply rising through-road above Guisando on its eastern side (coming from Arenas, follow the camping signs on reaching the village). Just before the sharp left bend at the Hostal Galayos, turn right on to a surfaced forestry road which heads round the wooded slopes of La Cuba to the turning circle and open stone hut of El Joyuelo. (The route description begins from here but by taking the left-hand of the two forestry roads leaving from the circle, it is possible to gain another 200m of height: take the left branch at the only junction and continue as far as the big stone fuente at Chorreras de la Lancha. The road surface is poor in parts.)

Starting from El Joyuelo, take the path up through the trees which leaves 50m along the right-hand forestry road. Higher up, this meets the left-hand one which is followed briefly across a stream to a fuente, where a steep track continues uphill in the trees behind it. Passing two branches to the left, the angle eases along a more open but boggy passage which

115

finishes on the forestry road near the stone fuente at **Chorreras de la Lancha** (1300m, *35mins*). It is from here that the original path line has disappeared. Instead, go left on the road across the stream and past a turning to a cabin, to reach a wide track leaving to the right which rises parallel to the stream until a rough platform is reached about 15mins later. Now the two approaches diverge:

1. If you take the rough path which leaves diagonally right up slope, it soon disappears but you can continue fairly easily up onto the crest of a lateral spur which is then followed without difficulties to join the main ridge at the lowest outcrop of a series called **Las Berroqueras** (1650m, *1hr*). Their eastern (right) slopes are a continuous line of steep slabs. Descend slightly to work along their base, then go steeply up a vegetated line with signs of a path, to the gap between the Berroquerras and the first conspicuous rock tower (*50mins*). Scramble through the difficult mixture of rock and broom to the right of the steeply rising crest until cairns and a poorly defined path are picked up. This leads to a small shoulder above the Portilla gap in front of Gran Galayo. Climb the shoulder the very short distance to the summit of **Punta Don Servando** (2180m, *45mins*).

2. From the rough turning circle, the forestry track continues upstream a little further, crossing one tributary stream but fizzling out in a fenced enclosure before the next. Climb the slope above the enclosure, badly chewed up by forestry machinery, parallel to the second streambed, until the latter opens out into a long series of slabs which can be climbed to reach the vegetated line to the right of the Berroqueras slabs. From there, follow Route 1.

From the summit of Punta Don Fernando, retrace Route 1 to the lower end of Las Berroqueras, and continue down the crest on easier ground, avoiding outcrops on the left. Arriving at the lowest point (1532m, *2hrs 30mins*) before the ground starts to rise again to Cobacho, head down the steep left-hand slopes through a mixture of vicious blackened broom stumps and new growth to reach a rough forest track (*25mins*). It winds down to a stream then joins the forestry road which, to the left, leads to **Chorreras de la Lancha** (*25mins*). Retrace the start of the route to El Joyuelo (*25mins*).

Canal de Gran Galayo

31. EL NOGAL DEL BARRANCO - LA APRETURA - CANAL DEL GRAN GALAYO - PUNTA DON SERVANDO (2180m) - COBACHO COL - EL NOGAL DEL BARRANCO.

Time: approx. $7^{1}/_{2}$-8hrs
Total ascent: 1020m

For experienced scramblers, a circuit is possible from El Nogal del Barranco which uses the Espaldar de los Galayos in descent. It follows Route 28 until level with the Victory hut then climbs the Canal del Gran Galayo, the huge gully between Gran Galayo and Punta Don Servando, to the Portilla gap. This involves climbing up small rock steps and unstable blocks and there is a steep section below the col which is divided into three by two rock towers. The middle gully is the least recommended. From there, work round the back of the towers then up a steep track to the shoulder below the summit of Punta Don Servando from where Route 30 is reversed to just before the Cobacho col. Cairns indicate the start of a trackless descent over rough but open ground to the Apretura path, just above the roadhead.

32. (DO)MINGO FERNANDO - PUERTO DEL PEON - PEÑA DEL MEDIODIA (2224m) - RETURN.

Time: 6¹/₂-7hrs
Total ascent: 1064m

The Peña del Mediodía is a long flat plateau section of ridge of no great interest as a summit, except for a jumble of outcrops on its southern side. However, it is the nearest summit for a reasonable day walk from the Mingo Fernando roadhead above El Hornillo. The Puerto del Peon is believed to be so called (peon - labourer) because it was the pass used by men from the southern villages who were working on the construction of the Hoyos del Espino-Plataforma track. The trail up to the pass was improved by the Gredos-Tormes Society in 1914 and the careful grading and long stretches of intact paving make it an easy climb, with the usual proviso about early starts in hot weather. It may possibly have been tidied up in the last year or two as many current guidebooks warn of struggles through overgrown sections, none of which materialised. Some of the same writers label the approach as tedious, but I found plenty of variety and changing views, as the path takes a rising line across three successive spurs and side valleys, all the time with the impressive backdrop of the eastern flank of the Galayos spur. It certainly compares well with the approach to the same summit across the northern moors (see Routes 19, 20 and 20a).

The Mingo Fernando roadhead is reached by taking the surfaced forestry road which starts on the right of the Guisando road about ¹/₂km outside El Hornillo (large sign Pista Forestal Monte no.11). It follows the Cantos valley up, on its western slopes, crosses the stream and comes a little way back down the valley to a T-junction. Go left and then left at the next fork to the Mingo Fernando turning circle and the ICONA refuge buildings.

(If your car suspension can stand it, you can gain another 100m or so of height by taking the right (Cebedilla) branch at the junction preceding Mingo Fernando to follow a dirt road, which, after a left then much later a right fork, arrives at a stone fuente and another turning circle. Behind the fountain, a track climbs the right-hand wooded slopes of a small valley to meet the main path in a couple of minutes.)

Starting from Mingo Fernando (1160m), follow the path leaving between the hut and the wooden gates, alongside an irrigation ditch. Pass a barn, but at the next building, a small open stone shelter on the right, take a right fork towards a cairn. Although the next section is confused by shortcuts, the original cairned path crosses an irrigation channel and leads to a stream trickling down steep slabs at the start of a side valley. Here, the track moves away right on a long rising traverse through the trees, followed by well-made zigzags leading up through what must have been agricultural terraces in pre-forestry days, to cross a dirt road (*25mins*).

On the wooded spur above the road, the path soon swings left (two possible shortcuts across the bend) to contour round into a valley, passing on the way the junction with the path coming up from the alternative start which can be seen just below. Crossing the streambed, the now partly paved track works up the opposite slope, out of the trees and across a shoulder for the first views of the upper Cantos valley and the Galayos spur beyond (*30mins*). After climbing the easy angled rock crest for a while, a rising traverse across the head of another side valley reaches the crest of the next shoulder (*20mins*).

Once more the crest is climbed, at first on rock then after passing a tuente, in big zigzags. These work left up steeper broom-covered slopes until the hollow immediately below the Puerto del Peon comes into view (*35mins*). The track initially drops into this depression, then contours across it to climb in good zigzags through the boulders and outcrops on the slopes leading up to the pass (2035m, *40mins*). There are two or three fuentes on this last section. From the pass, head right, following cairns into the broom, which initially keep well to the left of the rocky crest. They then lead round to the elongated summit of **Peña del Mediodía** (2224m, *45mins*) which has a survey post at the highest point.

33. EL ARENAL/PUERTO DEL PICO ROAD - COLLADO DE LA CENTENERA - PUERTO DEL ARENAL - PUERTO DE LA CABRILLA - ROAD. (see map p99)

(Highest point 1990m, just behind the 2008m Cabrilla headland)
   Time: **6¹/₂-7hrs**
   Total ascent: 1060m

This route covers a frankly uninteresting section of ridge although the contrasting views to north and south, as well as the eastern

*Boundary
post or
gibbet in
Mombeltran*

aspect of Los Galayos ahead, make it worth attempting. The two
passes visited on the route were formerly used to connect El Arenal
and Navarredonda and, on the steep south side, both carry well-
graded mule tracks. The circular route described here, written with
car drivers in mind, starts at the lowest point, which means there
is a 4½km walk along the road to the Collado de la Centenera on
the opposite side of the valley. The road, only surfaced in the last
ten years, carries negligible traffic and passes through terraces of
hazel trees and plantations of resin pine in a very pretty valley
backed by the rocky peak of Riscos de las Morrillas.

As a cross-range route, the Puerto de Arenal is the shortest
approach to the main ridge from anywhere on the south side if you

can start at the **Collado de la Centenera**. This is quite possible by taking a taxi from El Arenal. The onward track from the Puerto del Arenal to the Parador takes about 1³/₄hrs and the path joins Route 20 near the Tormes source. Alternatively, by climbing to the Puerto de la Cabrilla, you could reverse Route 20 to the Parador as well, although there seems little reason to choose to cross on the interminable and arid zigzags of that pass, when both the Arenal and Peón Passes are easier and more interesting. In reverse, though, coming from Navarredonda, it is the only southern descent to have the advantage of finishing so near a village.

The best place to park on the El Arenal-Puerto del Pico road is some ¹/₂km after the big hairpin above the village, in a large lay-by on the right and opposite a concrete block-like structure (1010m). (This point is shown on all maps as the start of the footpath up to the Puerto de la Cabrilla. However, relatively recent forestry clearance and new terracing means the path starts much higher up at the end of a winding dirt road.)

Walk up the Pico Pass road, eventually crossing the valley to reach the crest of the long wooded southern spur of Risco de las Morrillas at the **Collado de la Centenera** (1350m, *1hr*). A forestry road leaves to the left, behind a chain barrier. Wandering up the spur and out of the trees, it arrives at a concrete hut and stone animal pen at the **Collado Alto de las Campanas** (1560m, *30mins*). A cairn to the left, just before the hut, marks the start of the mule track which is heavily eroded at first, but later has several sections of good paving between passages which are entirely overgrown. The track contours to the left round the head of the El Arenal valley and climbs gently to a shoulder, from where it starts to zigzag (follow cairns carefully) up to the **Puerto del Arenal** (1815m, *1hr 5mins*). Go left along the crest on tracks through the dense short broom, linking up the well-spaced cairns. They keep more or less to the crest all the way except on the unnamed headland (point 2008m on most maps), where the line bears right just below the summit to drop the short distance to the **Puerto de la Cabrilla** (1950m, *1hr 10mins*).

The mule track down the southern slopes leaves from behind the signboard on the lip to the left. Unlike the track used in ascent, the many tight zigzags down the steep slope here are not at all overgrown, but nor are they paved, having a generally broken and loose surface. A useful fuente is passed after about 10mins. This first set of zigzags finishes on a level area of shoulder well down to the right. The path then crosses the valley head to the left to return to zigzagging, with plantation gradually thickening up during the descent. Lower down, recent forestry work has interfered with the original path, which is suddenly truncated by a rough cut running downhill. Follow it down to where it meets another, which in turn should be followed, but only for a few metres to where the original path leaves to the right. A few minutes later, the track meets the end of a drivable dirt road which winds down through terraced fincas to a surfaced road just above the concrete building and layby (*1hr 40mins*).

Roman road below the south side of Puerto del Pico

CHAPTER SIX

Eastern Gredos

TOPOGRAPHY

The eastern end of the range is the longest section, running for 54km from the Puerto del Pico to the town of San Martín de Valdeiglesias. Almost on a due west-east axis, it maintains for its whole length the familiar pattern of a broad crest, rising from time to time to rocky summits, some with south-facing crags and some sending out long lateral spurs to north and south. The rock scenery is at its most spectacular in the Riscos de Villarejo, which is the collective name for the series of crags at the west end of the zone, between the Puerto del Pico and the minor road pass of Collado de Serranillos (1575m). Here the cliffs reach 250m on the south face of El Torozo (2026m).

Between the Collado de Serranillos and the Puerto de Mijares, the only other road pass across the eastern range, the culminating rock summit is the Sierra de Cabezo with the double top of Los Niños de Cabezo (2190m) and Cabezo (2188m). East from the Puerto de Mijares, a long descending section of crest between Gamonosa (1915m) and the Puerto del Alacran (1776m) precedes the final significant section of crags above the south-draining valleys of the Cercela and Nuño Cojo streams. These centre on La Serradilla (2008m) and El Pulpito (2009m) on opposite side of the Portacho de las Serradillas (1869m). The ridge maintains its height to the east as far as Escusa (1959m) then gradually tapers off across the Puerto de Casillas (1477m) and down to San Martín de Valdeiglesias.

VILLAGE BASES

As the walking possibilities are more limited and less spectacular than in other parts of the range, it is unlikely that visitors would choose to base themselves in this area. Therefore, **Mombeltran**, already recommended as the best base for Central Gredos, is quite convenient for the few walks covered in the east. If you should wish to explore this end of the range in more depth, the quiet upper Alberche valley is very attractive, with its complicated hillocky terrain and patchwork of vineyards. **Burgohondo** and **Navalmoral de la Sierra** have one hotel each. The wooded south side of the range comes within weekend range of Madrid and is therefore more visited, but the village centres are still very rustic and agricultural

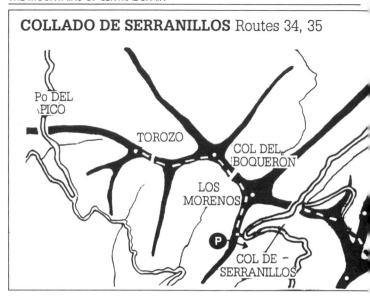

COLLADO DE SERRANILLOS Routes 34, 35

(map showing Po DEL PICO, TOROZO, COL DEL BOQUERON, LOS MORENOS, P, COL DE SERRANILLOS)

with perhaps **Pedro Bernardo** (one hotel) the most picturesque. **Gavilanes**, **Casavieja**, **Mijares** and **Piedralaves** also have at least one hotel each. The only campsite is at Navaluenga in the Alberche valley. There are no refuges or shelters in the range.

ROUTES

Walking in Eastern Gredos could be described as an esoteric occupation. Although the main ridge has height, views and a string of rocky summits, there is nothing to compare with the spectacular scenery of the Central zone or even the glaciated valleys further west, so there is not much incentive, especially for visitors, to undertake the 4hr ascents from the villages. This lack of interest means that the supposed approaches to the crest are in fact very hard work, being often overgrown and difficult to sort out among the maze of forestry tracks. Even many stretches of the crest itself are pathless and covered in dense mats of broom. Most walkers appear to be content to wander the forestry tracks in the valleys on the south side, which contain very attractive mixed woodland, small meadows and pretty streams. In view of all this, the four routes described here are confined to stretches of the main ridge between the two road passes and convenient high points.

34. COLLADO DE SERRAN-ILLOS (SOUTH SIDE) - LOS MORENOS - COLLADO DEL BOQUERON - PIEDRA CABALLERA - EL TOROZO (2026m) - RETURN.

Time:	5½-6hrs
Total ascent:	846m

This short section of the main ridge, sandwiched between two road passes and known as the Riscos de Villarejo, is the most spectacular in the eastern sector with its almost unbroken curtain of enormous cliffs to the south. If you could arrange to be dropped at one pass and picked up at the other, the traverse could be made in 3-4hrs, with the west-east direction being the easier. If not, the out-and-back alternative is much more satisfactory from the Collado de Serranillos. The crest is normally followed from the pass up the tedious broom slopes above a TV relay station, but the start described here takes instead the open upper section of the south spur of Los Morenos. This not only has easier terrain but also gives the best close-up views of the immense crags, buttresses and towers of the Riscos del Tio Pasito which plunge to the Placero stream. Once on the main crest, there is no real track but the route sticks as much as possible to the lip of the southern faces in order to avoid the broom and make the most of the rock scenery below. El Torozo is a fine summit perched at the apex of cliffs which carry the longest rock climbs in Gredos.

Park at the outside of the last hairpin bend (1540m) below the south side of the Collado de Serranillos. (Room for two cars with one further space a little higher up the road on the right.) The rough track up the slope above the outside of the bend leads immediately to the wide crest of the southern spur of Los Morenos. Follow it up through a small patch of mixed broom and then over bare stony ground, scattered with lavender. Higher

125

up, a line of low outcrops just in front of the main bulk of the summit rocks is reached (*25mins*), giving the first views of the crags lining the Placero valley. Follow this rib a little way until you can work left into a wide steep grassy gully which leads straight up to the summit plateau. (Gaps in the enclosing spine to the left can be used to look into the deep-cut gullies and buttresses of the Tio Pasito crags.)

The grass gully exits on to a wide plateau of broom. Follow the top of the crags round to the left, linking up climbers' paths to the unmarked highest point of **Los Morenos** (1880m, *30mins*). A little further on, a cairn can be seen on a headland above the Placero valley, but the direct route to the **Collado del Boquerón** (1785m, *10mins*) descends slightly right, through the broom and past some low slabby outcrops. Continue beyond the col and up into the outcrops above the vast cliffs on the west side of the valley. When the ground steepens, a scramble keeping to the crest looks possible. Otherwise, move onto the steep broom slope to the right, working back to the ridge line as soon as there is a gap in the rocks. Bits of path develop to the right side of the crest, linking up the terraces above the cliffs. Head for the two piles of stones in the broom which are on the summit area of **Piedra Caballera** (2005m, *45mins*).

Beyond it, a long gently descending plateau of rock and scattered clumps of vegetation lead to a small col (1930m, *20mins*). On the far side, climb to the right of the first outcrops then continue along the crest towards the rocks of El Torozo. On the way, pass to the right of a prominent cairn to cross slabs which lead to a tiny col below the rocky point of the summit (2026m,.*20mins*) with its survey point and small cross.

35. COLLADO DE SERRANILLOS - PUERTO DEL LAGAREJO - LOS NIÑOS DE CABEZO (2190m) - CABEZO (DE MIJARES)- RETURN.

Time:	6¹/₂-7hrs
Total ascent:	915m

The Sierra de Cabezo is the highest part of the crest which lies between the two road passes of Serranillos and Mijares. It is made up of two summits of almost the same height. (The SGE/IGN map give the western as the higher by 2m, but Cabezo has the survey point.) They are separated by a few hundred metres of narrow rock crest although the scrambling can be avoided. Unusually, the

Cabezo from Los Niños de Cabezo

steeper and longer faces are on the north side here. The approach from the Collado de Serranillos is on the whole less interesting than from the Puerto de Mijares (extension of Route 36) but is shorter. Some stretches are trackless and there is a steep 330m climb from the Puerto del Lagarejo to the Risco de Miravalles. Like the preceding route, if you can arrange to be dropped at one pass and picked up at the other it would make a more satisfactory day out.

Park at the Collado de Serranillos (1575m) and go through the broken fence to the right of a locked gate on the east side of the pass. A wide track begins there, rising to the right of the dirt road which starts at the gate. While the road contours round the north side of this section of crest (Los Mosquillos), the track goes along the top connecting a line of shooting butts, to rejoin it at a saddle. From there, follow the road to its end near the head of a stream which flows north (*35mins*). Although the crest line continues up the spur to the left, it is far quicker to cross that spur and struggle through the chest-high broom on the slopes beyond. This trackless traverse rejoins the descending crest line, which carries a fence, some way above the **Puerto del Lagarejo** (1670m, *35mins*).

The fence turns across the col and has to be climbed over to reach the

127

base of the long slope opposite. Take the easiest line through the vegetation to the first outcrops, from where a few cairns and traces of path appear alongside or among a rising line of intermittent low rock. Around where the Risco de Miravalles summit rocks come into view, cairns and a poor track head diagonally left through the broom and across a shallow streambed to join the crest just to the left of the summit (1999m, *55mins*). Continue along the gently rising wide crest on a clearer but not completely continuous track. As the ground steepens, avoid the first big outcrop on terraces to the right, then rejoin the crest to arrive at the piled blocks of the summit of **Los Niños** (2190m, *45mins*), with its crude metal cross. From there, follow the narrow continuation of the ridge, crossing a small saddle, to the cairn and survey point on **Cabezo** (2188m, *10mins*).

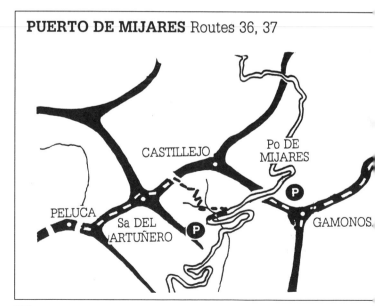

PUERTO DE MIJARES Routes 36, 37

CASTILLEJO

Po DE MIJARES

PELUCA

Sa DEL ARTUÑERO

GAMONOS

36. PUERTO DE MIJARES - SIERRA DEL ARTUÑERO - PELUCA (2053m) - RETURN.

Time: 5-5¹/₂hrs
Total ascent: 593m

The pyramidal summit of Peluca, poised above the village of Mijares, is a reasonable point to aim for on an easy and pleasant day-walk from the Puerto de Mijares. The crossing of the series of outcrops called the Sierra del Artuñero gives additional interest on the way. If starting from the pass, there is a stiff climb over El Castillejo, the first top on this section and, as the slopes face east, they catch the sun early. Instead, the route described here joins the ridge at the saddle beyond that summit, by way of a track used by local farmers to take the cattle to the summer pastures. There is no difficulty in extending the walk from Peluca along the crest to Cabezo if desired, although there appears to be little rock and much broom along the way. This would add approximately 3hrs to the whole walk.

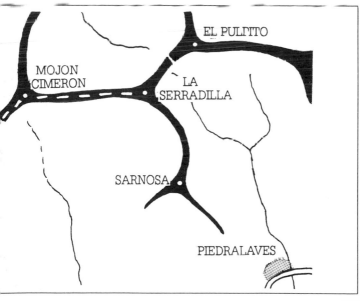

Driving up to the Puerto de Mijares from Mijares village, park next to a stream, on the inside of the last (right) hairpin (1520m) before the pass. Walk up the road and after rounding a small shoulder, start up a wide cattle track which leads back to the left. The track becomes less clear in meadows after a stone barn, but actually continues, visible here and there, across the stream then up a narrower strip of grass along the margins of a tributary stream to the left of the main one. At the top of the strip, head almost horizontally right into the broom to find the start of a wide zigzagging path which passes easily through the broom band to easier-angled higher meadows with the saddle beyond (1901m, *55mins*).

Turn left at the saddle and make for the scar of a wide stony track heading upslope, slightly to the right of the crest line. This leads to just beyond the first and highest of the Artuñero outcrops (2000m, *20mins*). A less clear path leads along the crest, avoiding outcrops on the right, but keeping to the crest over the last two, to arrive at the col (1970m, *30mins*) below Peluca. The slopes leading up to the peak are covered in dense broom and a path only develops below the summit rocks, from where it works up the right side of the crest to the survey post (2053m, *25mins*).

37. PUERTO DE MIJARES - GAMONOSA - PUERTO DEL ALACRAN - LA SERRADILLA (2008m) - RETURN.

Time:	approx. 9hrs
Total ascent:	711m

The final area of interest in this sector is the stretch of ridge between the Puerto del Alacran and El Pulpito (the easternmost point over 2000m), where once more crags plunge steeply into the wooded valleys to the south. The Serradilla summit is halfway along this section at the apex of the big Sarnosa spur. However, if a shorter walk is preferred, you could turn back at Mojon Cimera (6^1/$_2$-7hrs). The initial climb to Gamonosa is long and hampered by the broom, but once on its rocky summit, the walking becomes easier along a wide, stony, gently undulating balcony.

There is plenty of parking by the road at the treeless pass of Puerto de Mijares. Start up the eastern slopes to the right of the ridge wall, which later changes to a fence. There is a faint path as far as the the first big outcrop which is avoided to the right. Above it, the broom becomes very dense and it is easier to work across slope to the right, connecting up clear patches and rock, to reach the rocky crest of Gamonosa's southern spur. This can be followed up without difficulties to the survey point on the summit (1915m, *55mins*).

Torozo from the Puerto del Pico

PART THREE

The Sierra de Guadarrama

INTRODUCTION

These mountains are known locally as the Sierra de Madrid, although they are visible from only certain points in the north and west of the capital and lie 50km away at their nearest point, "at just the distance they ought to be" according to one local writer. This sentiment seems to be shared by many Madrileños, a significant number of whom have summer homes in the foothills or on the lower slopes. Thousands more are prepared to sit in interminable motorway traffic jams for the sake of a few hours' fresh air at weekends.

In fact the range is too close to Madrid for its own good and there is little point in pretending that there has not been some environmental damage: power lines, housing urbanisation and insensitive ski developments have all had a detrimental impact. More insidiously, the last twenty to thirty years in particular have seen the loss of many species of wildlife, some degradation of the natural vegetation as well as a chronic litter problem in the most popular areas.

However, the case must not be overstated: except for the three small ski areas, most of the visual damage is confined to the foothills, and some conservation measures are now being taken, such as the restriction of traffic in the most threatened areas. Furthermore, it appears that only a small proportion of visitors are interested in high-level walking as opposed to just being in the countryside. Thus, away from the valleys, the pressure of numbers is negligible compared to other European uplands so near to a major city. It is surprising how few parties we pass, even on Sundays or public holidays, once away from the roadhead. On weekdays, I rarely meet anybody. In one sense, the range's accessibility is an advantage in that the wide choice of convenient entry points to the ridges serves to spread people more evenly over the range than is possible in the Sierra de Gredos.

Although, like Gredos, the north side of the main watershed falls away as a gently rolling gradient while the southern slopes are more abrupt, there is no corresponding sharp contrast between the Segovian and Madrid scenery. Cattle farming and forestry shape the landscape on both sides of the range, and from the remnants of traditional drystone, pantiled housing still to be seen, the villages must once have resembled those on the north side of Gredos. Now, after so many years of extensive rebuilding, infill and expansion, rural picturesqueness has generally given way to metropolitan comfort, and the result is a haphazard mixture of vernacular and modern plus the range of services required by the sophisticated weekenders from Madrid. Nevertheless, if they lack the rural atmosphere of Hoyos del Espino or Guisando, Guadarrama villages are still very pleasant places to stay between walks. Their granite churches, town halls and other public buildings have a dignified quality and their focus is generally the South European necessity of a tree-shaded plaza with a drinking fountain and a collection of bars spilling out tables and umbrellas.

The 90km length of the Sierra de Guadarrama lies on a SW-NE axis between El Escorial and the Puerto de Somosierra, 50 and 75km respectively north of Madrid. In the west, the range takes the form of a single chain with a couple of long subsidiary ridges, the Sierra de Malagon and the Mujer Muerta/Sierra del Quintanar thrown out to the west from the Segovia side, but at the Puerto de los Cotos, it divides to enclose the long high valley of Lozoya. It is the northern, higher branch which carries the watershed and connects with the sierras further to the east.

ROUTES

This long, narrow chain offers mainly ridge-walking with some dramatic panoramas of the Meseta to north and south. Yet, in spite of the lack of individual summits, routes within the range are surprisingly varied. A ridge walk could mean Las Machotas with their wide grassy crests scattered with a jumble of gigantic, rounded granite boulders, or Siete Picos with its succession of chunky, flat-topped tors. It could be the harsh, dry, stony upland of La Cuerda Larga or the glaciated corries and tarns of Peñalara, while even in the heat of August, the shady but open scots pine forests of Fuenfría and Valsaín are a pleasure to walk in. Undoubtedly, though, the jewel in Guadarrama's crown is the beguiling chaos of towers and slabs, boulders and domes which make up the La Pedriza ridges. If the Sierra de Gredos appeals to those who like big walks in extensive, wild and remote scenery, the Sierra de Guadarrama is for walkers with a taste for variety and texture and constant changes of perspectives and terrain.

The smaller scale of the range, its generally amenable terrain and vegetation, numerous access points and dense network of good footpaths mean that the choice of circular day walks is enormous. For most individual ridges and mountains, it has been possible to describe several

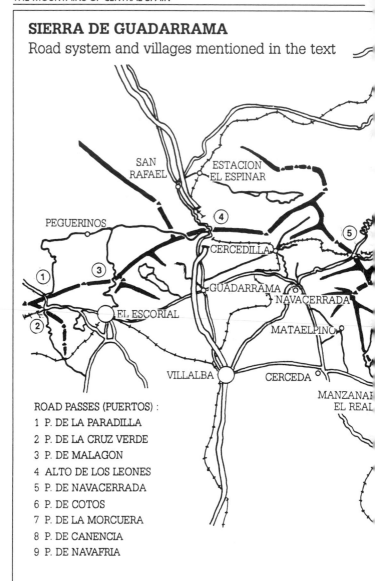

SIERRA DE GUADARRAMA

Road system and villages mentioned in the text

ROAD PASSES (PUERTOS) :

1 P. DE LA PARADILLA
2 P. DE LA CRUZ VERDE
3 P. DE MALAGON
4 ALTO DE LOS LEONES
5 P. DE NAVACERRADA
6 P. DE COTOS
7 P. DE LA MORCUERA
8 P. DE CANENCIA
9 P. DE NAVAFRIA

approaches, as well as to include **many routes which can be reached by public transport or a short taxi ride (marked *) or can be adapted to suit walkers without cars (marked §).**

I have divided the range into five sections:

a. **Western Guadarrama** from San Benito to Alto de los Leones.

b. **Central Guadarrama (West)** from Alto de los Leones to Puerto de Navacerrada.

c. **Central Guadarrama (East)** from Puerto de Navacerrada to Puerto de los Neveros (northern branch) and to Puerto de la Morcuera (southern branch).

d. **The Upper Manzanares Basin** which includes La Pedriza.

e. **Eastern Guadarrama** from Puerto de los Neveros to Puerto de Navafría (northern branch) and Puerto de la Morcuera to La Cabrera (southern branch).

Navacerrada village

CHAPTER SEVEN
Western Guadarrama

TOPOGRAPHY

The western end of the range forsakes the usual SW-NE axis for one running almost due south-north. The slopes on the Madrid side are characteristically steep, but on reaching the crest, instead of looking down the expected long gentle slopes to the Northern Meseta, the walker is confronted with a succession of jumbled ridges, some sharp, some rounded, stretching away to the west and the profiles on the horizon of the Sierras de Gredos and Paramera.

The chain begins with the isolated conical form of San Benito (1625m) which is separated from the main ridge by the Puerto de la Paradilla carrying the El Escorial-Avila road. Just below this to the southeast, the Puerto de la Cruz Verde connects San Benito with its lower offshoot, the Machotas Ridge (1461m) which projects SSE. Back at the Puerto de la Paradilla, the main ridge quickly rises to the northeast via the summit of Barranco la Cabeza (1680m) then is crossed by a minor road at the Puerto de Malagon. Just beyond, the outstanding viewpoint of Abantos (1753m) projects west from the broad divide which itself turns due north to continue over San Juan (1734m) and then a series of small undulations culminating in Cabeza Lijar (1824m).

This section forms the back wall of the Valle de los Caidos (Valley of the Fallen), where Franco built his grandiose memorial to the Civil War dead. He is now buried there in the huge underground basilica, topped by what is reputed to be the largest cross in the world (150m high not including the substantial outcrop it stands on, which contains the basilica). To say the least, it is highly visible from a surprising distance, and whatever one's opinion of its conception and positioning, it is now as much part of the landscape as any of the surrounding summits.

Cerro de la Salamanca (1789m), the top to the south of Cabeza Lijar, is joined by the Collado del Hornillo to a subsidiary ridge called the Sierra de Malagon, which extends due west for about 30km, reaching its maximum height just above the Collado del Hornillo, at Cueva Valiente (1903m).

From Cabeza Lijar, the crest drops away northeast to the lowest road pass in the range, the Alto de los Leones (or Puerto de Guadarrama, 1511m) and the limit of this western section. As the easiest crossing point in the Sierra, it carries both the National VI trunk road and a tolled motorway (the latter underground at the pass), connecting Madrid with the cities of Northwest Spain.

VALLEY BASES

Of all the bases recommended in this guide, **San Lorenzo de El Escorial** is the most atmospheric. It has a fine position on the pine-covered southern slopes of Abantos, looking across to the big bowl of deciduous woodland which is cradled by the craggy Machotas ridge. But it is the looming presence of Philip II's colossal, grey granite monastery/palace, sitting on a shelf above the hollow, which dominates the town and evokes some of the grim magnificence of 16th century Spain. There is nothing grim about the town centre, however, which has a number of elegant 19th century cafes off the tree-lined main street and terraced plazas. There is a lively, cosmopolitan feel, especially in summer as it is something of a cultural and educational centre as well as a tourist attraction.

San Lorenzo de El Escorial, the upper town around the monastery is separated from **El Escorial**, the lower part around the railway station, by the grounds of the monastery (about a 20min walk down an avenue of magnificent chestnut trees). There is a tourist office in the upper town on the main street (Calle de Floridablanca) and both parts have all necessary shops and services. There is a good range of accommodation in San Lorenzo, but the less fashionable lower town has one or two hotels/ pensions as well. There are good connections with Madrid by bus and train and some of the latter continue to Avila. In addition, there is a Sunday bus service through a few villages to the west of the main watershed which can be used to some advantage by walkers.

Another possible base for walkers with a car is the town of **Guadarrama**, to the south of the Alto de los Leones, which has the advantage of being well placed for some walks in both the central and western sectors. It has one or two hotels, the restaurants are well spoken of, and it is likely to be cheaper than the more touristy El Escorial. However, its great disadvantage is that the main street is the NV1 and the traffic is continuous.

There is a large campsite 5-6km to the northeast of El Escorial on the Guadarrama road. Much more isolated are two sites on the southern slopes of the Sierra de Malagon, the nearest village being Peguerinos. There are no wardened refuges, but open shelters with no facilities (and in some cases no nearby water source) are scattered around the range (see maps pp 157).

El Escorial

ROUTES

The routes selected are a mixture of circuits starting in El Escorial plus a small number which use public transport to distant points for walks back to the town, and others which require a car to reach the starting point. Although this end of the range is relatively low, the landscape is very varied and the views as good as anywhere, often with dramatic perspectives of the monastery. There is a scattering of Civil War remains, particularly at the northern end and, on the slopes above the town, various curious buildings are found connected with the complex water supply system for the monastery. The one small complaint I have about the area is its popularity with trailbike riders, which has resulted in some of the paths being badly eroded and broken up.

For the sake of brevity and following local usage, I refer to San Lorenzo de El Escorial as "El Escorial" in all the descriptions. In fact, none of the walks selected touches on the lower town.

38. *LAS MACHOTAS.*

Las Machotas, as El Fraile and La Machota Chica are collectively known, are the shaggy little clump of hills lying to the southwest of the town and to the east of the Puerto de la Cruz Verde which carries the Madrid-Avila road. Their isolated position protruding SSE into the Meseta means that,

139

in spite of their relatively low altitude, they form a wonderful platform from which to view a great sweep of mountains from La Pedriza in the east to Gredos in the west, as well as vast distances south across the rolling tableland.

Their lower height and detached position gives them an even sunnier climate than the main range, as they are often below the base of any cloud clinging to the watershed; but even in poor visibility, the route along the ridge is a fascinating walk through a continuous sculpture park of weathered rock groupings, at its most spectacular on the summit of La Machota Chica where a number of giant boulders are piled at the top of a huge sloping slab. The lower altitude and many sheltered sunny slopes also make this area a botanist's paradise in spring, with many species not found in the main range.

The multi-topped Machota Chica is sometimes called Los Tres Hermitaños (the Three Hermits) after the monks who looked after the hermitages in the area. The northernmost and highest point is known as El Fraile, after a distinctive conjunction of boulders on the summit, resembling a friar with a pointed cowl.

38a.* EL ESCORIAL - ERMITA DE LA VIRGEN DE GRACIA - ROMAN ROAD - LA MACHOTA CHICA - EL FRAILE (1461m) - ERMITA DE LA VIRGEN DE GRACIA - EL ESCORIAL.

Time: 6¹/₂-7hrs
Total ascent: 711m

This very fine circuit has a gentle, sylvan start as it crosses the monastery grounds then wanders through pastureland thickly scattered with a variety of deciduous trees, to link up with the course of a Roman road which leads to the southern end of the ridge. The road was apparently a branch from the more important one over the Fuenfría Pass and today is a pretty lane between drystone walls fringed with ash trees. There are glimpses of the original paving in one or two places.

The climb up the slabs and boulder fields of the southern end of the ridge is very enjoyable, but is continuously steep and at one point there is an unavoidable scramble up a 20m slab which would certainly present difficulties in wet or icy conditions. From the main summit of La Machota Chica, there are a variety of ways along the

LAS MACHOTAS, SAN BENITO AND BARRANCO DE LA CABEZA

Routes 38a, b, c, d, 39

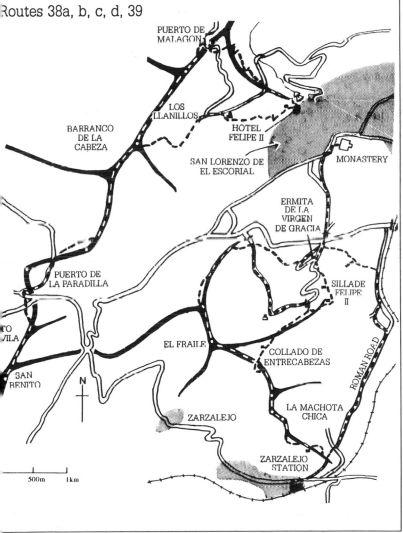

ridge, crossing or avoiding a couple of complicated little tops before a longer climb to El Fraile and its long whaleback summit, scattered with strange conjunctions of outcrops and loose boulders. The return route crosses the protected Herrería Woods with its rich variety of deciduous trees, principally oak and chestnut.

Pass through stone arches at the southwest corner of the monastery (1040m) and follow the road round to the gates of the monastery grounds. The surfaced but traffic-free road which crosses them (with GR10 red/white stripes appearing) leads to the **Avila road** (*20mins*). Start up the road directly opposite which is signposted Silla de Felipe II, but before reaching the little chapel of the Virgen de Gracia, leave on a dirt road to the left starting at a metal gate (sign to Granja Escuela y Deportes). Keep to the main track across a picnic area with a fuente and follow its windings, ignoring any minor branches, until a fork is reached. The left branch leads to some gates (Finca Herrería written on them) and farm buildings just beyond. Go to the left of the buildings to pick up a track leaving left from a cattle trough. It is only a faint trace at times as it wanders through the trees but it leads to a gate (*20mins*) giving onto a lane with a railway line running parallel to it. Follow the lane to the right, then take the right branch at a fork, which leads to the gates of another finca, and to the left of them the start of a narrow path running between drystone walls. This emerges onto the Roman road at a rising paved section. Follow it to its southern end, where it meets a wide dirt road (*50mins*).

Opposite and a few metres to the right, a track rises between stone walls for a short distance. As soon as it levels out, the yellow circles which mark the route to La Machota Chica can be picked up on the right. They start by crossing a stone wall to the right of a prominent outcrop then wander up, a little to the right of the crest of a small spur, eventually to climb a dry grassy streambed towards a roofless stone building (1100m, *20mins*) connected with the extensive quarries found on the other side of the spur.

Beyond it at the end of a broad grassy terrace, a wall on the left is crossed and the climb starts in earnest on a zigzagging route through a band of cistus. This gives way to a long rising traverse to the right, at first through boulders then across huge banks of slabs. At the end, a steep climb follows through another cistus band then up a grassy slope and into more boulders which culminate in a wide belt of steep slabs, some 20m high. The marks run straight up the face then climb through a wide,

Las Machotas from Reuben's Cross

chaotic boulder field to enter a grass-floored corridor above. Near its head, the markers exit to the left and cross easy-angled slabs to the summit of **La Machota Chica** (1404m, *1hr*). The highest point is a survey pillar on top of one of the massive boulders.

The way along the ridge runs to the left of the boulders, at the top of the big slab, and is well marked as it meanders down to a small saddle. The next top beyond it has a scrambling line over its crest and a couple of traverses to the right. At the next col, a traverse leaves to the left although again there is a marked route over the next high point. These alternatives converge on a grassy plateau area which falls away at its far edge in another chaos of rock. Various cairn lines run down to the **Collado de Entrecabezas** (1274m, *25mins*) below.

The traditional route crosses the wall at the angle it makes at the top of the pass and follows it up the slopes, on a clear if meandering path, but recently the Prohibido el Paso signs have appeared and you may feel more comfortable keeping to the left of the wall, where you will come across, about halfway up, the Fuente de Saltedero (which doesn't normally run all summer). The wall continues across the top of **El Fraile** (1461m, *30mins*), a wide grassy ridge scattered with boulder groups, and at the end of the summit area it turns left then sharp right down a spur pointing back towards the town. Follow motorbike tracks to the left of the wall all the way down the crest. Near the base of the spur, the landowner has fenced across the tracks, presumably to keep out bikers rather than walkers. Climb over the two stone walls which make an angle

143

on the right then continue right on a track into a small wooded valley which leads down to a surfaced lane (*55mins*).

Cross the road and follow a wide path through the woodland until it meets a farm lane. Two minutes to the left are the picnic sites around the Virgen de Gracia Chapel with the **Avila road** (*20mins*) just beyond. Reverse the beginning of the route back to the **monastery** (*20mins*).

38b.* ZARZALEJO STATION - LA MACHOTA CHICA - EL FRAILE (1461m) - ERMITA DE LA VIRGEN DE GRACIA - EL ESCORIAL.

> **Time: 5-5¹/₂hrs**
> **Total ascent: 691m**

This follows the same line across Las Machotas as Route 38a, but uses the Avila train to the station at the south end of the ridge to avoid the long walk out from El Escorial.

There is a regular bus service between the road junction at the bottom of the Calle de Floridablanca in the upper town and the railway station. Alternatively, you can walk down through the monastery grounds, entered through gates to the right of the main road below the monastery. Zarzalejo is the next stop along the line in the Avila direction. From the station there (980m), walk to the main road and follow it to the right, to the end of a long white building. On the other side of the road, a wide stony track climbs gently to the right, eventually heading away from the road and up onto a grassy saddle (*10mins*), with a heavily quarried ridge rising on the left. From there, follow Route 38a.

38c.* EL ESCORIAL - SILLA DE FELIPE II - COLLADO DE ENTRECABEZAS - MACHOTA CHICA - EL FRAILE (1461m) - ERMITA DE LA VIRGEN DE GRACIA - EL ESCORIAL.

> **Time: 5¹/₂-6hrs**
> **Total ascent: 697m**

If you don't wish to tackle the steep, rugged southern end of the ridge, this is the far more popular alternative which crosses the Herrería Woods and climbs to the Collado de Entrecabezas, the big

Ruins of the Casa de los Ermitaños, El Escorial and the central peaks

saddle at the halfway point on the ridge. A section of the long distance footpath GR10 is followed all the way from the monastery to the saddle. It passes on the way the Silla (Seat) de Felipe II, a carved rock platform made for the king to watch the progress of the monastery's construction. Situated on a low spur running northeast from Las Machotas, this popular spot has car parking and a bar (open in summer and at weekends).

Arriving at the mid-point of the ridge means, of course, that the route has to double back from La Machota Chica to continue to El Fraile, but this is no hardship, given the interesting scenery of the crest, the magnificent views and a choice of lines to vary the return to the Collado.

Follow Route 38a to the **Avila road** (960m, *20mins*) and start up the road to the Silla, but instead of turning off at the metal gate, continue along the road, still following the red and white stripes of GR10. Just opposite a picnic area with a fuente, they turn into the trees on the left in order to cut off a long bend in the road. The latter is rejoined higher up but only for a few metres, with the marks heading into the trees again, at the outside of the next bend. At an unmarked crossroads, just after leaving

145

the road, turn right to climb steeply into the rocks of the **Silla de Felipe II** (1080m, *20mins*).

Continue following the GR10 markings to the right of a small bar. Rocky steps lead up to a ruined building, called the Casa del Sordo. The path continues along its terrace, with fine views to the south and east, then round to the right, so bringing La Machota Chica into view. Turn left at a junction with a dirt road to arrive in a small clearing with a stone wall and metal gates to the left. The now narrow track meanders through bouldery woodland, keeping the stone wall to the left, until the latter meets another one coming down from the left across a small meadow. The traditional path and the GR10 crossed into the meadow but Prohibido El Paso signs have recently appeared and it is probably advisable to shadow the rising wall to its left, all the way to the **Collado de Entrecabezas** (1274m, *50mins*). Half way up on the other side of the wall you will see the ruined Casa de los Ermitaños. At the top of the pass, SENDA DE LOS 3 ERMITAÑOS is etched on the El Escorial side of one of the larger rocks with an arrow indicating the start of the track to the summit of La Machota Chica. From there, reverse Route 38a to La Machota Chica then continue on it all the way back to the monastery.

38d. SILLA DE FELIPE II - CASA DE LOS ERMITAÑOS - COLLADO DE ENTRECABEZAS - MACHOTA CHICA - EL FRAILE (1461m) - FUENTE DE LA REINA - SILLA DE FELIPE II.

Time: 4¹/₂-5hrs
Total ascent: 411m

The Silla de Felipe II, described in Route 38c, is in fact the nearest roadhead to the ridge and car drivers can make this shorter circuit from that point. Another possibility, if you would prefer to walk the ridge from end to end from here, is to take a very pretty track through the ashgroves and meadows on its eastern flank to link up with Route 38a at the end of the Roman road.

The Silla is reached in a car by following the Avila signs from the lower town which takes you to the main road to the Puerto de la Cruz Verde. After 2-3km in the Avila direction take a signposted turning to the Silla on the left. Immediately there is a fork and it is the left branch with the central white line which leads up through deciduous woodland to the viewpoint.

Although it is worth taking a look at the "seat" beyond the stone gateposts, cars can continue a little further up the road as far as a barrier (1080m).

The walk starts on the dirt road to the left of the barrier and links in with Route 38c at a junction, just before the clearing with a wall and metal gates. To link up with Route 38a, as mentioned above, take the track on the other side of the gates. Otherwise continue on 38c as far as the Collado de Entrecabezas, then on Route 38a to the surfaced lane at the base of El Fraile. Follow the road to the right on its sweep of the wooded Herrería basin, past the Fuente de la Reina and back to the barrier (*25mins*).

39.* PUERTO DE LA PARADILLA - SAN BENITO - PUERTO DE LA PARADILLA - BARRANCO DE LA CABEZA (1680m) - PUERTO DE MALAGON - EL ESCORIAL.

Time: 5¹/₂-6hrs
Total ascent: 615m

Although Barranco de la Cabeza is the highest point on this route, it is San Benito which is the more interesting summit. This conical mountain with a crinkly summit ridge enjoys an isolated position to the west of the pass carrying the Madrid-Avila road and is effectively the most westerly summit in the Sierra before the relief falls away into the lower ridges running towards the Sierra de Gredos. The views in all directions are therefore spectacular. The summit may well be an object of pilgrimage as there is a shrine and a cupboard with a visitors' book (although some of the comments in the book are unlikely to have been written by pilgrims).

Its position actually makes it difficult to put together a satisfactory route. At 45mins from road to summit, it clearly isn't a serious walk in its own right but any complete traverse of the mountain would have to include return stretches on the often busy Avila or Robleda de Chavela roads. This walk settles therefore for retracing the route from the summit back to the starting point at the Puerto de la Paradilla, then continues along the main watershed back to El Escorial. The crest on this section is broad and rolling with wide views to the west and plantation to the east. Coming from this direction you hardly notice crossing the long whaleback of Barranco

de la Cabeza. It is, however, worth a small detour at the summit to look down into the crags and gullies on the southeast slopes (which are explored in Route 40c).

The descent route from the Puerto de Malagon provides a striking contrast to the landscape so far: a well constructed, possibly ancient, footpath heads steeply down through very attractive mixed woodland, including a spectacular copse of Aspen.

As this isn't a circular route it is necessary to take a taxi or bus to the Puerto de la Paradilla. In fact, at the time of writing, the Herranz company run a bus service which crosses the pass on its way to the village of Peguerinos. It is, however, only the Sunday one which is useful to the walker as it leaves El Escorial at 10.00. The bus stop is on the small plaza on a terrace at the bottom of Calle de Floridablanca (the main street). Tickets have to be purchased before boarding, at the kiosk inside a bar, just round the corner in the Calle del Rey. Ask the driver to stop at the Restaurante La Ventalera, which is at the **Puerto de la Paradilla** (1345m).

From the restaurant, cross both the Santa Maria de Alameda and Avila roads, which meet slightly to the left, and start to follow some tyre tracks which leave the road to the right of the steep bank at the top of the pass. The tracks wind up the open grassy slopes of San Benito towards a shoulder on the skyline to the left. Before they reach a gate in a barbed wire fence head uphill towards the junction of the fence and a beautifully made stone wall which cuts horizontally right across the northern slopes of the mountain. At the junction, the wall turns uphill and can be followed on either side directly to the summit ridge, a series of small outcrops with the highest point marked by a survey post (1625m, *45mins*), at the far end.

You can slightly vary the return to the **Puerto de la Paradilla** (*35mins*) by heading straight down the open northern slopes when the pass comes into view. Then follow the road above the restaurant until a dirt road cutting into the side of the Cerro de la Gancha leaves to the right. It leads to the main crest at a saddle beyond that hill. Stick to the left of the stone wall which follows the crest, rather than the zigzags of the dirt road, to reach the summit of **Barranco de la Cabeza** (1680m, *1hr*). It isn't well marked but is to the right of the wall where it makes an angle on open ground.

Continue along the crest to the **Puerto de Malagon** (1534m, *30mins*) which is crossed by a metalled road. Moving over to the El

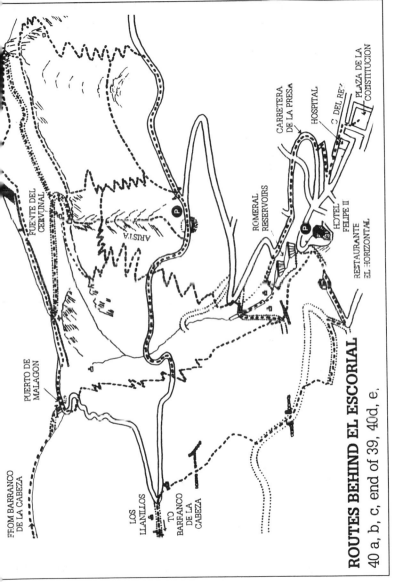

ROUTES BEHIND EL ESCORIAL
40 a, b, c, end of 39, 40d, e,

FROM BARRANCO
DE LA CABEZA

PUERTO DE
MALAGON

LOS
LLANILLOS

TO
BARRANCO
DE LA
CABEZA

FUENTE DEL
CERVUNAL

ARISTA

ROMERAL
RESERVOIRS

CARRETERA
DE LA PRESA

HOSPITAL

C. DEL REY

PLAZA DE LA
CONSTITUCION

HOTEL
FELIPE II

RESTAURANTE
EL HORIZONTAL

Escorial side of the pass, leave the road at the first curve, to continue downhill on a clear track into a sloping meadow. After an electricity pylon, take the fainter left-hand path to cross the road and enter some woods. The wide, well-made track descends the right-hand slopes of a wooded valley, passing high above a fuente in the valley bottom. About 10mins after crossing the metalled road again, take the right branch at a fork for the few metres before it meets another path. Go right and immediately left down to a gate made from a metal bed base. Beyond this the path drops steeply following the wire boundary fence of the Romeral Reservoir down to the driveway of the Felipe II Hotel, a few minutes' walk from the town centre (*55mins*).

40. *ABANTOS.*

More like a headland than a mountain, Abantos throws wide skirts eastwards into the Meseta dividing the El Escorial bowl from the Valley of the Fallen. Its position and steep southern and eastern slopes give it a more imposing appearance from the Madrid side than its height would suggest. To the west, it is connected by a short ridge to the main crest and the moorland scenery of both the valleys and the broad tops is chequered with patches of plantation.

It is possible to drive on a narrow, potholed road from El Escorial over the Puerto de Malagon to a point only 50mins walk from the summit of the mountain, but that misses the pleasures of the many fine approaches from the town to the balcony-like summit. The pine-covered slopes above El Escorial are crisscrossed with paths and forestry roads, some connecting up the elaborate fuentes which dot the hillsides. Out of the many possibilities, I have chosen two direct routes to Abantos and used three more in descent from longer walks taking in other summits on the ridge.

40a.* EL ESCORIAL - ARISTA DE ABANTOS - ABANTOS (1753m) - PUERTO DE MALAGON - EL ESCORIAL.

> **Time:** 5-5½hrs
> **Total ascent:** 650m
> **(or 4hrs - 434m ascent from base of the arête)**

One of the most striking features to be seen from the town is the

long, steep arête rising from the pine-covered slopes to the north and topped by a tiny stone building. In spite of the ridge's prominence, it is unnamed on maps, although one guidebook writer calls it the Arista de Abantos and the steep section below the hut is called the Risco de San Benito. The ridge is precipitous on the west side, less so on the east but the scramble along the crest over the succession of chunky towers is sometimes steep but neither difficult nor particularly exposed. An added attraction in May and June is the sea of french lavender which laps up against the rocks.

There are two routes from the summit to the Puerto de Malagon. One follows forest roads, passing Reubens' Cross on the top of a prominent outcrop where the painter was reputed to have sketched a view of the monastery. The other joins the main ridge and makes the most of the views towards the Sierra de Gredos. Both routes follow for part of the way a strikingly sculptural stone wall, one of many examples found in Guadarrama.

Walking from the town (1040m), start in the Plaza de la Constitución at the top end of the Calle de Floridablanca, and leave along the few metres of street at the highest corner which leads immediately into a triangular space in front of a hospital. Take the rising road on the right of the hospital which has a sign to the Hotel Felipe II, and at the top, turn right into a narrow steep lane which ends in an avenue of large detached villas. Follow it to the right and over a crossroads, past more villas and onto the signposted Puerto de Malagon road.

At a right hairpin bend, go straight on at the outside of the corner onto a track which runs beside a metal fence surrounding the tiny Romeral Reservoir. At the top corner drop steeply left into a small valley scattered with magnificent deciduous trees. Cross the streambed and head up the valley, past a couple of fuentes, to come upon a line of large stone slabs, which actually cover a water channel. Use them as a path until they meet a dirt road. A few metres along this to the right a track heads uphill and back on to the Puerto de Malagon road at another right hairpin. Again, leave it on the outside of the bend on a clear track climbing into a small grassy valley. It soon swings up the right-hand slopes to cross a stony forestry road before joining, a few metres higher, the GR10 (red/white stripes). Follow this uphill until it meets the surfaced road again. The base of the Arista is 5mins along the road to the right (1320m, *50mins*).

(For a shorter walk, it is possible to park at the base of the arête on the road to the Puerto de Malagon. To reach it by car, drive up the Calle del Rey, (the street parallel to and above the Calle de Floridablanca), passing a hospital to the left and a sign to Hotel Felipe II. At the top of the street, which merges with a parallel one to the left, continue uphill to a confluence of five roads with another sign for the hotel straight ahead. Double back into the first road to the right (Carretera de la Presa) which takes a rising curve to the left. Go straight over the crossroads and at the next junction follow the Puerto de Malagon signs. The road climbs for a few kilometres through pine woods past two more junctions. Immediately after the second, the slabby rock of the base of the arête can be seen to the right and a stone balconied viewpoint to the left. There is room for three or four cars opposite the terrace and a couple more back at the preceding junction.)

The route up the ridge from the road is neither marked nor shown on any maps. The best access is a little to the left of the layby as you face uphill and route-finding is a matter of picking a way through the rock and scrub until the first large outcrop is reached. Make for the crest and look for the easiest line over the alternating buttresses and cols to reach the stone hut at the top of the **Risco de San Benito** (1660m, *1hr*).

A dirt road starts behind the hut. Leave it after a couple of minutes where it makes a gentle curve to the left and go straight on across an open strip of ground, which is the continuation of the Arista spur, between a plantation to the left and steep slopes falling away to the right (some GR10 markings). Passing through a band of trees the path rises steeply to the left to reach the summit of **Abantos** (1753m, *15mins*) with its cross, aerial, dish and survey point. (The true summit appears to be a little to the northwest at the corner of a stone wall.)

If you want to return by the Reubens' Cross route, follow the dirt road behind the summit down to its junction with the one from Risco de San Benito. Turn right to follow it round the upper slopes of a wooded valley. (The cross can be seen slightly lower to the left where the road starts to curve to the right, away from the valley.) Continue into plantation to where a stone wall crosses the road then turn downhill on a wide track, badly damaged by motorcycles. It splits lower down, both branches leading to the metalled road just to the north of the **Puerto de Malagon** (1534m, *50mins*).

The alternative route from Abantos to the Puerto de Malagon follows the GR10 markings along the summit stone wall across a small col and up to the main crest beyond. Where the wall and markings head right towards San Juan, turn left onto a wide track along the open ridge to descend gently into plantation. Keeping to the right of a stone wall, the

Reubens' Cross dirt road is crossed and the surfaced road to the **Puerto de Malagon** (*55mins*) is joined a little lower down.

Return to El Escorial on Route 39 (*55mins*). If you are parked at the base of the arête, leave that route at the horizontal surfaced road, following the latter to the left and back to the layby (*45mins*).

40b.* EL ESCORIAL - GR10 - ARISTA (PORTICHUELO) - ABANTOS (1753m) - PUERTO DE MALAGON - EL ESCORIAL.

> **Time:** 5-5¹/₂hrs
> **Total ascent:** 650m
> **(or 4-4¹/₂hrs - 434m ascent from base of the arête)**

For those not interested in scrambling, this walk covers much the same ground as Route 40a but with the arête section replaced by a stretch of the GR10 which meanders up the forested valley just to the west of the ridge, then on a well-made zigzagging path which crosses the upper part of the arête at a small col, called El Portichuelo.

Walking from El Escorial, follow Route 40a as far as the point where the GR10 footpath meets the horizontal surfaced road (*45mins*). Car users, wanting a shorter walk, can park in the layby at the base of the arête as for Route 40a, then continue along the road as far as the same point (*5mins*).

GR10 crosses the road and climbs a forested bowl in big zigzags, with recently cleared areas on the right giving good views of the arête. After 20mins or so, GR10 goes straight on at the outside of a right hairpin (no paint marks at this point but a cairn at the junction). Continue instead up the shortening zigzags above, soon leaving the trees to head up steep rocky ground to the **Portichuelo** (*35mins*) on the arête.

The path on the far side of the col drops gently to the left to join another well-made mule path. Follow zigzags uphill then a straight rising section into a plantation. After a left hairpin the path disappears on the tree terraces just below the upper margin of the wood. The broom on the slopes above is extremely dense, so turn right, along the upper edge of the plantation, and at its corner pick up a rough cairned path running diagonally right through more open scrub than rocks, to join Route 40a on the ridge just below the summit of **Abantos** (*40mins*).

Stone wall near the Puerto de Malagon

40c.* EL ESCORIAL - ALTA HORIZONTAL - LOS LLANILLOS - BARRANCO DE LA CABEZA - PUERTO DE MALAGON - PISTA FORESTAL - ABANTOS (1753m) - EL ESCORIAL.

Time: 6-6½hrs
Total ascent: 872m

Barranco de la Cabeza is the long, curving top to the west of the Puerto de Malagon. The straightforward traverse of the summit along the main ridge has already been described in Route 39. A much more interesting approach starts from El Escorial, first picking a way through the dense mesh of paths and forestry roads in the band of trees on the lower slopes, then finding a rough steep line through the broad curtain of crags below the summit.

There could not be more of a contrast, emerging from the shelter of the forests and gullies of the El Escorial slopes to walk the broad, rolling, Pennine-like ridge to the Puerto de Malagon. From here, forestry roads are followed to the top of Abantos and the descent to El Escorial starts on an old mule track directly below the summit crags.

The walk starts at the Felipe II Hotel/conference centre and can be reached on foot or by car: start by passing the hospital as in Route 40a.

At the top of the street both cars and pedestrians should move left into the adjoining street which leads across a multi-junction, directly to the hotel. The car park to use is to the left of the hotel's approach road before it swings back on itself at the foot of the reservoir dam. Just as the curve finishes, a path rises left from stone steps set in the bank. It leads to the hotel boundary fence which is then followed to the right to the Restaurante el Horizontal.

Take the metalled road beyond the restaurant as far as a sharp left curve, from which point a dirt road leads back uphill past some villas. Follow it to a T-junction then go left until the dirt road peters out and a footpath continues up through the trees. When a dirt road is joined higher up, go left to pass soon after through some gates in a wall. When the road turns left and starts to descend, leave on a rough track uphill through a clearing. (Just to the right can be seen the Arca de Agua del Helechar - part of the once extensive water-collecting arrangements for the monastery.) At the top of the clearing, follow the track through trees to an open area of grass and boulders, where a slight trend to the left leads through a stone wall and eventually to the **Fuente de la Concha** (1340m, *40mins*).

The Puerto de Malagon road just above the fuente rises gently to the left to arrive at the branch to the Los Llanillos picnic site (prominent signs). Cross its pleasant terraces (another fuente) on a horizontal dirt road which continues beyond a barrier to curve to the right, round a broad shoulder. As it descends into a shallow valley, leave uphill on a narrow track (*20mins*), initially following a small pipeline.

In a few minutes, when this track disappears in the streambed, cross to the left bank to work up the more open slopes on that side - there is no path over the rough and broken terrain and the craggy spur descending from the summit of Barranco de la Cabeza is now in full view above to the left. Higher up it is easier to move back to the right bank, following cattle tracks up the steep grassy strip between the streambed and a stone wall with plantation beyond it.

Scramblers might like to explore the big gully splitting the lower cliffs on the left for early access to the spur crest, but this route continues up the streambed as far as a prominent cairn-like structure in the stone wall. From there make a direct line for another gully a little up to the left. The rocks in the lower part give way to grass which leads up to the crest of the ridge. Turn right and climb the broken rocks to the right of some large slabs then continue uphill over a mixture of grass and boulders to the summit of **Barranco de la Cabeza** (1680m, *50mins*). (All scrambling can be avoided by continuing to follow the stone wall to a saddle in the ridge just to the right of the summit.)

Behind the summit, cross the stone wall which follows the watershed and go right on the wide track running alongside it to the **Puerto de Malagon** (1534m, *30mins*). Staying on the Avila side of the pass, follow the road briefly to just beyond a layby at the first curve to the left. A wide track with yellow paint leaves on the right. From here, go either by Reubens' Cross or the main ridge, reversing sections of Route 40a, to **Abantos** (1753m, *50mins*).

For the descent to the town, leave to the left just behind the cross to drop steeply to a grassy platform. From there, a badly broken-up path descends in zigzags to the left. Lower down, it moves right below some outcrops and a ruined stone hut then returns to zigzagging down a shallow fold in the slopes (ignore one left branch). Much lower down and well after re-entering the pinewoods, look for a horizontal path leaving from the outside of a left hairpin. This crosses the enclosing rocky spur from where it drops gently below the arête to a metalled road (*55mins*). If the horizontal path is missed, the zigzags continue straight down to a more easterly point on the same metalled road.

From either point, go right on the road, past the barrier at its junction with the main Puerto de Malagon road and then round the base of the arête to the point where GR10 crosses the road. Follow the red and white stripes down into the trees, reversing the start of Route 40a as far as the stone slabs covering a water channel. Instead of turning onto them, continue on the dirt road which rises to the left to the crest of a spur. Leave it there for a track down to the left, which is blocked by an old bed frame in a stone wall. On the other side it leads directly back to the **Felipe II Hotel** (*45mins*).

40d.* PEGUERINOS - (PEÑA DE LA ESTRIBA) - CASA DE LA CUEVA - REFUGIO LA NARANJERA - SAN JUAN - ABANTOS (1753m) - FUENTE DEL CERVUNAL - EL ESCORIAL.

Time:	**6-6¹/₂hrs**
Total ascent:	**402m**

Peguerinos is a small village in the middle of the high valley system of Pinares Llanos to the west of the main watershed. A Sunday bus service from El Escorial makes possible a walk from the village back

PEGUERINOS AND THE SIERRA DE MALAGON

Routes 40d, 42a, b

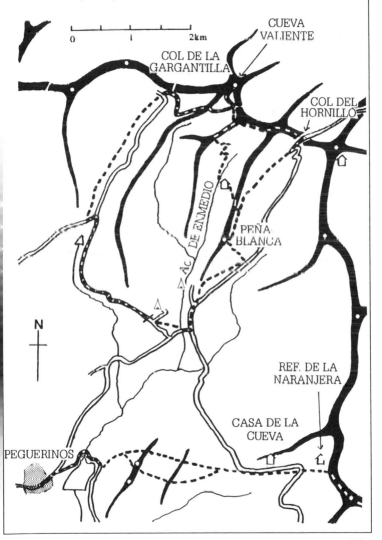

to El Escorial through an interesting cross-section of the countryside: a gentle climb from the village, through a parkland landscape of meadow and trees with occasional rocky interruptions, then the moorland and plantation along the main watershed, which, from the Refugio la Naranjera to Abantos, is more of an escarpment than a crest with a dramatic falling away to the east. In a dip between San Juan and Abantos there is a gap in the ridge wall and a wide track leads down through the forest to a Pozo de Nieve, an ice house which was built in 1603 and restored in the 1930s. It is an interesting building surrounding a deep pit, in a quiet and atmospheric spot.

Details of the bus service are given in Route 39. It stops at the Plaza de la Iglesia in Peguerinos (1352m). With the church to your left, take the street with shops and bars, leaving from the right-hand corner of the square. Follow this out of the village for 5mins then take a metalled road to the right just after the municipal cattle pens. This leads past the cemetery to a reservoir. Depending on the water level, either stay on the road round an inlet or take a short cut across a weir at its mouth to rejoin the road.

A minute or two later at a right bend, leave the road for a wide track which passes through a gap in a wire fence. There is an immediate fork but both branches re-emerge at the crest of the shoulder to the left. Used by trailbikes, the wide track climbs the shoulder between two stone walls. This path, which has occasional paint markings, can be followed all the way to a metalled road (*1hr 25mins*).

(Alternatively, a more interesting but untracked route can be taken over the Peña de la Estriba, the rocky knoll to the right of the main track. Once beyond the little summit, make for the next band of rocks on the other side of a slight depression. A convenient corridor through the outcrop emerges on to more parkland. Continue in the same direction, crossing a wide track and entering denser stands of trees. By moving gradually to the left, the original motorbike track is rejoined.)

Go right on the road, using parallel paths through the bordering trees, past the Casa de la Cueva refuge and its adjoining picnic site and fuente, to another meadow/picnic area. Here the road makes a sharp bend to the right and, behind another fuente on the outside of the bend, a path with yellow markings heads into the trees towards the semi-ruined Refugio la Naranjera (*45mins*) on the main ridge. It is worth a small diversion on to the outcrop to the left beyond the ridge wall, for the view across the

Valley of the Fallen.

Return to the hut and continue on rising ground through trees to the right of the stone wall which runs along the crest. The path, now marked with GR10 red and white stripes, eventually rises steeply to open moorland and the survey point at San Juan, which is hardly an impressive summit but a good viewpoint to the north and east. Continue to follow the wall all the way to the summit of **Abantos** (1753m, *1hr 5mins*).

Behind the summit rocks, descend beside the remains of a brick building down a steep eroded slope to a grass terrace. Turn right and look for the red and white markings which lead through a few trees to an open strip of land between plantation to the right and steep slopes dropping away to the left. At the end of the strip, turn right onto a dirt road. still following the GR10 markings. These soon leave to the left descending to the **Fuente del Cervunal** (*15mins*) in the centre of a sloping meadow. Continue downhill through scattered trees to the left of the emerging streambed where the markings and a track become clearer.

When they cross a small shoulder to the left, go straight down the other side in a confusing tangle of tracks and short cuts until the markings and the now wide zigzagging path can be picked up again as they drop into the wooded valley. Arriving at a horizontal surfaced road (*40mins*), reverse the start of Route 40a back to El Escorial (*35mins*).

40e.* ALTO DE LOS LEONES - CABEZA LIJAR (1824m) - CUERDA DE CUELGAMUROS - ABANTOS - EL ESCORIAL (see maps pp161 & 149)

Time: 7-7¹/₂hrs
Total ascent: 817m

This is one of the classic Guadarrama ridge walks, which follows the main watershed southwards and is of considerable interest and variety. The difficulty for the visitor is to reach the start at the Alto de los Leones road pass. In the last resort, car users could walk only the first half of the ridge, as far as Cerro de la Carrasqueta or the Refugio la Naranjera, then return on the little used surfaced road just to the west.

A taxi from El Escorial is the simplest if most expensive way to reach the Alto de los Leones Pass. Alternatively, take one of the Madrid buses as far as the village of Guadarrama (Autocares Herranz) and then a taxi for the few kilometres to the pass.

A surfaced lane, carrying the GR10 red and white stripes, leaves the top of the Alto de los Leones (1511m) to the right of a large restaurant. (Turn left immediately behind the lion statue if driving up from the Madrid side). The initially good road surface finishes a few hundred metres later at some military telecommunications installations. Continue on the potholed lane until, just after a cattle grid, the markings leave diagonally right, rising through pine trees. Motorists can park here.

As the route as far as Abantos sticks to the crest and is waymarked with the GR10 colours, there is little need for a detailed description. The principal features are:

Cerro Piñonero (or Gamonosa) 1649m, *15mins* from the road.

Collado Vaquero 1600m, *10mins*. The surfaced road touches this saddle on the east side.

Cabeza Lijar 1824m, *35mins*. The summit, an excellent all-round viewpoint, is topped by a Civil War bunker which is used as an overnight shelter.

Collado de la Cierva 1710m, *10mins*. The road crosses this pass.

Cerro de la Salamanca 1789m, *15mins*, with an open unwardened refuge.

Riscos del Palanco 1688m, *25mins*. The path goes to the left of this outcrop.

Cerro de la Carrasqueta 1640m, *25mins*. The actual summit is bypassed just to the right.

Refugio La Naranjera 1520m, *45mins*. From this point the route coincides with Route 40d. It is worth making the small detour across the ridge wall before reaching the refuge for the view into the Valley of the Fallen.

San Juan (survey point) 1734m, *25mins*.

Abantos 1753m, *30mins*.

There are three equally attractive routes back to El Escorial from Abantos: the direct route from the summit (Route 40c), the continuation of GR10 via the Fuente del Cervunal (Route 40d) or the one described here which lies between the two.

Leave the summit on the steep eroded path to the left of the remains of a brick building to arrive at a grassy platform behind another rocky headland. Follow the GR10 markings to the right through a band of trees then across open ground as far as the first sizeable rock outcrop. Descending the steep rocky ground to the left of it, look for cairns cutting half right across a band of broom to the top corner of a plantation. Work

La Maliciosa in winter
Zabala Refuge from the slopes of Dos Hermanas

Laguna Grande and Dos Hermanas
La Maza from the Collado de las Vistillas with La Maliciosa in the distance

CUERDA DE CUELGAMUROS
Routes 41 and the beginning of 40e

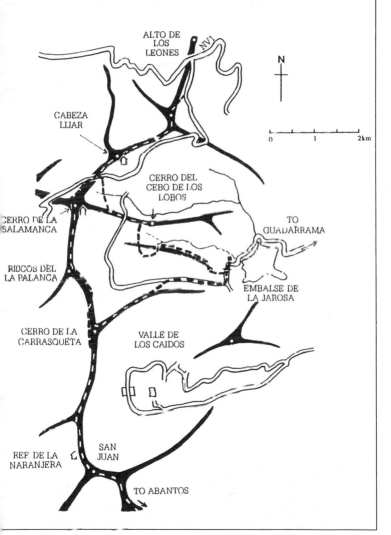

right, through the trees without a clear track and without loosing much height, until a well-made mule track is reached. Follow it downhill. After emerging from the plantation, it zigzags down open ground to the left of the rock towers of the Arista de Abantos, then enters the main band of trees. When it meets a horizontal path (*50mins*), turn right to descend to a surfaced road which is followed to the right, past a junction and round the base of the Arista to where the GR10 crosses it. Rejoin GR10 to reverse the beginning of Route 40a back to **El Escorial** (*50mins*).

41. EMBALSE DE LA JAROSA - CERRO DEL CEBO DE LOS LOBOS - COLLADO DE LA CIERVA (OR MINA OR LIJAR) - CERRO DE LA SALAMANCA (1789m) - CERRO DE LA CARRASQUETA - PISTA FORESTAL - EMBALSE DE LA JAROSA.

Time:	**5¹/₂-6hrs**
Total ascent:	**743m**

This circular route is another good alternative to Route 40e for those with a car, as the section of the Cuelgamuros ridge which it includes, from the Collado de la Cierva to the conical little top of Cerro de la Carrasqueta, is perhaps the most attractive part - a succession of rocky knolls with a scattering of trees, rising from the wooded valleys on either side. Even the long forested ascent from the Jarosa Reservoir is enjoyable and varied, with plenty of breaks in the typically loose Guadarrama planting patterns and constantly changing perspectives as spurs are crossed or rocky promontories reached.

The return route down the northeast spur of the Cerro de Carrasqueta has its own interest as well. The upper section gives striking views to the south, of the cross, basilica and monastery of the Valley of the Fallen. Lower down, although pathless in stretches, the crest carries a double row of large cairns (probably fencepost bases) which run practically the whole length of the spur. These, along with all the other ruins and foundations passed on the walk, are Civil War remains.

To reach the reservoir, take the NVI through the centre of Guadarrama, heading towards the Alto de los Leones. Just after the main run of shops and a left bend there are some traffic lights with a Chinese restaurant on the left. Turn left here, then right at the end of the road. Continue past blocks of flats and under a viaduct carrying the A6 motorway to approach the low dam of the reservoir. Turn right onto the lane which runs below the barrage then round the western bank. Where the asphalt finishes, three dirt roads fan out and the wide right branch leads in 200m or so to a bar/restaurant (open weekends and holidays), gravelled parking area and picnic tables scattered in the trees (1100m).

Behind the bar to the left, a wide unsurfaced road rises into the forest. Just beyond a metal barrier, turn right on to a narrower road which climbs gently through cistus thickets scattered with pines. First crossing a spur then heading left up a valley, the road gradually narrows into a footpath. (Ignore cairned branch to right when the head of the valley is reached.) Recrossing the spur at a wooded col, the track climbs a clearing of grass and bracken, swinging right near the top to merge with a horizontal path. A few minutes later it meets another track which, followed to the right, leads immediately to the rocky headland and viewpoint of the **Cerro del Cebo de los Lobos** (1392m, *1hr 5mins*). This sits on a wide spur which runs down from the Cerro de la Salamanca on the main crest, now seen clearly above.

Return to the junction of the paths but continue along the crest of the spur to arrive shortly at a horizontal forest road. On the far side, a path badly damaged by trailbikes heads up the steepening spur through cistus, rocks and trees to a more open section with some Civil War remains. It is possible to continue straight up to the Cerro de Salamanca, but a pleasanter way leaves to the right through a broken wall and into the head of a wooded valley. After crossing the streambed, the tracks zigzag up the right-hand slope to a small quarry in the trees just below the crest. Leave the track a few metres beyond the quarry on a short cut up to a metalled road, which to the left leads to the **Collado de la Cierva** (1710m, *1hr*).

Leave the road and the pass diagonally left on the GR10 (red/white paint). As far as the **Cerro de la Salamanca** (1789m, *20mins*), it keeps below the west side of the crest, although a rougher route along the top can be followed if preferred. From the refuge there, the heavily eroded path descends to skirt left of the next outcrops on the ridge (Riscos del Palanco), then climbs towards the shapely point of the **Cerro de la Carrasqueta** (1640m, *55mins*). (GR10 avoids the summit rocks, so leave the path to follow a fence which leads directly to the top.)

The broad back of the northeast spur is seen below pointing straight towards the reservoir and can be reached by crossing the fence then either scrambling down the steep rocks below the summit or by taking easier ground round to the left of them. The double line of cairns which then appear are occasionally lost in dense bands of cistus and broom. Pass a prominent rocky knoll which has the foundations of a circular building and continue into the trees to reach a wide forestry road (*35mins*). To the right, this leads back to the car park (*40mins*).

42. *SIERRA DE MALAGON.*

The Sierra de Malagon is the longer of the two spurs running back WSW from the Segovia side of the main watershed and stretches nearly 30km from the Collado Hornillo, where it leaves the main spine, to the village of La Cañada on the El Escorial-Avila road. For much of that length it is a succession of rounded and totally forested tops, but there is a compact area at its eastern end and centred on the summit of Cueva Valiente where the rock erupts above the tree line and three long spiky fingers descend southwards into the Peguerinos valley. The resulting combination of woodland, meadow, rock forms and wide views to Gredos, the North Meseta and the central Guadarrama mountains makes very attractive walking country.

The area is of such a size and the network of forestry roads and footpaths so dense that anyone with a reasonable sense of direction could have a good day just wandering in and out of the ridges and valleys, without becoming hopelessly cut off from their starting point. The two routes described here are longer and shorter ways of linking the main attractions, using the principal paths.

42a. COLLADO DEL HORNILLO - CUEVA VALIENTE (1903m) - VALLE DE ENMEDIO REFUGE - PEÑA BLANCA - COLLADO DEL HORNILLO.

Time:	**4hrs**
Total ascent:	**405m**

This is the shorter of the two rounds, the Collado del Hornillo being a conveniently high starting point. The cave, after which Cueva Valiente is named, is found on the slopes above San Rafael at about 1700m and is 20m deep. Peña Blanca is a large column of rock situated at the end of the easternmost of the subsidiary spurs.

There is local legend that the Devil placed a sack of gold on its summit to tempt people to climb it. Today it is popular with rock climbers because it is easily reached from a road.

Coming up from the Madrid side on the NVI, take a lane to the left at the Alto de los Leones, turning immediately behind the stone lion. After 6km of atrociously potholed road, the Collado del Hornillo (1640m) is reached, a wide meadow between forested slopes, with plenty of parking.

Take the wide track which heads straight up the right-hand slope into the trees and is another multi-stranded, motorbike-eroded mess. After 10mins or so the angle eases and when the now single strand of path forks once more, take the left branch which continues through woods across the upper part of the Peña Blanca spur. Arriving at the head of the Enmedio valley, which separates the Peña Blanca spur from the middle one, the views open up towards Gredos. Further along on an open part of the middle spur, it joins the path coming up from the Enmedio valley. Follow it to the right, ignoring any branches, to climb gently to a col carrying a surfaced lane closed to traffic, which winds up to the summit of **Cueva Valiente** (1903m, *1hr*). The top is a large area of meadow with a number of big outcrops, the highest of which shelters a small locked stone hut.

Retrace the route as far as the junction on the middle spur mentioned above. Continue on the track marked with yellow stripes which descends the crest then leaves it to the left to plunge into the forested Enmedio valley, reaching the streambed at the **Valle de Enmedio Refuge** (*50mins*). Take the path up the opposite slope beyond the hut which goes directly to the crest of the Peña Blanca spur. Follow the cairns to the right, which keep to the right of the rocky spine, as far as a small dip in front of a striking group of sculpted rocks. A track drops off the crest to the left and a few minutes later meets a horizontal one. Continue to the right and after passing through a clearing enclosed by rocks, take the left branch at a fork. This leads to a steep drop into a gully with a chockstone, and **Peña Blanca** (1600m, *35mins*) just beyond.

Retrace the yellow markings where they swing sharply up to the crest but, continue on the horizontal track which in a few minutes joins a clearer one taking a gently descending line across the slopes to the road just below the **Collado del Hornillo** (*40mins*).

42b. CAMPING PEGUERINOS - COLLADO DE LA GARGANTILLA - CUEVA VALIENTE (1903m) - REFUGIO ENMEDIO - PEÑA BLANCA - CAMPING PEGUERINOS.

> **Time:** 5^1/$_2$-6hrs
> **Total ascent:** 683m

While it covers much the same high ground as Route 42a, this walk takes a lower and more distant starting point - the campsite at the foot of the most westerly spur. Both the approach to the Collado de la Gargantilla and the return from Peña Blanca pass through very pleasant scots pine woods with grassy clearings (covered in pinky-purple merendera flowers in September).

Drive to the Collado del Hornillo as for Route 42a, but continue by car down into the Peguerinos valley. Follow the Camping Peguerinos signs and park on open land at the junction where the campsite has come into view and there are gates across the road ahead.

Cross the broken wall to the right of the gate and continue on the surfaced road, (open only to forestry vehicles), as far as a T-junction with a sign Camino de Gargantilla (*35mins*), just beyond a small reservoir. You can continue on the road to the right, but, by going left for 3mins then right on to a dirt road, a more attractive parallel route through trees and clearings can be followed. The road is rejoined at the **Collado de la Gargantilla** (1620m, *40mins*) and its continuation to the right leads over a small spur to a wooded col on the main ridge, then on to the summit of **Cueva Valiente** (1903m, *40mins*).

Return to the wooded col and, after the road swings left, leave it diagonally left across a rising slope of grass to find the start of the path to the Enmedio valley. Follow Route 42a as far as **Peña Blanca** (1600m, *1hr 25mins*). The yellow markings peter out as the tower is approached but a steep cairned track leaves down the left-hand wooded slopes to the Collado del Hornillo-Peguerinos road. Instead of making straight across the clearing between the edge of the trees and the road, go diagonally right to join a wide track heading back into the forest, occasionally marked with white stripes and faded numbers in circles. Follow number 10, by taking the left branches at two forks. (In spite of the numbers and some cairns, sections of the path are not very clear and might be difficult to follow under snow.)

When the road is rejoined after 20mins follow it to the right, past the

166

Enmedio valley branch, and then right at a T-junction with a Camping Peguerinos sign. Leave it to the right after crossing the Enmedio stream. At the top of the sloping picnic ground is the junction at the start of the route (*1hr*).

CHAPTER EIGHT

Central Guadarrama (West)

TOPOGRAPHY

From Alto de los Leones the ridge continues northeast rising to La Peñota (1945m) then swinging north to form the western side of the Fuenfría valley with three summits all over 2000m. The most northerly of these, Cerro Minguete (2023m), drops away on its east flank to the Puerto de la Fuenfría (1792m) at the head of the valley, an historically important pass with quite well-preserved remains of a Roman road on the south side.

Cerro Minguete is also the starting point of a subsidiary ridge which runs north to Montón de Trigo (2155m) then swings northwest then southwest to enclose the valley of the Río Moros. This last southwestern section is made up of three summits: Pinareja (2193m), Peña del Oso (2196m) and Pasapan (2003m) which are known collectively as La Mujer Muerta (The Dead Woman) because of the ridge's evocative profile.

From the Puerto de la Fuenfría, Cerro Ventoso (1965m), Segundo Pico (2088m) and Pico de Majalasno (or Primer Pico, 1938m) form the eastern side of the Fuenfría valley. The last two summits are also counted as the first of the seven distinctive tors which make up the Siete Picos Ridge, although Primer Pico is much lower and offset to the south of the east-west axis of the other six. The distance from Segundo Pico eastwards to Séptimo Pico (2138m) is little more than 1 ½km but the ridge continues less dramatically for another 2km over Cerro de Telégrafo (1985m) to the Puerto de Navacerrada (1860m). This is a ski station and carries the most direct road connection between Madrid and Segovia.

VALLEY BASES

For the walker without transport, **Cercedilla** has more to offer as a base than any other mentioned in this guide. Firstly, there is direct access to the Fuenfría skyline from the village, and many more possibilities open up by taking a 6km taxi ride to the Chalet de Peñalara at the head of that valley. Secondly, because it is a stop on the Madrid-Segovia railway line, not only are connections with the capital excellent, but two of the mountain stations towards Segovia can be used to good effect for cross-country routes. Thirdly, it is the starting point of a narrow-gauge branch line to the Puertos of Navacerrada and Cotos, both starting points for a number of high mountain walks. Similarly, for the car driver with only a limited amount of time to spend in the range, Cercedilla is the most convenient base not only for the rich variety of walking in the Central section but also for routes from El Escorial and in La Pedriza, both a 25min drive away.

The village itself is large and, although it has a messy mixture of vernacular granite architecture and second home eclecticism, there is an alpine feel to the place, surrounded as it is by pinewoods and meadows and backed by the steep southern crags of the Siete Picos ridge. There is one hotel and a range of shops, banks, restaurants and bars.

Only 5km to the southwest is the attractive village of **Navacerrada**, nestling in a high basin on the shores of a reservoir and backed by the impressive bulk of La Maliciosa. Although there are no walks which start

Cercedilla church

from the village, it has a better choice of hotels than Cercedilla, with more in the adjoining village of Becerril, and would therefore be a good alternative base for motorists. Although there is a regular bus service to Madrid and Segovia via the Puerto de Navacerrada and, at weekends, a walkers' bus to Puerto de los Cotos (extended in the winter to Valdesquí), an independent walker based here would have to rely heavily on taxis.

If you prefer to be based as high in the mountains as possible, there are two hotels at the **Puerto de Navacerrada**, which is a very good centre for walking but has the rather uncompromising architecture of a typical Spanish ski station. At the less developed **Puerto de los Cotos**, a few kilometres away, the Club Alpino Español have a big comfortable refuge open all the year round - dormitories but a full restaurant and bar service. There is nothing else at the pass apart from two more restaurants.

ROUTES

This is probably the most popular sector in the range with hundreds of backpacks pouring off the Friday night trains at Cercedilla and Puerto de Navacerrada, either to camp in the Fuenfría valley or to fill the various hostels at the pass. Fortunately, the camping and hostelling often seem to be an end in itself and numbers are rarely overwhelming out on the ridges.

The relief in this area is a system of handsome interconnecting ridges with numerous enjoyable approaches to them from the adjacent wooded valleys. Because of the wealth of possible combinations, you will find more overlap and duplication in the routes described in this sector. This is in order to do justice to the variety available and to provide a choice of long and short outings as well as circuits and point-to-points.

43. *LA PEÑOTA.*

When looking northwest at the long section of the main watershed which divides the Río Moros valley from the upper Guadarrama basin, it is always La Peñota which draws the eye in spite of it being lower than the three peaks to the north of it. This is partly due to its position, thrusting forward from the general axis of the ridge, which produces a more mountain-like form than that of the tops to either side. In addition, the southern face has steep crags below the three distinctive crenellations of the summit ridge. (The mountain's other name is Tres Picos.)

El Espinar from the southwest ridge of La Peñota

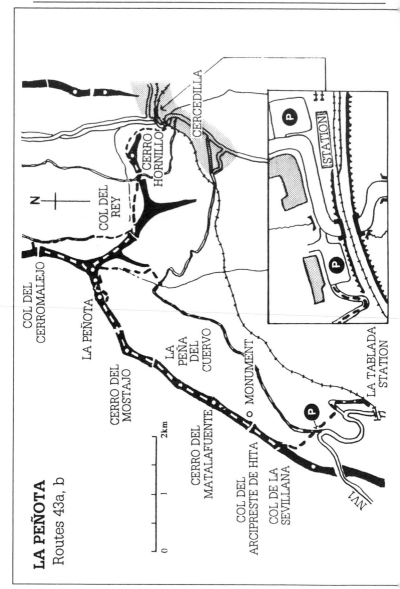

LA PEÑOTA
Routes 43a, b

43a.* LA TABLADA - COLLADO DE LA SEVILLANA - PEÑA DEL CUERVO - COLLADO DEL ARCIPRESTE DE HITA - CERRO DEL MATALAFUENTE - LA PEÑA DEL CUERVO - CERRO DEL MOSTAJO - LA PEÑOTA (1945m) - COLLADO DEL REY - CERCEDILLA.

Time: 5^{1}/$_{2}$-6hrs
Total ascent: 806m

This route takes advantage of Cercedilla's rail connections to complete a traverse of La Peñota, starting at La Tablada station just below the Alto de los Leones and following the ridge on to the rocky southwest shoulder of the mountain, by far the best approach to it. The line of relatively low, broad tops between Alto de los Leones and La Peñota are more interesting than they look from below, having plenty of rock exposed and a scattering of twisted and stunted scots pine as foreground for the fine views of the Meseta to the south and the tree-filled valley of the Río Moros and the Mujer Muerta Ridge to the north. Once the main rocks of La Peñota are reached, the nature of the walk changes from easy ridge-walking to a semi-scramble on a fascinating line, partly out on the steep south face. The descent to Cercedilla has the merit of being direct rather than enjoyable as the terrain on the southeast shoulder is often steep and loose. However, things improve in the woods lower down.

The ridge has a great deal of historical interest: the second col north of Alto de los Leones has been named after the 14th century poet Juan Ruíz, better known as Arcipreste de Hita. His book, *El Libro de Buen Amor* has many descriptions of these mountains. In consequence, a group of Spanish intellectuals succeeded in having a curious rock formation at the col dedicated to the poet and designated a Natural Monument of National Interest for the sexcentenary of his birth in 1930. Two quotations from the book are engraved on the rocks. The monument survived the Civil War in spite of being right on the front line - many remains of republican bunkers, gun positions and trenches are passed on this walk.

(The col, incidentally, appears to be wrongly placed on the IGN Guadarrama sheet, to the south rather than the north of the slight undulation called Peña del Cuervo.)

If you are driving to Cercedilla to catch the train, the station car park is invariably full. Coming in on the Los Molinos road, the best place to park is on an open space to the left, immediately after passing through the tunnel under the tracks. This also happens to be the **end** of the walk. La Tablada is the next station along the line in the Segovia direction and, at the time of writing, there are a couple of trains which stop in the mornings (weekdays only).

Follow the surfaced road rising to the right of the station buildings (1270m). After a big curve to the left, take a path leaving straight uphill opposite a white water tank. It immediately meets a wide horizontal track. Go right on this following its windings up a wide forest ride with electricity pylons. When the track disappears, continue up the ride on whatever footpaths there are. Not long after crossing a horizontal forest road, the firebreak finishes at a level area. Wheel tracks go diagonally right into the trees and lead in a few minutes to the **Collado de la Sevillana** (1496m, *40mins*) and the barbed wire fence which runs along the crest of the ridge.

Go through the gate and turn right on to the track following the fence, which has the red and white GR10 markings. After wandering through low rounded outcrops and boulders over the slight rise known as Peña del Cuervo, the path drops to the Collado del Arcipreste de Hita. (A path starts from a gate there, leading to the monument which lies slightly upslope from the col and just to the right of the fence.) Meanwhile GR10 continues out of the trees up broad open slopes. The stripes are faded and difficult to follow, but cairns lead up to the rocks of **Cerro de Matalafuente** (1642m, *35mins*) which has a survey point on its summit.

The wire fence was possibly constructed after the GR10 was marked out, as it appears sometimes to cut straight through the windings of the path. However, there is no problem in following the crest over **La Peña del Cuervo** (1700m, *20mins*), where the fence changes to a stone wall, then the **Cerro del Mostajo** (1715m, *20mins*). The markings start up the slopes of La Peñota to the left of the wall, but cross to the right at the base of the main rocks taking at first a not very obvious line round the back of a perched horizontal slab then steeply up to the right of a big buttress. Thereafter, the clearer track crosses the crest twice more, passing to the right of the middle summit and to the left of the third and highest point (1945m, *1hr*).

Leave GR10 just beyond the summit where a track branches off right, heading for a point below, where two stone walls meet. At a gap just to the left of the corner, the cairned path down the southwest shoulder begins, keeping to the left of a wire fence which heads straight down the crest. When the trees thin out the track breaks up into several loose and steep alternatives but all heading for the **Collado del Rey** (1610m, *35mins*), a level bare section of the shoulder rather than a pass. (A pleasanter but longer alternative, by about 15mins, is to continue from La Peñota on GR10 to the Collado de Cerromalejo, descend to the right to the forestry road and follow it right, directly to the Collado del Rey.)

From the Collado, start out across the level ground but, well before reaching the lip, follow cairns heading gently down the left-hand slope above a streambed. Lower down as the trees thicken, multiple paths develop. Keep straight down the slope to come out at a swimming pool above a dirt road with some summer camp buildings to the right. Cut down between the buildings to a saddle with the Cerro La Hornilla beyond it. A path starts, indistinctly at first, to the left of the copse of pine trees at the saddle. It drops gently across the wooded northern slopes of the Cerro to meet a horizontal old road with the remains of granite paving. Follow it to the right (waymarked with blue solid circles), back to the car park below **Cercedilla Station** (*1hr*).

43b. NV1 TRUNK ROAD AT km56 - FOREST ROAD - COLLADO DE LA SEVILLANA - PEÑA DEL CUERVO - COLLADO DEL ARCIPRESTE DE HITA - CERRO DE MATALAFUENTE - LA PEÑA DEL CUERVO - CERRO DEL MOSTAJO - LA PEÑOTA (1945m) - FORESTRY ROAD - km56.

Time: 5½-6hrs
Total ascent: 686m

Instead of completing the traverse, car owners can make the same approach to La Peñota but return to the car by the dirt road which runs from Cercedilla to the NV1 a kilometre# below the Alto de los Leones, gently rising back across the southern slopes of the ridge already completed. The drawback is an hour stumbling down the steep, loose trackless south face of La Peñota to reach the road. A longer but easier alternative is suggested.

Drive north from Guadarrama on the NV1 and park at the start of a

---

\# This main road, like many in Spain, is marked at kilometre intervals with the distance from the bigger of the two cities it connects - in this case, of course, Madrid.

forestry road, on the right at km56. There isn't much warning - just a break in the crash barrier immediately after a 50kmph sign and an emergency phone. There is also a kind of decorative column assembled from three or four large slabs of rock. PR30 is written on it in large letters, indicating that this is the start of one of the local marked footpaths. After a few minutes' level walking, the forestry road enters the ride carrying the path to the ridge. Continue on Route 43a over the summit of La Peñota and down to the continuation of the ridge wall.

Cross it near the base of the summit rocks and head straight down into the steep shallow gullies which coalesce lower down into a streambed, although it is generally easier going on the ribs of rock and mixed ground between the gullies. When the outcrops along the enclosing ridge to the left give way to easier angled slopes and before reaching a small band of pines, work horizontally left using cattle tracks onto the slopes. Progress is much quicker down between the broom and thorn patches than in the scrub-choked streambed. Arriving at a dirt road (*1hr 10mins* from the summit), turn right to follow it back to the car (*50mins*). The alternative descent from the summit continues on Route 43a until just above the Collado del Rey. From there, cross the ridge fence at one of the outcrops which interrupt it, then take a slightly descending line across open scrub and boulder slopes to join the dirt road.

44. *LA MUJER MUERTA RIDGE.*

A small collection of legends and poems have been inspired by the Mujer Muerta - the Dead Woman. The profile of the three tops which make up this elevated and isolated ridge suggest the ghostly but unmistakable silhouette off a recumbant woman's body and the winter snow provides the shroud.

These resonances are better appreciated from, say, the tower of Segovia's Alcazar than from walking the crest itself, but even without them, this would still be one of the finest ridge walks in the Sierra. Each of the three tops has its own distinctive character, there is the usual interesting mixture of smooth slopes and rocky outcrops, and with relatively steep northern slopes this is more of a true ridge than the edges of the escarpments found in some parts of the range. But what really distinguishes it is its offset position to the northwest and parallel to the main range, giving spectacular views towards Gredos, the whole Northern Meseta, Peñalara and the long spine running up to Somosierra, as well

Southern profile of the Mujer Muerta Ridge

as a very different perspective to the other central summits to the east and south.

I have chosen four ways of approaching the ridge: long and short circuits from the Río Moros valley and two long cross-country routes. Once again there is plenty of evidence of the Civil War front, particularly on Pinareja and at the Collado de Tirobarra.

44a. VADO DE LAS CABRAS RESERVOIR (RIO MOROS VALLEY) - COLLADO DE TIROBARRA - MUJER MUERTA RIDGE (PEÑA DEL OSO, 2196m) - FOREST ROADS - RESERVOIR.

Time: 5-5½hrs
Total ascent: 861m

This is the shortest possible circuit which includes the whole ridge, and needs a car to get to the starting point high up the Río Moros valley. The climb to the Collado de Tirobarra is very attractive as it follows the Río Moros then a tributary all the way to the pass. The descent to the car links up forestry roads on the ridge's southern

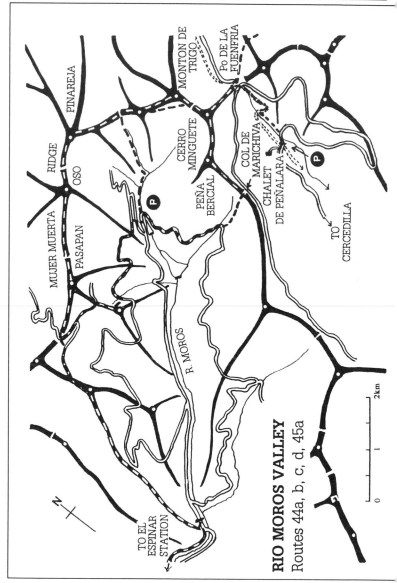

RIO MOROS VALLEY
Routes 44a, b, c, d, 45a

slopes.
    N.B. The forestry road up the valley is open to cars only between 8.30 and 17.30 and is closed altogether between mid-June and mid-September because of the fire risk (although it is still possible to walk - 7km from the gates to the Vado de las Cabras Reservoir).

The quickest way to the head of the Río Moros valley from the Madrid side of the range is to take the A6 motorway and leave it at the San Rafael exit, just after the tunnel (toll to pay). Turn left immediately onto the parallel N603 San Rafael-Segovia road, then again in a minute or two, into a lane signposted to Estación El Espinar. (Alternatively, you can use the slightly slower NV1 to cross the range at the Alto de los Leones Pass, branching right onto the N603 at traffic lights in San Rafael, to arrive at the same Estación El Espinar junction.)
    The lane leads through the small settlement around El Espinar railway station and into the Río Moros valley. After some picnic zones, turn right at a T-junction to pass through the gates, from where the car restrictions mentioned above begin to operate. The forest road is mostly unmetalled but well-compacted and leads to the head of the second reservoir, the Embalse de Vado de las Cabras (1560m). There is space for parking by the road just before the road swings right across the bridge over the stream above the reservoir.
    Take the level grassy path to the left of the stream, which leaves the road just before the bridge. Although the track is discontinuous, follow the left bank, crossing a couple of tributaries (the first smaller one may be dry) as far as the point where two equal-sized tributaries join to form the main river (*20mins*). Stay on the left bank of the left-hand one and follow it upstream, without a continuous path and mostly through pine forest then juniper and heather, to the **Collado de Tirobarra** (1979m, *50mins*).
    Turn left at this level bare saddle to take the clear path up the wide treeless slopes to the mound of shattered blocks which form the summit of **La Pinareja** (2193m, *25mins*). The route along the ridge can be seen to the southwest. In misty weather, the various paths are clear and there are cairns through the rock sections, which present no difficulties. The next top, **Peña del Oso** (2196m, *35mins*) has a rather dilapidated sculpture of a bear. After crossing the much lower summit of **Pasapan** (2003m, *30mins*), descend to the forestry road which crosses the **Puerto de Pasapan** (1845m, *10mins*). Turn left onto the road to head back up

the valley on a gently falling line. When the road turns left and starts to rise again, look for a narrow path leaving down to the right, just before the bend. It leads straight downhill between tall bushes and small pines to arrive in a plantation of widely spaced mature pines. Leave the path to head down through the trees, steeply but without difficulty until another horizontal forestry road is reached (*25mins*).

Turn left and follow it up the valley. This will eventually lead back to the reservoir if you turn right at the only branch. However a pathless short cut can be taken down to the reservoir (*35mins*) before that junction is reached. The forest obscures any views of the water but the time to turn off is about 25mins out along the road in the middle of a long straight stretch.

44b. VADO DE LAS CABRAS RESERVOIR - PUERTO DE PASAPAN - MUJER MUERTA RIDGE (PEÑA DEL OSO, 2196m) - COLLADO DE TIROBARRA - MONTON DE TRIGO - CERRO MINGUETE - PEÑA BERCIAL - COLLADO DE MARICHIVA - RESERVOIR.

> Time: 7-7¹/₂hrs
> Total ascent: 927m

For a longer day out, this route combines the traverse of the Mujer Muerta Ridge with the three tops at the head of the Río Moros valley. Because of the restricted hours of access, mentioned in Route 44a, a reasonably early start is advisable if you don't want to be locked in the valley with your car.

Park in the same place as for Route 44a and reverse it all the way to the **Collado de Tirobarra**. Crossing the Collado (1979m), paths start up the slopes ahead towards a group of rocks on the skyline, below which are the remains of some buildings from the Civil War. After a small rise behind them, cairns lead along a broad grassy crest towards the jumble of rocks which is the top of **Montón de Trigo** (2155m, *30mins*). From the summit, follow the cairns steeply down the southern slope to a small col then straight on in a few minutes more to the summit of **Cerro Minguete** (2023m, *25mins*). Continue southwest along the now very broad ridge, soon picking up a good track with cairns. This skirts just to the left of the summit rocks of **Peña Bercial** (2001m, *15mins*).

You can stay with the cairns, which descend through a confusing mixture of tree heather and fine old stunted and twisted scots pines, to join the forestry road at the **Collado de Marichiva** (1750m, *25mins*). (Alternatively, it you want to follow the short summit ridge of Peña Bercial, you can descend to the left at the end of the main rocks down cattle tracks through knee-high broom, taking a few minutes longer. In clear weather the long Marichiva saddle, with a stone wall and forestry road running along it, is always in view from these slopes.)

Go to the far end of the long level section where there is a gate in the ridge wall and take the forestry road which drops to the right into the Río Moros valley. After only 50m, leave on a wide track to the left just after a Prohibido el Paso sign and a yellow arrow. Lower down, it widens even more as it descends the left-hand slopes of a side valley to join the principal valley loop road at a bridge (*15mins*). Follow the road to the right through forest back to the reservoir (*30mins*).

44c.* CHALET DE PEÑALARA - PUERTO DE LA FUENFRIA - CERRO MINGUETE - COLLADO DE TIROBARRA - LA MUJER MUERTA RIDGE (PEÑA DEL OSO, 2196m) - El ESPINAR STATION.

> **Time:** 7-7½hrs
> **Total ascent:** 907m

The starting point for this walk is at the top of the Fuenfría valley, to the southeast and parallel to that of the Río Moros. More details about the valley and the Chalet de Peñalara are given on p 183. There is no public transport operating in the valley but taxis can be taken from Cercedilla village or station. Trains to Cercedilla from El Espinar are at the time of writing about every 2hrs, but not at weekends and holidays.

The descent from the Puerto de Pasapan as far as the Río Moros is on the GR88, a long distance footpath from the Puerto de Somosierra. It passes through Segovia then crosses the end of the Mujer Muerta Ridge at this point, to continue to San Rafael and finally join the GR10 on the Cuelgamuros Ridge.

Follow Route 45b as far as the **Puerto de Fuenfría** (1792m, *40mins*). Turn left up the bank to pass the metal sculpture and start the climb of the eastern slopes of **Cerro Minguete** (2023m, *30mins*). There are numerous paths between the scattered dwarfed and contorted pines, leading to the group of rocks on the rounded summit. Leave the top to the right to descend very slightly to the small saddle dividing Cerro Minguete from the rocky pyramid of Montón de Trigo. Just where the ground starts to rise again a cairned track leaves diagonally left and makes a rising traverse across the southwest slopes of the mountain to reach its northwest ridge at a small rise, the Cerro de Tirobarra. The path continues over it and through some small outcrops and Civil War remains, down to the **Collado de Tirobarra** (1979m, *35mins*).

Continue on Route 44a as far as the **Puerto de Pasapan** (1845m, *1hr 40mins*). Cross the forestry road at the pass, to pick up in the broom one of the rough paths leading down a streambed to a horizontal dirt road. Follow it right, around the head of a forested hollow then along the crest of a small spur to a grassy knoll (*20mins*). A firebreak leaves to the right which, occasionally marked with the red and white paint, is the direct route down to the river and main valley road. It meets them at a gate with stone pillars (*50mins*). Follow the tarmac road to the right for 4km to **El Espinar Station** (c.1200m, *50mins*).

44d.* PUERTO DE NAVACERRADA - CAMINO SCHMID - SENDA DE LOS COSPES - PUERTO DE LA FUENFRIA - MINGUETE VALLEY - COLLADO DE TIROBARRA - LA MUJER MUERTA RIDGE (2196m) - EL ESPINAR STATION. (see maps pp204 & 199)

Time:	7^1/$_2$-8hrs
Total ascent:	610m

This is another good, varied, cross-country walk, made possible by using the rail network. Although longer than Route 44c it starts so high at the Puerto de Navacerrada (1860m) that the overall effort involved is probably about the same. It first crosses the forested northern slopes of Siete Picos and Cerro Ventoso using the well-made and almost horizontal Camino Schmid and Senda de los Cospes.

Take the mountain railway from Cercedilla to Puerto de Navacerrada. Follow the road behind the station building as far as the start of a short chairlift which leads directly to the pass proper. (When the lift is closed, walk up by the chairs, otherwise there is a path to the left of the enclosing fence.) Emerging onto the main road, it is only a few metres to the top of the pass and the start of a lane leaving to the left (after the Venta Arias Hotel), which leads past the base of another chairlift then to the foot of a ski slope. Cross the latter to find the start of **Camino Schmid** (1880m, *20mins*), marked with yellow circles, alternating with green bands, which descends gently to the left into the forest, crossing a langlauf (cross-country skiing) piste.

About 40mins along the track, the path splits with Camino Schmidt starting to climb the slopes to the meadows of Collado Ventoso, while the Senda de los Cospes continue straight ahead. Keep to the markers as another path branches off to the right almost immediately. It is a gentle walk round the northern slopes of Cerro Ventoso to join a wider path which leads up in a few minutes to a fuente then the **Puerto de la Fuenfría** (1796m, *1hr 10mins*).

Route 44c can be followed from here over Cerro Minguete, but an alternative is to climb the attractive Minguete valley to the col south of Montón de Trigo. To do this, leave the Puerto de la Fuenfría on the forestry road to the right of the metal monument, beyond a barrier. Branch left on to the Roman road after a few minutes, then leave that in turn where the Minguete stream crosses it. Climb the valley to the col passing through woods, meadows, then on a choice of several tracks through broom and other scrub. At the col (1989m, *35mins*) continue on Route 44c to El Espinar Station.

THE FUENFRIA VALLEY

The Fuenfría valley runs north from Cercedilla for 6kms and in spite of the extensive pine forests and a plethora of picnic sites scattered among them, the area seems neither oppressive nor overrun with trippers. ICONA seem to have targeted this valley for visitor management schemes: there is an information centre on the road in and a number of marked paths exploiting the dense network of forestry roads and tracks on the slopes of the valley - alternatives worth bearing in mind if low cloud makes the ridge routes described here less attractive. The Chalet de Peñalara at the foot of the Fuenfría Pass runs residential courses for school groups but the cafe/restaurant is open to the public at weekends and holidays.

At the time of writing the last section of road to the chalet is closed to cars at exactly those times. Part of it, anyway, is unsurfaced and deeply eroded, often becoming impassable in icy conditions. Therefore, to reach the highest parking point when the restrictions apply, drive north along the valley road from Cercedilla as far as the ICONA Information Centre where the road forks. Take the right branch and follow it to its end at a barrier and the Majavilán car park. From there, continue on foot beyond two barriers and across the Descalzo Bridge which marks the start of a preserved section of the Calzada Romana (Roman Road), waymarked with white solid circles. It leads to a car park/clearing just below the chalet. This walk-in adds 20mins to either end of the routes starting there.

In good conditions during the week, there is no reason not to drive up to the chalet car park. Take the left branch at the ICONA Information Centre, then at a left hairpin soon after, follow the upper of the two roads which start on the outside of the bend. Continue through the pine forest to the chalet (ignoring a right branch signposted to car parks). The road crosses the car park and continues beyond a barrier at the far side. The chalet can be seen slightly higher to the left at the end of a curving drive.

To walk to the chalet from Cercedilla Station, follow the car directions to the Roman road given above. There is unfortunately no way of avoiding this long stretch on the road without adding considerably to the time, which as it is takes 1hr 35mins. Although there are usually taxis at Cercedilla Station for rides to the start of the Roman road, the problem, of course, is the long walk back at the end of the circular routes. Where it is possible, I have suggested ways of adapting these routes to finish in the town rather than at the chalet.

45. *MONTON DE TRIGO.*

Although the mountain has already been included in a partial tour of the Río Moros valley skyline (Route 44b), it actually merits its own small section, as much for its fine conical rocky summit which gives it its name (Pile of Corn) as for its position at the head of the Río Moros valley to the west, and above the forested bowl of Valsaín to the east. It is in fact one of the finest viewpoints in the Sierra. The first two walks explore each of these flanks: one is a relatively short round of the head of the Río Moros valley, while the second starts in the Fuenfría valley, crosses into Valsaín, using the old Roman road, then climbs the attractive but little used northeast ridge of the mountain. The third route is a longer ramble through the extensive area of forest which clothes much of the northern side of the range.

MONTON DE TRIGO Routes 45a, b, c,

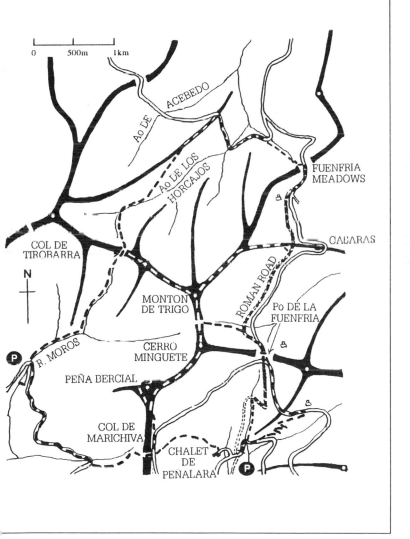

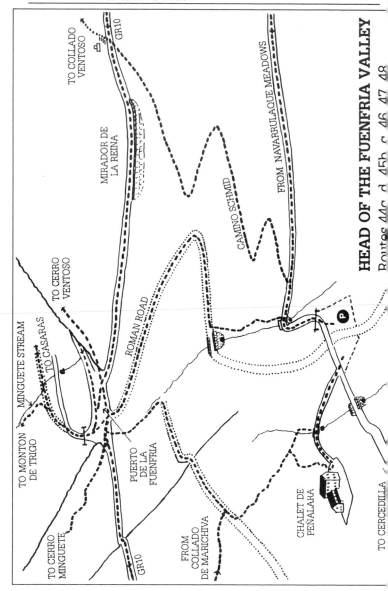

HEAD OF THE FUENFRIA VALLEY

Routes 44c, d, 45b, c, 46, 47, 48

TO COLLADO VENTOSO

GR10

MIRADOR DE LA REINA

FROM NAVARRULAQUE MEADOWS

CAMINO SCHMID

TO CERRO VENTOSO

ROMAN ROAD

MINGUETE STREAM

TO CASARAS

TO MONTON DE TRIGO

PUERTO DE LA FUENFRIA

TO CERRO MINGUETE

FROM COLLADO DE MARICHIVA

GR10

CHALET DE PEÑALARA

TO CERCEDILLA

45a. VADO DE LAS CABRAS RESERVOIR (RIO MOROS VALLEY) - COLLADO DE TIROBARRA - MONTON DE TRIGO (2155m) - CERRO MINGUETE - PEÑA BERCIAL - COLLADO DE MARICHIVA - EMBALSE.

Time: 4¹/₂-5hrs
Total ascent: 675m

While most of this walk is included in Route 44b, it provides a shorter alternative while still sampling something of the Río Moros valley and its skyline. The ridge section is confined to the three peaks arranged around the head of the valley. See Route 44a for details of entry restrictions for cars into the Río Moros valley.

Park as for Route 44a and follow it as far as the Collado de Tirobarra. From there follow Route 44b for the rest of the walk.

45b.§ CHALET DE PEÑALARA - PUERTO DE LA FUENFRIA - CONVENTO DE CASARAS - MONTON DE TRIGO (2155m) - CERRO MINGUETE - PEÑA BERCIAL - COLLADO DE MARICHIVA - CHALET DE PEÑALARA

Time: 5-5¹/₂hrs
Total ascent: 709m

The route takes the best preserved part of the Roman road to the Puerto de la Fuenfría at the head of the valley, joining it at the well-restored Enmedio Bridge. The road was the main connection between Madrid and Segovia until well into the 18th century when the Puerto de Navacerrada road was opened. The original surface is recognisable but broken up, except for the last 200m or so before the pass.

From the Puerto de la Fuenfría, a much frequented col where several routes and forestry roads meet, the walk continues on the Roman road into the extensive pine forests of Valsaín until it crosses a grassy spur with the ruins of the Casarás, one of Philip II's hunting lodges (mistakenly called a Convento). The ruins, the meadow scattered with tall scots pine and a backcloth of forested slopes topped by the crenellations of the Siete Picos Ridge make this a very atmospheric spot and a fine setting for a Gothic novel.

From there the route follows the spur up on to the northeast

ridge of Montón de Trigo. Although there is no clear track, the climb through forest then on open ground is not difficult. The reward is an easy but enjoyable scramble along the broken and tilted blocks of the crest, which can be avoided if preferred to one side or the other, albeit on a rough mixture of broken rock and juniper. The route continues along part of the western crest of the Fuenfría valley to the Collado de Marichiva, from where there is a wooded descent to the Chalet de Peñalara. However, from the col, a direct return to Cercedilla could be made by continuing on the forestry road to the Collado del Rey, then following the end of Route 43a down to the railway station.

The Roman road starts its climb to the Fuenfría Pass to the left of the road barrier in the chalet car park (1500m) and is clearly marked with white solid circles, but for the first 20mins the surface is very broken and loose. It is pleasanter instead to follow the forestry road beyond the barrier as far as a small stone bridge, then climb beside the stream on its wooded right bank until the Enmedio Bridge is reached. Turn right along the Roman road which makes a big dog-leg on the lower slopes of Cerro Ventoso to reach the **Puerto de la Fuenfría** (1792m, *40mins*). (There is a good fuente 150m down the path leaving to the right on the far side of the pass.)

From the pass, take the forestry road which leaves to the left on the far side, beyond a barrier. A few minutes along it, the Roman road branches off to the left, cutting across the forested eastern slopes of Montón de Trigo. In the form of a grassy terrace, it takes a line slightly above the forestry road, to arrive at the top of an open grassy spur which has the ruins of **Casarás** (c.1700m, *30mins*) at the lower end. This is a good place to rest, but the route actually leaves the Roman road just before it emerges from the trees on to the spur: look for forestry vehicle wheel tracks leaving steeply to the left into the trees. Where they finish, continue uphill on cattle tracks out of the forest and on to slopes of low broom and juniper. Head for the nearest rock outcrops above and from there take more cattle tracks towards the much bigger formations on the upper part of the ridge. Follow these to the summit of **Montón de Trigo** (2155m, *1hr.5mins*).

From the summit continue in the same direction of travel down the steep boulder-strewn southern slopes with a variety of cairn lines to follow. They all arrive at an unnamed col with the summit of **Cerro Minguete** (2023m, *25mins*) just beyond. Now follow Route 44b as far as the **Collado de Marichiva** (1750m, *40mins*). From the far end, where there is a gate in the wall, left drop into the trees from the forestry road on a wide path but leave it almost immediately to the left again at a yellow paint mark. Follow the yellow circles and narrow path on a diagonal descent through the forest to come out on a horizontal terrace marked with yellow/white stripes. A few metres along to the right, the yellow markings continue steeply downhill (metal signboard) to the stream slightly uphill from the chalet car park (*35mins*). For the Majavilán car park, stay with the wide path leaving Marichiva (red circles) which comes out on the valley road a few minutes south of the car parks.

45c. CHALET DE PEÑALARA - PUERTO DE LA FUENFRIA - CASARAS - FUENFRIA MEADOWS - TESTEROS DE LOS HORCAJOS - COLLADO DE TIROBARRA - MONTON DE TRIGO (2155m) - MINGUETE STREAM - PUERTO DE LA FUENFRIA - MIRADOR DE LA REINA - CAMINO SCHMID - CHALET DE PEÑALARA. (See maps pp 185 & 186)

Time:	6-6½hrs
Total ascent:	738m

Here is a long circuitous route to the mountain, through the rolling forests of Valsaín. Spanish guidebook writers are extremely fond of this area and describe numerous walks based on permutations of the forestry roads which crisscross it. When snow is lying or during hot weather, it is very enjoyable to wander through the tall, well-spaced scots pines, connecting up the numerous fuentes and quiet little meadows which are scattered across these northern slopes.

This route combines a taste of these pleasures with more open walking on the ridges above. The Roman road forms a balcony across the eastern slopes of Montón de Trigo, giving a wide panorama of the bowl of trees with Peñalara and the Cuerda Larga beyond, as well as linking up the clearings at the Fuenfría Pass, Casarás and Fuenfría (or Venta) Meadows. The latter has the hardly distinguishable remains of a Venta (roadside inn), once mentioned by Cervantes. The route turns back at the Testeros de los Horcajos spur, to start the climb to Montón de Trigo. A diversion can be taken from that point to see the fine stands of trees, mixed with hollies, in the Acebeda Pinewoods, a protected Site of National

189

Interest. This would add about 45mins-1hr to the walk.

After crossing Montón de Trigo, the return to the Puerto de la Fuenfría can be made by a traverse of Cerro Minguete or by descending the valley of the Minguete stream, which is described here, a good place to see a variety of flowers in the spring. From the pass, the quickest way back to the chalet car park is down the Roman road, but the horizontal forestry road around the southern slopes of Cerro Ventoso is the interesting alternative used in this walk. One section of the road is balustraded with extensive views down the valley. The descent to the chalet, through the forest, is on the carefully graded zigzags of the Camino Schmid.

A scots pine

Follow Route 45b as far as the **Casarás meadows** (c.1700m, *1hr 10mins*). Continue on the Roman road to where it joins a narrow surfaced forestry road at the Fuente de la Reina. This in turn leads in a couple of minutes to the attractive **Fuenfría Meadows** (1630m, *15mins*). Halfway across, take a dirt road leaving on the left but turn immediately right on to another one which descends into a wooded valley following the left bank of a small stream. Narrowing to a footpath at times it eventually meets a horizontal forestry road. Follow it left across the Horcajos stream and steeply up to the right on to the crest of the **Testeros de los Horcajos spur** (1640m, *35mins*).

At this point the road forks: the right branch is the Acebeda Pinewoods diversion, the other climbs left up the spur and soon divides again - go right on a steep and churned up section which leads to the long, almost level, open crest of the spur. Eventually, the track starts to drop gently across the left-hand slopes to end in the bed of the upper Horcajos valley (*45mins*). Continue to follow the stream up-valley out of the trees, taking the left branch at a confluence, then the channel farthest to the left at a fan of streamlets at the very head of the valley. Above is the bare, windswept **Collado de Tirobarra** (1970m, *30mins*).

A path to the left leads up to rock outcrops then continues over the slight rise of the Cerro de Tirobarra and straight up the open northwest slopes of **Montón de Trigo** (2155m, *30mins*). The descent starts behind the summit rocks on a path which drops steeply to the right, splitting into several strands lower down. All of them arrive at an open unnamed saddle. At the lowest point move left to find the start of a path dropping into the Minguete valley. The track is vague, lower down at times, but the entrance to the valley is crossed by the Roman road. Turn right on it to rejoin the forestry road which leads back to the **Puerto de la Fuenfría** (*45mins*).

Take the horizontal forestry road leaving on the far side of the pass, to the left of the Roman road. In less than 15mins, shortly after re-entering the forest after the balustraded section, the continuation of the Camino Schmid from the Collado Ventoso crosses the road (yellow solid circles on the trees, Fuente R. de Velasco up to the right). Follow it down to the left through the forest (large zigzags later) back to the **chalet car park** (*40mins*).

46.§ CHALET DE PEÑALARA - PUERTO DE LA FUENFRIA - CERRO MINGUETE (2024m) - PEÑA BERCIAL - PEÑA DEL AGUILA - LA PEÑOTA - PISTA FORESTAL - COLLADO DE MARICHIVA - CHALET DE PEÑALARA.

Time:	7-7$^{1}/_{2}$hrs
Total ascent:	925m

This is a complete traverse of the western skyline of the Fuenfría valley giving good views of the Río Moros valley and La Mujer Muerta to the northwest. The tree line reaches the ridge at some points but only enough to add variety. Although La Peñota is the lowest top on the ridge, its summit above a precipitous southwest face and the consequent unimpeded view across the Meseta is a fitting culmination. Another attraction in April are the acres of crocus found along the ridge, particularly on the eastern slopes of Cerro Minguete. The Roman road to the Puerto de la Fuenfría from the Chalet de Peñalara, described in Route 45b, is the most direct approach but the alternative offered here, after an admittedly steep start, follows the course of another old road, through the forest but with open views. Without a car, the walk is possible by taking a taxi up the valley and returning to Cercedilla from the top of La Peñota on Route 43a, in marginally less time than it takes to return to the chalet.

From the chalet car park (1500m) walk up the drive to the chalet forecourt and take a path marked with yellow paint which starts at the top of stone steps on the right. It winds across a streambed then climbs steeply through the forest to meet a track running along a wide terrace (the course of the old Segovia road) (*20mins*). Turn right on to this and follow the yellow and white stripes which mark its course as it contours around to the streambed at the head of the valley. After following the latter up for a short distance, the marks move diagonally right over piles of shattered rock to join the Roman road a few metres below the **Puerto de la Fuenfría** (1792m, *25mins*). Climb the small bank to the left and go straight up the slopes behind the metal monument on any of a variety of tracks to the summit of **Cerro Minguete** (2023m, *30mins*). From here, follow Route 44b to the **Collado de Marichiva** (1750m, *40mins*).

El Yelmo from Hueco de las Hoces. (Routes 58, 59, 60)

Collado de la Ventana and Cerro de los Hoyos

Eastern end of the Sierra de la Cabrera from the summit of Cancho Gordo

FUENFRIA VALLEY Routes 46, 47, 48

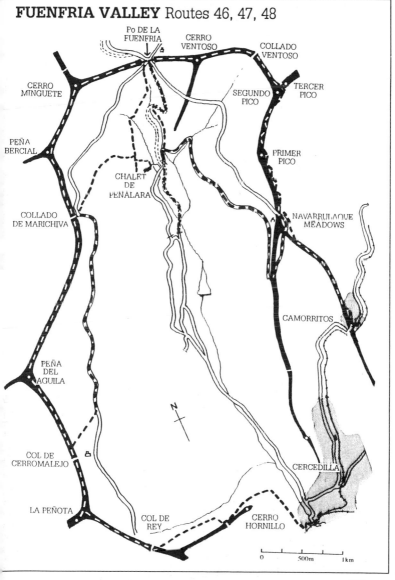

A broad rocky path, to the right of the stone wall and marked with the GR10 red and white stripes, rises from the Collado into scattered pines. The track climbs the long whaleback of Peña del Aguila, sometimes through pine trees but mostly with open views. From the summit (2012m, *50mins*) continue to follow the markers and occasional cairns down the southern shoulder of the mountain, very soon crossing to the left of the wall. Lower down, the path enters plantation then recrosses the wall just before the **Collado de Cerromalejo** (1778m, *40mins*). The final climb to **La Peñota** (1915m, *30mins*) continues along the wall but leaves it just below the summit, where the markings move diagonally right to go straight to the summit rocks.

Return to the point where the wall was last crossed, just north of the Collado de Cerromalejo. At the back of the small clearing to the right, a wide path starts, marked with solid red circles. This leads down to a horizontal dirt road (*30mins*). Follow it left, rising gently, back to the **Collado de Marichiva** (*40mins*) from where Route 45b is followed back to the **Chalet de Peñalara** (*35mins*). For the Majavilán car park, continue with the red circles to join the valley road system at the Fuenfría Sanatorium.

GR10 above the Fuenfria Pass

47.§ CHALET DE PEÑALARA - PUERTO DE LA FUENFRIA - CERRO VENTOSO - COLLADO VENTOSO - SEGUNDO PICO (2089m) - PICO DE MAJALASNA - MIRADOR DE V. ALEXANDRE - CHALET DE PEÑALARA.

Time: 4¹/₂-5hrs
Total ascent: 676m

This excursion is a mirror of Route 46 in that it links up the tops on the eastern side of the Fuenfría valley. However, there the similarity ends as this side of the valley has none of the continuity of profile of a classic ridge walk, being made up of two quite disconnected tops followed by a long low shoulder running south to Cercedilla, broken by one prominent step at Primer Pico. The first top is Cerro Ventoso, the gently rounded and completely forested hill to the east of Puerto de la Fuenfría, whose southern slopes divide the head of the valley. To the south and separated from it by the meadows of Collado Ventoso (covered in crocus and narcissus in spring) is the dramatic rocky fortress of Segundo Pico which lives up to the promise of its precipitous appearance from the valley. The summit, gained by a short scramble from a col to the east, gives impressive views down into Fuenfría and also back along the steep south face of the Siete Picos ridge, of which it forms a part.

From here it can also be seen that the next top on the walk, Pico de Majalasna (or Primer Pico) is merely a large tor rising some 40m above the broad southern spur of Segundo Pico, on which it sits. Another drop through pine forest brings you to the meadows of Navarrulaque and the interesting Mirador (viewpoint) over the Navelmedio valley just beyond. Like the last route, this one could also be turned into a linear one by taking a taxi to the chalet and following Route 49c from Navarrulaque Meadows back to Cercedilla.

From the chalet car parking area (1500m) take the Roman road, as for Route 45b, to the **Puerto de la Fuenfría** (1792m, *40mins*). At the pass turn right and follow the wide track which rises straight up through the pine trees on the western slopes of Cerro Ventoso. Picking its way over a band of large scree, cairns appear and it arrives at the highest point on an elongated summit ridge (1965m) just above the tree line. Follow the track along the top then down to the attractive meadows at the **Collado Ventoso** (1892m, *35mins*).

Cow on the meadows at the Collado Ventoso

The paths up the opposite tree-covered slope rising to Siete Picos leave from a couple of carved stone posts. Bear slightly right up the slope to find the most used route which leads to the col between 2nd and 3rd Picos (2058m, *25mins*). (There are various confusing cairn lines and the ones furthest left lead to the col between 3rd and 4th Picos.) The unmarked route to the upper rocks of Segundo Pico is along connecting terraces starting at the far (south) side of the col. The onward route also continues down that side in the form of a line of cairns straight from the col across a hollow then over a lip into the trees. Multiple lines develop when the angle eases but they all end at different points along a path marked with yellow circles and yellow and white stripes (*15mins*) at the top of the meadows of Majalasna. Follow the path left, down to the prominent rocky tor of Primer Pico, then continue with the markings across the grassy meadows to the left of the outcrop and into the trees. Soon the two types of marking split, the yellow and white stripes taking a steep direct line down the ridge and the yellow circles working further east for good views of the Siete Picos south face. They reunite at a level open section of the crest, called the meadows of **Navarrulaque** (1660m, *35mins*).

A forestry road runs north-south on the right of the meadows. (To the right of that, a fuente can be found a little further down the slope.) Follow the road south to the **Mirador de Vincente Alexandre** (*10mins*), just to the left. Apart from the view across the Navalmedio valley and of the south face of Siete Picos, you can also see another viewpoint, the Mirador de Luis Rosales, further down the slope. Return to the road which soon makes a U-turn to the right to begin a long gentle descent to the **chalet car park** (*50mins*). For the Majavilán car park, take a trail marked with red circles, which crosses the road after 25-30mins descent.

48.* FUENFRIA HORSESHOE: CAMORRITOS - NAVARRULAQUE MEADOWS - PRIMER PICO - SEGUNDO PICO (2089m) - COLLADO VENTOSO - CERRO VENTOSO - PUERTO DE LA FUENFRIA - CERRO MINGUETE - PEÑA BERCIAL - COLLADO DE MARICHIVA - PEÑA DEL AGUILA - COLLADO DE CERROMALEJO - LA PEÑOTA - COLLADO DEL REY - CERCEDILLA.

Time:	9¹/₂-10hrs
Total ascent:	1420m

This is a big walk amalgamating several routes in order to traverse almost the whole Fuenfría valley skyline. It is not quite circular as it starts at Camorritos, a leafy urbanization 3km from and 150m above the centre of Cercedilla and reached by the Puerto de los Cotos train or taxi.

Walk back towards Cercedilla from Camorritos Station (1320m) and turn right into a road rising behind a damaged stone monument. It leads into a villa development and is also part of GR10 (the red and white markings soon begin). Where the houses finish, the track continues beyond a road barrier, climbing steeply into the forest and eventually reaching the meadows of **Navarrulaque** (1660m, *50mins*) on the crest of the ridge. (There is a fuente a few metres down the the western slopes, beyond a forestry road.)

You then have the choice of following the PR7 (yellow and white stripes) which more or less follows the crest, or a path which wanders up the eastern flank and is marked with yellow circles. Either of them reverse Route 47 as far as Collado Ventoso, from where you continue over Cerro Ventoso to the **Puerto de la Fuenfría**. From there, climb the slopes on the opposite side of the col to the top of **Cerro Minguete** then follow Route 44b to the **Collado de Marichiva**, where Route 46 takes over as far as the summit of **La Peñota**. Return to **Cercedilla** on Route 43a.

49. *SIETE PICOS (SEVEN PEAKS) RIDGE.*

Seen from the south, the serrations of Siete Picos are the most instantly recognisable and dramatic section of the Guadarrama skyline. This inviting crescent of roughly flat-topped but heavily fractured and eroded outcrops is perched above vertiginous rocky southern slopes. There are only six bumps visible from a distance as the first peak is some way to the southwest, lying part way down the long spur from the westernmost of the Picos on the main ridge. Although the crest is not exactly a knife-edge, the wooded northern slopes are sufficiently steep to give a feeling of airiness on some parts if a high enough line is maintained. The path mostly follows the north side of the Picos and has only one short section where hands are needed, but the choice is there to scramble over any or all of them. The outcrops are numbered First (Primer) to Seventh (Séptimo) from west to east.

There are various ways of tackling the ridge: the first two described here are circular walks from the Puerto de Navacerrada which explore the very different north and south slopes respectively. The third route takes advantage of the rail connection with Puerto de Navacerrada to walk back along the ridge to Cercedilla, and the fourth is a circuit from Cercedilla.

49a.* PUERTO DE NAVACERRADA - SIETE PICOS (SEPTIMO PICO, 2138m) - SENDA DE LOS ALEVINES - COLLADO VENTOSO - CAMINO SCHMID - PUERTO DE NAVACERRADA.

> **Time:** 4¹/₂-5hrs
> **Total ascent:** 278m

This route traverses the ridge east-west, by far the more popular direction because of the high start at the Puerto de Navacerrada. It may at first appear awkward to have to drop from Segundo Pico southwest to Primer Pico then to double back north to the Collado Ventoso but, apart from the satisfaction of 'doing' all seven peaks,

SIETE PICOS Routes 49a, b, c, d, start of 44d

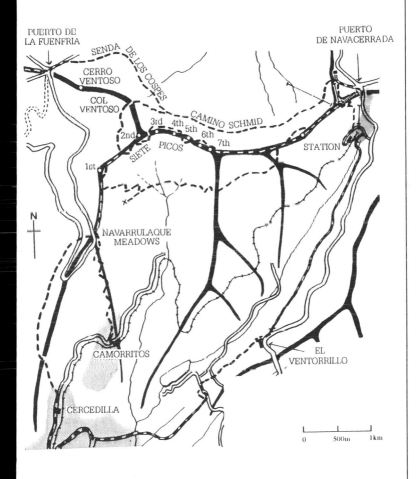

the rocky wooded traverse back to the Collado (the Senda de los Alevines) is more interesting than the direct route down from Segundo Pico.

The return route is along the Camino Schmid, marked out early this century by one of the pioneer explorers from the Peñalara Society. The purpose of the path was to link the Society's refuge at the Puerto de Navacerrada with the one in the Fuenfría valley. Señor Schmid was in fact warden of the chalet in Fuenfría for many years and his Camino is one of the best marked paths in the range, taking an easy line across the pine-forested northern slopes. With an early start, this combination of the breezy ridge and shady return is enjoyable even on hot summer days.

At the Puerto de Navacerrada (1860m) there are three ways to start the walk:

Coming from Cercedilla, car drivers should, at the very top of the pass, take the asphalted road to the left, immediately after the Venta Arias restaurant, which heads into the pine trees past a chairlift station. Park where the lane turns to the right at the foot of the Escaparate ski piste. (This is in fact where Camino Schmid finishes so the walk back to the pass is saved.) Climb straight up the ski slope.

However, at weekends in the ski season it is impossible to park there, as well as dangerous to climb what must be the most crowded ski piste in Spain. Instead park at the pass, either by the road on the south side or in the big skiers' car park next to the Puerto de los Cotos road. Start the walk by crossing the car park below Venta Arias then climbing steeply left on to a ski piste, which can be followed up on its left-hand side.

If arriving at the Puerto by train, the station is situated some way below the pass on the south side. Take the road which leaves behind the station building as far as a chairlift which goes directly to the main road at the pass. Walk up beside it, or outside the fence to the left if it is in operation, to just above the top station. Go left on a path which rises slightly to a small white building then climb the steep rough slopes behind it onto the ski piste (15mins - not included in total time). Climb the slope to the top of the chairlift.

The top of the pistes, where three chairlifts converge, is called **Alto del Telégrafo** (*10mins*). Beyond the machinery, a wide track heads southwest over level and now treeless terrain towards the rocky eminence of Cerro del Telégrafo. Branches to the left lead to the summit while the main path contours to the right of it. The paths rejoin at the Siete Picos meadows, a level section of the ridge. At the far end, go to the right of a large boulder with PR8 and 28 painted on it then cross a small dip (*25mins*) to start up the long pine-covered slope which leads to the ridge proper. As so often, there are numerous tracks beaten up it and they all eventually converge on a bouldery slope just above the tree line. At the top of the slope, a grassy rise is crossed and the first view is seen of the curious, masonry-like granite block of **Séptimo Pico** (2138m, *30mins*).

The scramble to the top, from the right-hand side where the path passes close to it, is steep but easy and worth the effort for the 360 degree panorama and the first view of the complete ridge curving ahead. It can also be seen from there that the ridge path continues across intervening meadow towards Sexto Pico, but splits before reaching the rocks. The left branch heading up to a small col is a dead end for all but scramblers while the right branch, which drops into a hollow before climbing round the right side of the Pico, is the through route. Thereafter the track keeps to one side or other of the crest until it reaches a col between the last two tops on the ridge. Scramble up the grassy ramp on the left side of the last one, **Segundo Pico** (2089m, *35mins*), for good views into the Fuenfría valley. Return to the col and descend to the right (south) following cairns steeply down into pinewoods. Several tracks develop, all of which eventually meet a path marked with yellow and white stripes and yellow circles edged. Go left on it to drop to the Majalasna meadows and the isolated outcrop of **Primer Pico** (or Majalasna 1938m, *25mins*).

From there, retrace the route to the top of the meadows then stay on the marked path which picks a way across the rocky, wooded western slopes of Segundo Pico to the meadows of **Collado Ventoso** (1892m, *30mins*). The yellow solid circles continue across the saddle to become Camino Schmid. Follow them down to the right on a wide path through the pine forest which leads back to the foot of the Escaparate ski slope (*50mins*). Train users and walkers with cars at the Puerto will have to turn right onto the surfaced road to reach the **Puerto de Navacerrada** (*10mins*).

49b.* PUERTO DE NAVACERRADA - CERRO DE TELEGRAFO - SENDA HERREROS - SIETE PICOS (SEPTIMO PICO, 2138m) - PUERTO DE NAVACERRADA.

Time:	**5¹/₂-6hrs**
Total ascent:	**438m**

This tackles the ridge in the opposite direction from Route 49a by first dropping diagonally across the steep southern slopes, on the path known as Senda Herreros (the Path of the Blacksmiths), to reach Primer Pico. This is a more varied and exciting route than Camino Schmid and, with its southern sheltered aspect, a good choice on a cold winter's day.

Follow Route 49a to the far end of the **Siete Picos meadows** (*35mins*). In the small dip at the foot of a long wooded slope, a path marked PR8 turns off to the left. Follow the yellow and white stripes at first across pine-covered slopes. A couple of spurs are crossed, then there is a long drop into the spectacular bowl of the Hoyo de Terradillo beneath the southern cliffs of the Picos. The tree cover is broken by large outcrops of slabby rock which the track generally avoids and two streambeds are crossed: first the steep treeless upper course of the Río Pradillos then, lower down, a tributary hidden in trees and dense thickets of white heather. This stream is followed down a few metres before the markings turn upslope to the right, soon to be crossed by a rough ascending path. Leave the PR8 here and follow the new path up a short distance to meet a better horizontal one (*1hr 15mins*). Go right on it on a wandering course up through the forest to where it joins a much broader path marked with solid yellow circles. Follow this uphill. After merging with the PR7 (yellow/white) the track comes out on the crest of the spur enclosing the Fuenfría valley and, soon after, reaches the meadows of Majalasna in front of **Primer Pico** (1938m, *25mins*). From there reverse Route 49a back to **Puerto de Navacerrada**.

49c.* PUERTO DE NAVACERRADA - SIETE PICOS (SEPTIMO PICO, 2138m) - NAVARRULAQUE MEADOWS - HERREN DE CEBRIAN - CERCEDILLA.

Time:	**5-5½hrs**
Total ascent:	**278m**

Take the train to Puerto de Navacerrada and follow Route 49a as far as the **Primer Pico**. Continue to follow the markings into the trees and, where they split, follow either branch down to where they meet again at the **Navarrulaque meadows** (*40mins*). Cross the forestry road which runs north-south on the right-hand side of the meadows and descend in a wide clearing, past a fuente, to cross again the returning road on to a path marked with orange dots. After dropping quite steeply through the forest, the wide path heads south across the slopes, keeping fairly horizontal (spots changing to faint yellow/white paint). It runs along the upper stone boundary wall of the Herrén de Cebrián finca then crosses a meadow to gain the left side of the ridge. At a fork there, take the right-hand branch which gradually descends the eastern slopes to join the road from Camorritos to Cercedilla just on the outskirts of the latter (50mins).

49d.* CERCEDILLA - CAMORRITOS - SIETE PICOS (2138m) - PUERTO DE NAVACERRADA - EL VENTORRILLO - CERCEDILLA.

Time: 7-7½hrs
Total ascent: 978m

This route takes the most direct line from the village to the ridge. It then returns from the Puerto de Navacerrada through the woods and meadows of the Navalmedio valley on a route which was much used by the pioneer explorers at the beginning of the century. At that time, of course, there was no mountain railway and all exploration started with a walk-in from Cercedilla.

Follow Route 48 as far as the meadows at **Navarrulaque** (1660m, *50mins*), then reverse Route 47 as far the col between Segundo and Tercero Picos (2058m, *1hr 20mins*). From there reverse Route 49a to Puerto de Navacerrada (1860m). If refreshments aren't needed at the bars on the pass, minutes can be saved by dropping to the right from the ski piste to join the path to the **railway station** (*1hr 40mins*). At the right-hand end of the platform opposite the station building is a small chapel and the lane below it swings left to the gates of a villa. Drop down a short bank here onto another lane and turn right on it to pass a metal barrier on the way down to the Regajo del Puerto streambed. On the other side, the wide track leads down-valley through the pinewoods, keeping left at the only fork. It emerges onto the main road to Puerto de Navacerrada just above the research station, called **El Ventorrillo** (*50mins*).

Go to the right of the main buildings on a wide lane which is crossed by a fence with a small opening for pedestrians. On the other side the dirt road descends through pinewood then across a mixed terrain of grass, cistus and scattered trees, gradually narrowing to a footpath. Cross a horizontal dirt road and follow less clear tracks down, soon to merge with a wider path coming from the right. This leads to a metalled road with a reservoir dam to the right (*25mins*). Go left on the road then diagonally right on a dirt road which gradually descends to cross a stream before climbing to the outskirts of Cercedilla (picking up GR10 markings along the way). Follow the wide and at first unmade street to a T-junction which to the right leads to the town centre (*40mins*).

PUERTO DE NAVACERRADA

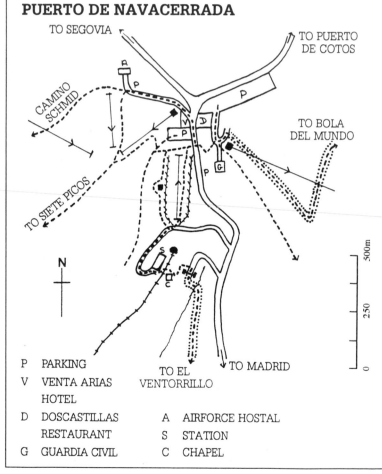

P	PARKING		
V	VENTA ARIAS		
	HOTEL		
D	DOSCASTILLAS	A	AIRFORCE HOSTAL
	RESTAURANT	S	STATION
G	GUARDIA CIVIL	C	CHAPEL

CHAPTER NINE

Central Guadarrama (East)

TOPOGRAPHY

The 18km of continuously high ridge to the east of the Puerto de Navacerrada is known as La Cuerda Larga. Usually snow-topped for five months of the year, it is the most visible and striking section of the range to be seen from Madrid. The first two summits, Las Guarramillas (2178m) and the Bola del Mundo (2258m), are at either end of an elongated plateau area, and there is some confusion in naming them (see Route 50d). Beyond them, the ridge continues east through the main heights of Cerro de Valdemartín (2278m), Cabezas de Hierro (2383m), Asómate de Hoyos (2230m), Los Bailanderos (2126m) and Najarra (2106m) to reach the high road pass of Puerto de la Morcuera (1796m).

Two very different ridges project south from the Guarramillas Bola del Mundo plateau: to the southwest the low rocky spur of Las Cabrillas, and to the southwest a much larger one culminating in the peak of La Maliciosa (2227m). Connected to the Bola del Mundo by the high Collado del Piornal (2073m), La Maliciosa is more than a high point on a subsidiary spur. Viewed from the south, it has the impressive appearance of a free-standing mountain with a precipitous, pyramid-shaped south face and four long rock ridges of its own. The other significant area of high ground on the southern side of the Cuerda Larga is the ridge and valley system of La Pedriza, connected to the main chain at Alto de Matasanos to the south of Asómate de Hoyos. This is a small area but, because of its complexity and interest, merits its own chapter (The Upper Manzanares Basin).

Also included in this east central section is the first 5km of the northern branch of the range, starting at the Puerto del Paular de los Cotos, usually shortened to Puerto de los Cotos (1830m and another ski station). This takes in the four summits of Dos Hermanas (2268m and 2284m), Peñalara (2430m - the highest in Guadarrama) and Los Claveles (2390m), working northward from the pass. The connection between the two arms of the range is the Peña del Aguila Ridge (or Loma de Noruega) which runs NNW from the Bola del Mundo down to the Puerto de los Cotos.

VALLEY BASES

The bases described in the West Central chapter are equally good for this sector. In addition on the north side of the range, **Segovia, San Ildefonso (La Granja)**, and **Pedraza de la Sierra** are outstandingly atmospheric and interesting places in which to stay. However, as no routes are included which start from that heavily forested Segovia side, these northern bases are not so convenient for people who intend to walk most days. For car users on a mixed walking and sightseeing holiday, the first two (only a 30 and 20min drive respectively from the Puerto de Navacerrada) are well worth considering.

ROUTES

This sector is the hub of the range with most of the tops above 2200m. Paradoxically it is also the most accessible with a railway and good roads to the high passes of Navacerrada and Cotos and then chairlifts up from both those points. This doesn't really detract from the serious walks - while there are certainly more than enough people on the Bola del Mundo and at the Laguna Grande (above Cotos) at weekends, you could still find yourself almost alone on the nearby celebrated peaks of La Maliciosa and Peñalara. As with the rest of the range, mid-week walking is very solitary indeed.

The area has many splendid high mountain walks plus some good scrambles. Furthermore, because of its overall height, it is the one part of the range with guaranteed snow cover on the ridges, at least from January to April and often longer. With the tendency at that time of year for the weather to be clear, calm and sunny for long spells, winter walking is often memorable.

More rarely, the snow is deep enough for skiing. This means that for maybe ten weekends a year the traffic at the three ski stations (Puerto de Navacerrada, Puerto de los Cotos and Valdesquí) is nightmarish - the police often start turning cars away by 10.00. During the week in the ski season there are no parking problems, except at Valdesquí.

50. *CUERDA DE LAS CABRILLAS.*

This enticing castellated ridge is the southern spur of Las Guarramillas and separates the valley of the Navalmedio from that of the Barranca de Navacerrada. It also carries the Puerto de Navacerrada road on its western flank. With the highest point on the ridge rising only 100m above the

LA BARRANCA VALLEY FOR LAS CABRILLAS AND LA MALICIOSA Routes 50a, b, c, d, 51a, b, c

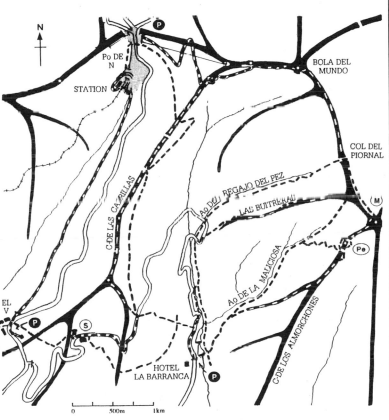

Po DE N - PUERTO DE NAVACERRADA M - LA MALICIOSA
Pe - EL PEÑOTILLO S - REAL SANATORIO C - CUERDA
EL V - EL VENTORRILLO

Puerto and all but the craggy crest swathed in forest, this is not nearly as popular an expedition as Siete Picos. Nevertheless, the rock section is longer and the scrambling as interesting. All it lacks is a big mountain atmosphere. A good path along the eastern slopes makes a tight circular route possible, but also included are two longer, more varied rounds as well as a line from Puerto de Navacerrada Station back to Cercedilla.

50a. EL VENTORRILLO - REAL SANATORIO DE GUADARRAMA - LAS CABRILLAS (1958m) - REAL SANATORIO DE GUADARRAMA - EL VENTORRILLO.

Time: 5¹/₂-6hrs
Total ascent: 475m

The crest of the ridge is the familiar Guadarrama configuration of a series of fractured and eroded granite blocks separated by small cols. It is possible to keep to the top all the way without any real difficulty although every col offers an escape onto a rough way round the next outcrop.

On the N601, about 2¹/₂km after the road interchange above Navacerrada village, the sign for El Ventorrillo (1483m) appears on the right below the Banco de Central-Hispano's holiday residence. Park a little further on at the entrance to the latter.

Just beyond the residence, the road bends sharply right and about 150m beyond that there is a metal gate on the right at the start of a private unmade road to some holiday homes behind and above the bank residence. Follow the road to just beyond the chalets and take a left fork which rises gently through pines eventually narrowing to a footpath. After crossing a streambed, it meets a forestry road. Climb the wooded slopes between the streambed and the road, but following the former, until a long single storey, roofless building is reached. Go to the right of this to rejoin the forestry road which passes between the various buildings of the abandoned **Real Sanatorio** (c.1640m, *25mins*).

Continue up the forestry road which crosses a spur to swing left onto a wide grassy terrace above the Barranca valley with spectacular views of La Maliciosa on the far side. Behind the terrace is a small wooden hut and to the right of it a track starts steeply up into the pines. This leads directly to the first top on the ridge, **Peña Pintada** (1856m, *35mins*). From there, the full sweep of the bristling Cabrillas crest can be seen, backed by the bulk of Las Guarramillas. Take a line over or round the succession of towers to reach the rather insignificant col beyond the last big outcrop (1910m, *1hr 50mins*).

The continuation of the ridge is broader now with only small scattered outcrops and it rises gently to meet the southern slopes of Las Guarramillas. Just beyond a prominent cairn, a wide path leaves diagonally left, heading for the Puerto de Navacerrada. Opposite that junction, but not quite in view from the crest, is the start of the track which traverses the eastern slopes. It begins by descending diagonally left then doubles back to cross open slopes with occasional groups of pines. Rejoining the crest at a col, cairns lead round the right side of a small rock formation then take a diagonal line down the eastern slopes again, into the forest. From there the path follows the course of a pipeline which drops gently across the slopes, to emerge from the trees onto the terrace above the Barranca valley (*1hr*). From there reverse the route to **El Ventorrillo** (*35mins*).

50b. EL VENTORRILLO - REAL SANATORIO DE GUADARRAMA - LAS CABRILLAS (1958m) - PUERTO DE NAVACERRADA - EL VENTORRILLO.

> Time: 5-5¹/₂hrs
> Total ascent: 475m

This is possibly a more varied walk than Route 50a, as it combines the mountain scenery of the crest with the forest and meadows of the upper Navalmedio valley. It is also more truly circular. One minor disadvantage at weekends is that the variety includes crowds and traffic at the rather dismal Puerto de Navacerrada.

Follow Route 50a to where it leaves the ridge to the right. Instead, take the wide track leaving to the left, gently descending to the bottom station of a chairlift at the **Puerto de Navacerrada** (1860m, *15mins*). Take a path with a stone balustrade down to the left and cross the main road to follow a chairlift down to another road, which to the right leads to the railway station. Cross the track then follow Route 49d back to **El Ventorrillo** (*55mins*).

50c.* PUERTO DE NAVACERRADA STATION - LAS CABRILLAS (1958m) - EL VENTORRILLO - CERCEDILLA.

Time: 5-5¹/₂hrs
Total ascent: 128m

This line is included for walkers based in Cercedilla without a car, or anyone who would prefer a cross-country route to a circle. Although it is mostly downhill, the sustained scramble along the ridge means that it is a more strenuous outing than it might first appear.

From the station (1830m) below the Puerto de Navacerrada, reverse Route 50b to where it arrives on the Cabrillas Ridge. From there, reverse Route 50a to El Ventorrillo then follow the end of Route 49d back to Cercedilla.

50d.* HOTEL LA BARRANCA - REAL SANATORIO - LAS CABRILLAS - LAS GUARRAMILLAS - BOLA DEL MUNDO (2258m) - COLLADO DEL PIORNAL - REGAJO DEL PEZ - HOTEL LA BARRANCA.

Time: 6¹/₂-7hrs
Total ascent: 858m

Because the Cabrillas Ridge is the southern spur of Las Guarramillas, it seems appropriate to include a route which uses it as an approach to that summit. The latter is in fact only a rocky protuberance at the western end of the extensive high plateau known as the Bola del Mundo#, so the most satisfactory round is to continue across this short section of the Cuerda Larga to the southeastern corner and highest point on the plateau, then return to La Barranca by the Piornal Pass. Admittedly, these summits are arguably two of the least attractive in the Sierra, being windswept, bare and much

---

There seems to be some confusion both on maps and in guidebooks surrounding the naming of this summit: Las Guarramas, Alto de las Guarramillas, Bola del Mundo are applied interchangeably to the whole elongated plateau area or to the highest points at either end. For the purposes of this guide, Las Guarramillas refers to the western summit with the restaurant and ski lift top stations, and La Bola del Mundo to the higher eastern end with the TV relay station.

interfered with by ski lifts and telecommunication buildings. Nevertheless, the views are good and the route, with its succession of forest, rock and high moorland scenery, makes an interesting day out.

The round could be extended to complete the Barranca valley skyline by following Route 51a from the Collado del Piornal to the top of La Maliciosa then returning to the hotel on the descent in Route 51b. It includes some steeper, rougher ground, but takes very little longer than the descent of the Regajo del Pez described here.

The Barranca valley is reached along a narrow surfaced road which branches off to the north from the N601 a kilometre east of the interchange above Navacerrada village. There is a car park at the end of the surfaced road, opposite the La Barranca Hotel (1400m). (Alternatively, it is only a short taxi ride from Navacerrada and a return taxi can be phoned for from the hotel.)

Walk along the unsurfaced continuation of the road, passing two small reservoirs. Just beyond the head of the second one, look for an unmarked but wide track leaving to the left climbing straight up into the tall, widely spaced pines. At the only fork, take the right branch which leads to a crossroads (*25mins*). Go left on a good path which contours mostly through trees well above the hotel, then works round to the right and over a spur. Just after crossing a streambed (*25mins*), a fork to the right leads up to the sanatorium ruins. Take the path to the right on reaching the building to come out on a horizontal forestry road. Go right on it until it reaches its highest point on an open terrace (1740m, *25mins*). (A rougher, trackless but more direct route to the terrace can be taken by going straight on at the crossroads. *40mins*.)

From the terrace, follow Route 50a to where it leaves the ridge to the right (*2hrs 10mins*). Continue instead on a clear path directly ahead up the shoulder to join the concrete service road coming up from the Puerto de Navacerrada. It leads to the main ridge and the huge TV relay station with its collection of red and white striped, rocket-like aerials which sprawl across the top of the **Bola del Mundo** (2258m, *35mins*). Pass round either side of the compound and continue down the bare slope beyond to look for the start of a wide track through low broom directly below the back fence of the station. 50m further down at a fork, take the curving right branch which descends very gently to the **Collado del Piornal** (2074m, *25mins*), passing first a ruined stone refuge and then a branch to the left.

Follow the path, which crosses this broom-covered saddle, to the right descending into the Regajo del Pez valley. It keeps to the left of the stream and is loose and steep at first but once in the trees is a beautiful walk, passing a good fuente just before reaching the forestry road. Either follow the left bank all the way back to the dam of the lower reservoir (*1hr 35mins*) or move on to the forestry road the second time it crosses the stream.

51. *LA MALICIOSA.*

Towering 1200m above the wide upland valley of the Navacerrada River and dividing the Barranca valley from the headwaters of the Río Manzanares, this splendid mountain is really the southern spur of the Bola del Mundo. Although it is 31m lower than that rather dreary plateau on the Cuerda Larga, it overshadows it in every other respect. From its shapely summit radiate five ridges. Four of these can be seen from the south as long inviting rocky staircases which give La Maliciosa's western and southern aspect a complex and imposing appearance. The view from the Cuerda Larga of its short northeast slope is, of course, less impressive but even here it displays a classic triangular profile with two converging rock-studded ridges. In fact La Maliciosa is probably the most rewarding individual summit in the range because of the variety and quality of the ascents, the rock scenery of the summit area and its unrivalled position as a viewpoint.

(The long and, from a distance, attractive-looking south ridge (Ladera de Matas) is not included in any of the itineraries because that approach to the summit is a 4hr struggle on discontinuous goat tracks through acres of cistus thicket.)

51a.* PUERTO DE NAVACERRADA - LAS GUARRAMILLAS - BOLA DEL MUNDO (2258m) - COLLADO DEL PIORNAL - LA MALICIOSA - RETURN.

Time:	4-4¹/₂hrs
Total ascent:	541m

Although the intervening summit of the Bola del Mundo has to be

crossed, this is still the easiest and by far the most popular ascent (even without taking the Guarramillas chairlift). If you ignore the 'development' in the Guarramillas-Bola del Mundo area and avoid Sunday crowds, this is a pleasant open walk with good all-round views, especially of the Barranca valley and the Buitreras Ridge. It is the one viable approach for those relying on trains or buses.

From the Puerto de Navacerrada railway station, reverse Route 50b to the bottom station of the TAGSA chairlift (open June-mid Sept and Dec-May if there is enough snow for skiing). If using a car, park in the big car park to the right at the top of the pass and walk up the lane behind the buildings to the lift. A concrete service road starts to the left of it, winding in big zigzags up the western then southern slopes of Las Guarramillas to the TV relay station on the summit of **La Bola del Mundo** (2258m, *55mins*). Loose, rubbly short cuts can shorten this time slightly. Chairlift passengers will find themselves deposited just below the summit of Las Guarramillas and can join the service road behind the bar/restaurant.

From the relay station, follow Route 50d to the **Collado del Piornal** (2074m, *25mins*). At a clearing in the broom on the saddle, a path starts on the far side making for a very prominent cairn, set almost at the upper limit of the vegetation. Above, more cairns lead over progressively rockier terrain towards the northwest ridge. The path curves gently left just below the rocks on the crest heading directly to the summit of **La Maliciosa** (2227m, *25mins*).

51b.* HOTEL LA BARRANCA - CUERDA DE LAS BUITRERAS - LA MALICIOSA (2227m) - LA MALICIOSA (OR LAS TIJERILLAS) STREAM - HOTEL LA BARRANCA.

Time:	5-5½hrs
Total ascent:	827m

La Cuerda de las Buitreras is the westernmost ridge on La Maliciosa and separates the Regajo del Pez valley from that of the Maliciosa stream. The tightly packed rock towers which sprout from the crest make this a scramble rather than a walk and the route is generally unmarked. An undeviating line along the crest would require a rope but there are plenty of ledges and terraces along the sides of the outcrops which are neither exposed nor committing.

La Maliciosa from the Collada de las Vacas

Park in the car park opposite the Barranca Hotel as in Route 50d. Take the forestry road to the first pronounced left bend then leave to the right to gain the river bank. Follow it upstream, either staying on the left bank or, when the water is low, crossing it at a ford and following a wide path up the opposite slope, away from the stream. Either way the forestry road is rejoined near one or other of two bridges. In both cases follow the road to the right beyond a sharp left-hand bend (*35mins*).

The first rock buttress of the ridge can now be seen up to the right - take the most direct line through the trees to its base (no tracks) then scramble round its left side on to the ridge proper. Cairns lead over the next outcrop, beyond which is a short section of open ground before the continuous series of towers which make up the bulk of the ridge. The line taken is a matter of personal choice and the highest point is marked by a large cairn (*1hr 30mins*) on the top of the last outcrop before the wide slope leading up to the northwest shoulder of the mountain. On reaching the rocks of the shoulder, the cairned path coming up from the Collado del Piornal is joined, leading to the summit of **La Maliciosa** (2227m, *20mins*).

There are various ways of descending into the Maliciosa valley. The quickest but least interesting is to return to the slope between Las Buitreras and the northwest shoulder then drop left down steep, open ground to the head of the Maliciosa stream, following its left bank until a clear path is picked up. It is worth, however, an extra 15mins to reverse

Route 51c from the summit, either completely, or leaving it at a wide col below El Peñotillo from where a cairned path descends to join the one following the stream. Lower down there is a confusing tangle of tracks, all eventually merging in the cistus scrub and leading back to the dam of the lower reservoir and the car park (*1hr 30mins*).

51c.* LA BARRANCA VALLEY - LOS ALMORCHONES (SIERRA DE PEÑA PINTADA) - EL PEÑOTILLO - LA MALICIOSA (2227m) - COLLADO DEL PIORNAL - REGAJO DEL PEZ - LA BARRANCA.

Time: 5¹/₂-6hrs
Total ascent: 827m

From the car park in the Barranca valley, the impressive rock buttress of El Peñotillo is often mistaken for the summit of La Maliciosa, as its huge bulk rears up out of the long Almorchones Ridge. In fact, the real summit can just be seen behind to the right of it. The walk starts in the lower valley of the Maliciosa stream, where the cistus thickets shelter acres of early purple orchids in May. El Peñotillo is a complicated outcrop and there are several ways round or over it. All of them involve some scrambling, although the easiest involves only a passage over large blocks up a reasonably gentle slope. The descent from La Maliciosa used here, following the Regajo del Pez and Navacerrada streams, is actually the second easiest and most popular ascent route after the Bola del Mundo route.

Park as for Route 50d. Cross the small dam at the top of the car park and take the upper right-hand path which rises a few metres into a dense, tall cistus thicket. After about 20mins when the vegetation starts to thin out a little and there are various strands of path, head for the lower end of a broad rocky spur running down from the Almorchones Ridge then start to climb it up the easy ground, with or without the help of vague paths, to where it joins the parent ridge (c.1560m, *55mins*).

Continuing upwards, a line of cairns appears on the ridge crest. Move out on to the right-hand slope to avoid the first big outcrop. Out on the slope, the lines become confusing: one leads back to the ridge beyond the outcrop, from where El Peñotillo can be bypassed on the left by scrambling up slopes, piled with shattered blocks, to reach a small col directly behind the tower. From there a line of low outcrops on the continuation of the ridge leads directly to the summit of **La Maliciosa** (2227m, *1hr 15mins*).

That is the most direct and easiest line to the summit, but it is more interesting, back at the confusing area, to take one of the lines of cairns which climb straight up the slopes to the main buttress of El Peñotillo. From there, there is another choice of routes: to the right, terraces can be linked to follow the base of the outcrop until a steep slope of large blocks is reached. This leads up to the col and the line of outcrops leading to the summit (*1hr 35mins*).

The other option is a scrambling line leaving left from the main buttress, on terraces which lead into a wide grassy gully with the exit

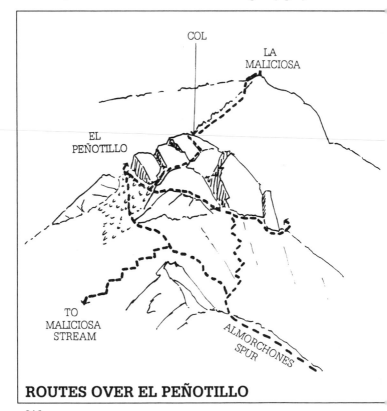

COL

LA MALICIOSA

EL PEÑOTILLO

TO MALICIOSA STREAM

ALMORCHONES SPUR

ROUTES OVER EL PEÑOTILLO

above left onto a small shoulder. Cairns then cross a sloping terrace, rising slightly to pass behind the next buttress. Continue out on to the lower blocks of a long steep gully coming down from the right. This is the key to a harder scramble over the summit of El Peñotillo (**see diagram**). Otherwise, cross the gully mouth and scramble over blocks below the crags to merge with the first route (*1hr 35mins* to La Maliciosa summit).

The descent from the summit follows cairns to the right of the small outcrops on the northwest ridge. Where the latter starts to drop to join the Buitreras Ridge the cairns turn right and head straight down to the **Collado del Piornal** (*25mins*). From there, follow the end of Route 50d back to the car park (*1hr 35mins*).

51d. FUENTE DE LAS CASIRUELAS - LA MALICIOSA CHICA - LA MALICIOSA (2227m) - RETURN.

Time:	7-7$\frac{1}{2}$hrs
Total ascent:	1049m

Although this is the longest approach to the mountain and takes in the intervening top of La Maliciosa Chica, it is actually my favourite. Starting in the La Pedriza Regional Park, a well-made path works gently up the eastern side of La Maliciosa's long southeast spur (called La Sierra de los Porrones or Cuerda del Hilo), with arresting views across the upper Manzanares basin to the La Pedriza rock formations. It joins the crest at the foot of La Maliciosa Chica and it is halfway up the slopes to that summit that the first views of the crags and buttresses of La Maliciosa's south face suddenly appear. After La Maliciosa Chica, the route has a big mountain feel, with the long wall of the Cuerda Larga rearing up across the Manzanares valley to the north, the deep corridor of the Gargantilla valley dropping away to the south and a hard-won summit to be reached, some 340m above the Collado de las Vacas.

The Fuente de Las Casiruelas can be reached only through the entrance to the Parque Regional de La Pedriza. The road into the park is described on page 237, and the way to the Fuente in Route 68.

From the layby opposite the fuente (1260m), cross the road and head straight uphill in a firebreak. In less than 10mins it finishes at a large clearing, from the extreme right end of which a wide path heads up into

Cuerda de los Porrones from the summit of La Maliciosa

the trees. Marked at the start by a small cairn, this gains height in large zigzags before starting its traverse of the upper slopes. (The zigzags can be missed out by continuing straight uphill from the clearing, keeping to the right of a stone wall for another 15mins, until some outcrops force the track to make an arc to the right. Before it returns to the wall, a horizontal path leaves to the right to link in with the top of the zigzags.)

Rising gently through alternating blocks of pine and stretches of open ground, the path reaches the crest of the Sierra de los Porrones at the foot of La Maliciosa Chica (1668m, *1hr 15mins*). There are a number of cairned ways up the broad slope ahead, weaving in and out of the outcrops and boulders. They lead to the crest of the southwest spur of the mountain, where the angle eases and both the south face of La Maliciosa and the summit of La Maliciosa Chica come into view. The track trends slightly right to the latter summit (1939m, *45mins*), then continues diagonally left, down the short northwest ridge to the **Collado de las Vacas** (1888m, *15mins*). Several cairned tracks lead up the long, steep shoulder to the right of the cliffs, with the angle easing just before the summit of **La Maliciosa** (2227m, *55mins*) is reached.

Return to the Collado de las Vacas and start up the northwest ridge of La Maliciosa Chica once more, but move to the right of the crest about

218

halfway up to look for the start of a cairned traverse across to the crest of the **southwest ridge** (*1hr*), thus saving a few minutes. From there reverse the outward route back to the **Fuente de las Casiruelas** (*1hr 30mins*).

52. *LA CUERDA LARGA*

PUERTO DE LA MORCUERA - NAJARRA - LOS BAILANDEROS - ASOMATE DE HOYOS - LOMO DEL PANDASCO - CABEZA DE HIERRO MAYOR (2383m) - CABEZA DE HIERRO MENOR - CERRO DE VALDEMARTIN - BOLA DEL MUNDO - LAS GUARRAMILLAS - PUERTO DE NAVACERRADA.

Time:	7$^{1}/_{2}$-8hrs
Total ascent:	approx. 1120m

High, harsh and bare, this 18km classic ridge walk is Central Spain at its most uncompromising, with no water and little shade or shelter to temper the Castillian sun or wind. It is a big high-level walk, dropping below 2000m only at one point apart from the slopes above the passes at either end. The views are consistently spectacular with the Lozoya valley and the craggy face of Peñalara to the north and the towers of La Pedriza, the upper Manzanares basin then the Barranca valley to the south. In spite of the smooth, rolling, treeless profile it presents from the valleys on either side, this is no plod, as the terrain changes as often as the views with high pasture, big and small rock outcrops, small scrambles, and wide slopes of bare soil or shattered rock.

The route is equally good in either direction but, walking west to east, it must be tempting at the end of a long day to leave out Najarra and head straight for the Puerto de la Morcuera. Without a car to leave at each end of the route or someone willing to drop and pick up, the logistics are difficult whichever valley base you are using. This is because the Puerto de la Morcuera is distant from villages and without any facilities or public transport, except for a wardened refuge a kilometre down the Rascafría side. An expensive solution, given the distances by road, is to leave a car at one end and telephone for a taxi back to it at the other (telephones in the hotels at Puerto de Navacerrada and the refuge at Puerto de la

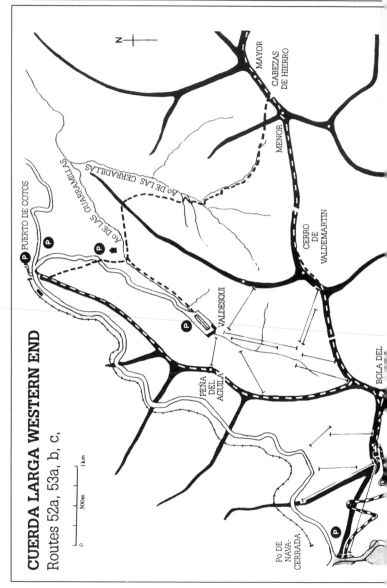

CUERDA LARGA WESTERN END
Routes 52a, 53a, b, c,

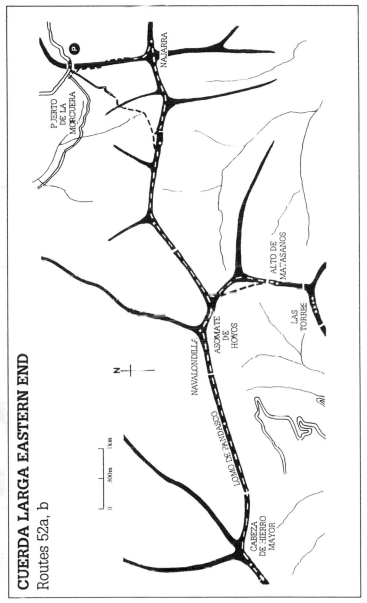

CUERDA LARGA EASTERN END
Routes 52a, b

Morcuera; nearest taxis in Navacerrada village and Miraflores respectively).

Another solution is to make it part of a two-day expedition: train/car to Puerto de Navacerrada - Cuerda Larga - (night at Morcuera refuge) - GR10.1 to El Paular then Puerto de los Cotos (described in Part Four) - train to Puerto de Navacerrada. If you prefer a hotel to a refuge, the above could be reversed with the night spent at one of the hotels at Puerto de Navacerrada. If, in the end, the transport problems are insuperable, day walks along each half of the ridge are described in Routes 52a and 53a.

Park in the large layby/viewpoint on the Miraflores side of the Puerto de la Morcuera (1796m). On the far side of the pass, a dirt road starts to the left but, once through the gate, leave it to pick up one of the faint tracks heading up the broom-covered slopes. They follow a wire fence up to the prominent crag on the skyline. The easiest line then is to cut through the outcrop on its left and take to the mixed ground to the left of the fence and further rock formations. Where the fence ends, continue over open ground to the big outcrops ahead which are the summit rocks of **Najarra** (2106m, *50mins*).

Najarra has a long, level summit ridge, at the western end of which is a tiny stone refuge perched on an outcrop. The track then drops away steeply, with close views to the left of the buttresses and towers on Najarra's western slopes, to arrive at a col (1970m, *30mins*). To the right of the next outcrop, the track merges with the one coming directly from the Puerto de la Morcuera and, from that point on, red and white paint and/or cairns mark the route along the rest of the ridge, all the way to the Bola del Mundo. The main features of the ridge are:

Los Bailanderos (2135m, *40mins*) at the end of a long, fairly level section with small outcrops. There is a steeper rise to a rocky summit with steep cliffs to the south.

Collado de la Peña de los Lobos (2047m, *20mins*).

Asómate de Hoyos (2239m, *30mins*). The wide slopes leading up to this summit merge into the spur running left down to Alto de Matasanos and La Pedriza. The summit is again an elongated plateau with the subsidiary summit of Navalondilla (2223m) at its western end.

Collado de las Zorras (2177m, *20mins*).

Lomo del Pandasco (2243m, *25mins*). A long ridge, bare of vegetation, with a couple of undulations along the top.

Collado de la Peña de los Vaqueros (2216m, *20mins*).

Cabeza de Hierro Mayor (2380m, *20mins*). The second highest summit in Guadarrama with fine views from the survey point.

Small unnamed col (2326m, *5mins*).

Cabeza de Hierro Menor (2374m, *10mins*) - there is a short scramble up to this summit.

Collado de Valdemartín (2148m, *20mins*).

Cerro de Valdemartín (2278m, *20mins*). Although the well beaten path appears to skirt the summit to the left, it makes in fact for the western end of the summit ridge, crossing it at an aerial just above the top of a ski tow. Follow the fence down the side of the ski piste until the markings move to the left.

Collado de Guarramillas (2161m, *10mins*).

Bola del Mundo (2258m, *15mins*) with TV relay station.

Follow the concrete road down, with the choice of shortcutting some of the lower zigzags, to reach the **Puerto de Navacerrada** (1860m, *40mins*).

52a. PUERTO DE LA MORCUERA - LA NAJARRA - LOS BAILANDEROS - ASOMATE DE HOYOS (2239m) - ALTO DE MATASANOS - RETURN.

Time:	6-6½hrs
Total ascent:	892m

Although it is necessary to lose height to reach the rock pyramid of Alto de Matasanos which lies just to the south of Asómate de Hoyos, it is worth it for the outstanding views from there of the Cuerda Larga, the Manzanares Basin and the north side of the Circo de la Pedriza.

Follow Route 52 as far as the wide slopes rising to Asómate de Hoyos. Strike off left just before the summit towards the curving ridge, studded with outcrops, which lead down to a col. You can follow the ridge for the views or short cut across the broom-covered but cairned western slopes. **Alto de Matasanos** (2107m, *20mins*) lies just beyond the col. Return the same way until just below the 1970m col at the foot of Najarra, where the direct path to the Puerto de Morcuera branches left.

53. *CABEZAS DE HIERRO.*

As the highest point on the Cuerda Larga and the second highest top in the range, the bulky top of Cabeza de Hierro Mayor, with its more elegant subsidiary summit of Cabeza Menor, is a very worthwhile mountain expedition in its own right. The normal approach is over the Bola del Mundo from the Puerto de Navacerrada, and there are also circular possibilities along a couple of the substantial subsidiary spurs of the Cuerda Larga. The ridges leading directly to the Cabezas themselves, however, are without tracks because of the blanket afforestation to the north and the inaccessibility of the southern slopes above the source of the River Manzanares.

53a.* PUERTO DE NAVACERRADA - LAS GUARRAMILLAS - BOLA DEL MUNDO - CERRO DE VALDEMARTIN - CABEZA DE HIERRO MENOR - CABEZA DE HIERRO MAYOR (2380m) - RETURN.

Time:	5^1/$_2$-6hrs
Total ascent:	1059m

From the big skiers' car park at the Puerto de Navacerrada (1860m), at the start of the Puerto de los Cotos road, take the lane behind the buildings which leads up to the TAGSA chairlift station or, if arriving by train, reverse Route 50b from the station. Then follow the concrete service road to the top of the **Bola del Mundo** (2258m, *55mins*). Leave the road on a wide stony track to the left across level ground, just before the relay station is reached. It quickly reduces to tyre tracks - go right at two successive forks to pick up the red/white markings which run along the length of the Cuerda Larga. Reverse Route 52 to **Cabeza de Hierro Mayor** (2380m, *1hr 25mins*).

53b.* PUERTO DE LOS COTOS - PEÑA DEL AGUILA RIDGE - CERRO DE VALDEMARTIN - CABEZAS DE HIERRO (2383m) - LAS CERRADILLAS VALLEY - PUERTO DE LOS COTOS.

Time:	6-6^1/$_2$hrs
Total ascent:	1057m

Two long ridges running northeast, one from the Bola del Mundo and the other from the Cerro de Valdemartín, enclose the Guarramillas valley with the ski bowl of Valdesquí at its head. The first, which is described here, is a more straightforward if longer approach to the Cabezas than the second. The long, open switchback over the Peña del Aguila provides a very enjoyable start to the route with the quick progress and views towards the Mujer Muerta and Segovia compensating for the less elevating sight of the ski bowl. The descent from the Cabezas into the little visited, possibly glacial, hollow of Las Cerradillas is rough, partly trackless and occasionally boggy. For a short time in the spring, when the snows in the bowls are melting, it can be difficult to cross the Guarramillas stream and a detour upstream to the Valdesquí car park may be necessary, adding 40mins to the walk.

At the Puerto de los Cotos (1830m), opposite the road leading to the chairlift, some stone steps mark the start of a wide track leading up through the scattered trees. This climbs directly along the crest of the Lomo de Noruega ridge, crossing several times the twists and turns of a dirt road, before coming out onto open slopes. From here can be seen the full extent of the spur ahead, leading over the **Peña del Aguila** (2003m, *35mins*), then an intermediate unnamed hill before a final steeper pull up in the direction of the rocket-shaped aerials on the Bola del Mundo. Before reaching the latter, turn off left behind the top station of a chairlift and follow a fence to its corner. Straight ahead among some rocks can be seen a cairn on the **Cuerda Larga track** (*50mins*). From this point, which lies between the Bola del Mundo and the Collado de las Guarramillas, reverse Route 52 to **Cabeza de Hierro Mayor** (2380m, *1hr 20mins*).

Return to the small col between the summit and Cabeza de Hierro Menor, then leave the ridge to the right down an open slope of small stones. Work slightly to the left, making for the grassy upper section of a spur coming down from Cabeza Menor. Cross this shoulder to drop quite steeply down grassy slopes into the big circular hollow of the upper Cerradillas valley. Although trackless, you are funnelled into a deepening streambed which curves down to the right. This has been formed by one of a fan of small streams which have cut into the floor of the hollow, before converging around the upper limit of the plantations which fill the lower valley. Before the trees are reached, a cairned path leaves to the left (*55mins*), opposite some ruined stone enclosures higher up the right-hand slope.

Just a few metres along the path, take the lower branch of a fork to head downslope. Look for faded yellow markings starting some way above the tree-line and follow them downhill. Once in the trees, they work left across three deeply cut and occasionally boggy streambeds to arrive on the wooded eastern slopes of the spur which encloses the valley. The now clearer track heads on a more or less contouring line for the crest of the spur which is crossed to drop to the **Guarramillas stream** (*45mins*). Cross the stream and take the path up a wooded side valley, at the top of which is the Valdesquí road. On the far side, a forestry road starts beyond a barrier and leads back to the **Puerto de los Cotos** (*10mins*).

53c.* PUERTO DE LOS COTOS - VALDESQUI ROAD - ARROYO DE LAS GUARRAMILLAS - NE SPUR OF CERRO DE VALDEMARTIN - COLLADO DE VALDEMARTIN - CABEZAS DE HIERRO (2383m) - LAS CERRADILLAS - VALDESQUI ROAD - PUERTO DE LOS COTOS.

Time: 6-6½hrs
Total ascent: 780m

The northeast spur of the Cerro de Valdemartín is a more direct approach than Route 53b, but altogether rougher than the good track on the Peña del Aguila Ridge. The route passes the former site of a Falange Youth summer camp (the old cookhouse is now the Pingarrón Refuge) and crosses the Guarramillas valley, which at this point is quite enclosed and a pretty mixture of rock, pine and meadow. The route along the crest of the Valdemartín spur is mostly pathless. There are some skirmishes with chest-high broom on the lower section and an easy scramble over a large outcrop higher up.

The start at the Puerto de los Cotos is for the benefit of train or bus users, while motorists can park by the side of the Valdesquí road at the old camp. They also have the advantage of being able to start and finish at the Valdesquí car park on the few occasions when the Guarramillas stream is uncrossable below the camp.

From the Puerto de los Cotos (1830m), climb the wooded slope to the right of the start of the Valdesquí road. The rough track joins a forestry road which soon forks. Follow the left branch which descends gently through denser forest to a layby on the Valdesqui road (*10mins*).

Opposite is the site of the old camp: a grassy knoll, crossed by a dirt road starting at a metal barrier.

Start to follow the dirt road but, level with a stone arch, drop into a grassy valley to the right. Descending into pine trees, a wide path emerges to arrive in a few minutes at the Guarramillas stream. Cross it and take the track heading downstream and marked with yellow stripes. It soon starts to climb the wooded lower end of the Cerro de Valdemartín spur. Where the pines thin out at the crest (*20mins*), start uphill into the mixture of broom, rock and scattered pine. Clear hunters' tracks disappear as the trees give way to a solid thicket of broom with discontinuous cattle tracks to follow. Higher up, the vegetation descends to ankle level, scattered rock starts to appear and a reasonable path develops which finally leads over a sizeable outcrop to drop to a saddle at the top of a chairlift (*1hr 5mins*).

It is not necessary to go to the summit of Cerro de Valdemartín, the mountain immediately beyond the chairlift. Instead, cross the saddle and start up the rough, bouldery ground, heading for a point about halfway down the left-hand skyline. With luck a line of scattered cairns will be picked up in a few minutes. With or without them, once the shoulder is reached, a clear path can be located contouring across steep loose ground above a hollow to join the Cuerda Larga just above the **Collado de Valdemartín** (2148m, *25mins*). From there, continue on Route 53b.

54. *THE PEÑALARA RIDGE.*

It is less than 5km from the Puerto de los Cotos to the Puerto de los Neveros, but within that distance lies a glaciated landscape on a scale unique in the Sierra de Guadarrama. Like the rest of the range, this ridge already displayed, pre-Ice Age, a steeper face on the Madrid (here east-facing) side, but the permanent ice produced a continuous line of high, steep crags, below which are found hollows and terraces carrying high meadows, bogs and circular tarns dammed by lines of moraine.

The area was declared a Site of National Interest in 1929, not only because of its geomorphology, but also because of the unusual vegetation and wildlife of its boggy ecosystem - frogs, newts, toads and some insectivorous plants in particular. The tarns and streams swarm with huge tadpoles and, in the summer, rangers permanently guard the Laguna Grande to discourage would-be swimmers. Unfortunately, the area's special status was not enough to protect the southern end from the

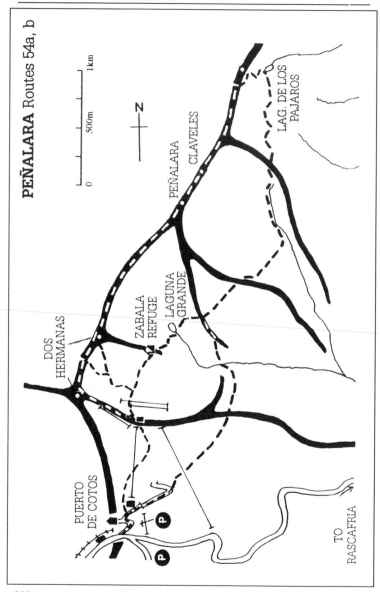

PEÑALARA Routes 54a, b

disastrous Cotos ski development. Because of its south-facing slopes, the station is in operation for only a few weeks in the winter, but as already mentioned, the main chairlift works in the summer and at weekends, pouring people into this fragile environment. In spite of that and the lack of shade, Peñalara is still the best walking area in the range during hot weather because of its height, green meadows, running water and cooling breezes.

54a.* PUERTO DE LOS COTOS - DOS HERMANAS - PEÑALARA (2430m) - LOS CLAVELES - LAGUNA DE LOS PAJAROS - (LAGUNA GRANDE) - PUERTO DE LOS COTOS.

Time: 5-5¹/₂hrs
Total ascent: 603m

If you are a keen scrambler, the curtain of crags and buttresses on the eastern flank offers several days of interesting exploration. As far as walkers are concerned, the area is small enough to take in most of its attractions in one glorious round. The ridge is a beauty: a wide balcony as far as the Peñalara summit (the highest in the range), from where it abruptly and surprisingly narrows to a rocky crest. This culminates in a short exposed, but avoidable, section of jumbled blocks leading to the sharp little peak of Claveles. From here there is a steep descent to the peaceful Laguna de los Pajaros set on a grassy terrace with spectacular views down the Lozoya valley. The return route works along the complicated terrace system below the cliffs, picking a way between the little tarns and bogs.

At the Puerto de los Cotos (1830m) it is often possible to park in spaces along the short road leading up to the Cotos chairlift and the Zabala Restaurant, thus saving a few metres' climb. Alternatively, there is the huge car park on the other side of the main road.

The route starts by following the line of the chairlift, on the ski piste. (You can take the lift in the summer holidays or the ski season, but it is not open until 10.00.) Alternatively, the yellow and white stripes of PR36 which traverses the crest of this massif can be followed a little way to the left of the chair, but it is easier keeping to the curving piste to reach the top station (2025m, *25mins*), where there is a bar/refuge (open only in

The Claveles Ridge, Peñalara

the ski season and weekends). The direct way up the broad shoulder is to follow the draglift starting above the chairlift but it is loose, stony and quite steep. Alternatively, the PR36 follows the very long easy zigzags of a narrow ski piste which starts to the left of the drag and is a comfortable, if long route up the broad treeless slope. Either way, PR36 is followed from the top of the drag on a wide track rising to the right of the machinery. At a left curve soon after, two paths continue uphill, with the left-hand one leading to the first summit of **Dos Hermanas** (2268m, *25mins*). (The other contours slightly to the right of it.)

The way to Peñalara can be seen clearly along the wide stony crest with a thin broken skin of turf and scattered low cushions of broom and juniper. There is a gentle slope towards the Segovia side with all the steep rock and interesting features to the right of the line of cairns and paint markings. The ridge also switchbacks a little, crossing a saddle at the head of the corrie used in the alternative approach (54b), climbing behind the rocky headland of the second summit of Dos Hermanas and traversing well above the back wall of the Laguna Grande corrie to the left of a prominent outcrop. Beyond it start the final and slightly steeper slopes to the summit, the mixed ground giving way eventually to a pure rock landscape. The ridge narrows dramatically as the summit of **Peñalara** (2430m, *40mins*) is approached, making the survey point a wonderful all-round viewpoint, although the Segovia slopes don't approach the steepness of the crags plunging to the east.

Beyond the summit, the ridge narrows further and, after a rock passage with a descent of an easy gully, a saddle is reached at the foot of the pyramid of **Los Claveles** (2390m, *25mins*) with its Madonna statue. Only the last section up the shoulder presents any real exposure and can be avoided on a path traversing across the left-hand slopes. No hands are needed for the rest of the ridge although it continues to be relatively narrow, finally dropping steeply down a wider shoulder to a small col. Turn off diagonally right on a clear path in a small grassy depression which leads to a steep eroded slope with cairns running down it to the southern end of the **Laguna de los Pajaros** (2170m, *30mins*).

With your back to the southern end of the lake, look for a distant cairn which marks the start of the routes along the terraces. There are various lines leading through the complicated terrain of shattered rock, moraines, bogs and tarns. The most direct one in summer sticks to the base of the Claveles crags and screes, but earlier in the year snow patches and wetter bogs can impede progress there. All the lines converge anyway, after passing below a great buttress thrown out from Claveles, to drop over a rocky step onto a narrow boggy terrace carrying a string of tiny tarns (dried out in late summer). On the lip of the terrace, a stream descends in a steep-sided bed to cross a lower terrace then drops steeply once more to the next level area. Leave its course diagonally right here to make a straight line for the prominent rock outcrops running along the lip of the platform.

At the far end, the lower part of a big spur from Peñalara has to be climbed. There are various cairned routes which converge on the crest at a prominent cairn, built round a boulder. This marks the start of a path which leaves the shoulder to the left to contour across slopes of broom to the crest of another ridge (*1hr*) above the Laguna Grande hollow. From here there is a choice of routes: the first keeps to the high mountain environment and affords a close look at the perfect little corrie lake of Laguna Grande. The second is a gentler finish on a fine contour path with good views across the upper Lozoya valley and has the further advantage in hot weather of passing two excellent fuentes.

1. Cross the ridge and take the path which drops diagonally right to the Laguna Grande. Continue along the lip of the corrie to scramble across large blocks then up to the Zabala Refuge perched on a high ledge.

Beyond this locked stone shelter, a clear path heads across a grassy terrace then round a hollow to the top of the chairlift, from where the start of the route can be reversed to the **Zabala Restaurant** (*45mins*).

2. Descend the crest of the ridge, following yellow and white stripes, which after a few minutes turns down the right-hand slopes to a small concrete dam and hut where the stream issues from the Laguna Grande hollow. On the far bank, go left on a wide level path which soon narrows to contour right, across broom-covered slopes then through pine forest. Finally it drops to a dirt road which leads down to the Zabala Restaurant (*40mins*).

54b.* ASCENT VARIATION TO THE COL BETWEEN THE DOS HERMANAS.

Although Route 54a is the normal approach to Peñalara, the variation described here, which climbs the corrie between the two tops of Dos Hermanas, passes through more interesting terrain.

Follow Route 54a as far as the chairlift top station (*25mins*). There the track to Peñalara and Laguna Grande is signposted: it contours across the wide basin to the right of the Dos Hermanas draglifts. After passing under two more tows which serve the basin, and just after a "no camping or swimming" sign, turn left on a small level grassy meadow and head up a boulder slope on faint tracks to arrive in a grass and juniper-filled hollow.

Behind this little glacial basin, a dry streambed leads to a cairned path coming in from the right from the Zabala Refuge. The cairns continue up through rocks and scrub then diagonally right across the scree slopes above, to reach the ridge (*45mins*). This top section may hold snow into June and can be avoided, if preferred, by taking to the rock bands on the right - there is a sparsely cairned diversion from the main path just before the scree is reached. From the ridge, continue on Route 54a.

CHAPTER TEN

Upper Manzanares Basin

TOPOGRAPHY

Between the central section of the Cuerda Larga and the Santillana Reservoir to the south lies the system of ridges which enclose the headwaters of the River Manzanares. Bounded by the Cuerda de los Porrones on the west and falling away to lower land around Soto del Real to the east, the area forms the northern end of the Parque Regional de la Cuenca Alta del Manzanares and has been protected since 1929 when it was declared a Picturesque Site of National Interest.

The River Manzanares and one of its tributaries, the Arroyo del Cuervo, bisect the high basin north to south. The western half (which I have called the Western Basin) includes some of the remotest areas of Guadarrama, but it is the eastern sector, known as La Pedriza, which has a totally unique character in the range. It covers a rough semicircle with the line of the Manzanares/Cuervo forming the base and has a radius of no more than 5km. Small though the area is, it yields a wealth of fascinating walks because geology and climate have combined to produce a spectacular three-dimensional labyrinth of sculpted rock.

This semicircular area is itself bisected by the valley of the Arroyo de la Dehesilla (Arroyo de la Majadilla lower down). These streams flow west then SSW to the Manzanares, from the Collado de la Dehesilla (or de la Silla), which is the only prominent break in the arc of rock towers. To the north and west of the Dehesilla-Majadilla valley lies the horseshoe, or rather an inverted and reversed 'j' shaped ridge enclosing the Circo# de la Pedriza Posterior. This circular basin contains the Los Pollos (or Poyos) and Ventana streams, which flow south into the Arroyo de la Majadilla. The highest point in the area is Las Torres de la Pedriza (2030m) which lie at the northernmost point of the horseshoe. The basic valley form of the Circo is complicated by the underlying northeast-southwest grain of the geology which results in numerous transverse ridges, a few of which form continuous rock bars across the depression.

The compact area of high ground to the south and west of the

For conciseness, I have translated "circo" as "cirque" throughout, although the term is more usually applied to glaciated hollows like the Circos de Cinco Lagunas and Gredos.

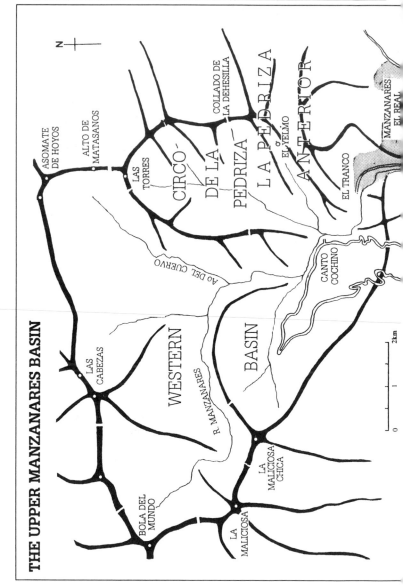

THE UPPER MANZANARES BASIN

Majadilla valley, known as Pedriza Anterior, is a system of tightly packed parallel spines of rock following the general northeast-southwest fault lines. The highest point, roughly in the centre of the mass, is a huge dome of rock called El Yelmo (1714m). While the successive ridges fall away in height north to south, the general structure is complicated by other domes, such as Cueva de la Mora, Peña Sirio and La Tortuga, as well as many connecting ribs between the spines and numerous small spurs, producing an amazing repertoire of eroded forms. The impression from nearly all directions is of an impregnable rock fortress.

Only from the southwest can a clear breach be seen in the form of the steep valley of Hueco de los Hoces which runs straight down from the western end of El Yelmo. The lower end of this canyon is suspended above a large hollow called the Barranco de los Huertos and the stream that flows from one to the other turns west there to drop to the Majadilla valley. Although the structure is invisible from the valley, the whole area is a labyrinth of grass-floored, narrow corridors between the vertical rock spines. In some places these widen out, as in the meadows around El Yelmo and in the virtually horizontal kilometre-long balcony, called La Gran Cañada, to the east of the Barranco de los Huertos.

BASES
Situated below the southern slopes of La Pedriza Anterior and the northern shore of the Santillana Reservoir, the large village of **Manzanares el Real** is another favourite weekend resort for Madrileños. This means there are rather a lot of second-home estates, which are particularly obtrusive towards the entrance to the Manzanares Gorge. Nevertheless, the centre is attractive, with a pleasant main square, storks on the church tower and an eccentric but genuine 15th century castle. The year-round weekend trade again ensures a good range of bars, restaurants, shops and other services. There is a direct bus service to Madrid, augmented at weekends.

There are a couple of hotels in the town as well as rooms to be had at two of the restaurants at **El Tranco**, 3km behind the centre and convenient for some walks in the park. A big campsite can be found 5km along the road to Soto del Real and another one with good facilities at El Tranco behind the village. There is also an official but basic campsite inside the park itself, 1.6km after the main car park, although it doesn't have drinking water. Rough camping is banned within the park but you see tents everywhere at weekends and many climbers use the numerous natural shelters found among the rock formations. This puts intense

The stork colony at Manzanares el Real

pressure on this small and fragile environment and increases the already high risk of fire.

In addition, you can stay at weekends and in the summer holidays at the **Giner Refuge** in the heart of the park. It is wardened, provides simple meals and is open to the public although members of the society which runs it have priority.

ROUTES

Beyond these bare facts of its geology and topography described above, La Pedriza has a special quality which stems from a combination of less tangible factors. The whole upper basin of the Manzanares is completely contained by higher ground and the river has been forced to cut a gorge to escape to the south. So whether arriving by the road over the Collado de Quebrantaherraduras or on foot through the Manzanares Gorge, there is always the feeling of entering a secret place. Added to this, the pink, orange and yellow tones of the rock are more reminiscent of the Dolomites than other granite scenery and they soften the violence of the tortured rock landscape. The combinations of colours can be breathtaking against the intense blue of Castillian skies.

In the 1950s, large areas of the basin, including the Cirque, were planted with pines and cypresses. Carried out sympathetically, it has actually enhanced the landscape as well as producing a more humid microclimate, which in turn has led to a more diverse ecosystem. It means also that many walks are alternating passages of forest and intricate rock scenery, so that for much of the time it is impossible to see where the path leads beyond a few metres ahead. This adds to the impression of wandering in a vast labyrinth with a constant succession of arresting cameos made up of ever-changing combinations of fantastic rock forms, pine and oak trees, water and sky.

By car, there is only one way into the park: by a lane leading from the Cerceda road and signposted Parque Regional La Pedriza. It starts just west of Manzanares el Real and leads to the park gates. At the time of writing, 800 cars are allowed in the park at any one time, so an early start is advised on fine weekends and holidays, when queues build up by mid-morning. In spite of the limit and the fact that most of the car occupants are intent on a very short walk followed by a very long picnic, there is growing concern about the damage being done to this unique area. It has long been proposed that all private cars should be excluded and a shuttle bus service operated from the entrance instead.

Most of the walks start at Canto Cochino, a large parking area near the confluence of the River Manzanares and the Majadilla stream. It has two makeshift bars which are open weekends and holidays and serve simple meals. To reach it, take the sharp right uphill fork at the only road junction about a kilometre after the park gates. This leads to a small pass, the Collado de Quebrantaherraduras, after which big hairpins lead down in a couple of kilometres to the car park.

Once the car limit is reached, "Cerrado" notices are fixed to the park signs at the turn-off from the main road. All is not lost, however, as it is possible to park instead at El Tranco, 3km behind Manzanares el Real at the entrance to the gorge. This is also the direct walk into the La Pedriza for those arriving in the town by bus. El Tranco is reached from the centre by going west on the road beside the church, i.e. away from the castle. Just before the road crosses the Manzanares River on the outskirts of the town, turn right into the Avenida de la Pedriza which follows the river (ignore left branch to El Tranco restaurant and right fork to campsite) to finish at an unsurfaced parking area and a collection of bars and restaurants.

A route called C1 has been marked out with yellow and white stripes to take in all the highest ground in both La Pedriza Anterior and the Cirque, starting at Manzanares El Real and finishing at El Tranco (or vice versa). It is too long to complete in a day, but many of the routes described below include sections of it. In addition, part of the GR10 long distance footpath crosses the park on its way to Manzanares el Real, but doesn't take in any of the high ground. The web-like nature of the path system in La Pedriza lends itself to an immense number of combinations. I have tried to include virtually all the main marked paths plus a selection of the less clear climbers' tracks and scrambling routes. Nothing is included on the little-visited eastern slopes and ridges because access problems on that side make it difficult to put together good circular routes.

55.* EL TRANCO - CANTO COCHINO.

Time: 25mins
Total ascent: 80m

The track, which is marked intermittently with yellow, white and red stripes (C1 and GR10), starts beyond the rough parking area and the various bars and follows the right bank of the river past a small reservoir and through the narrow gorge section. At the far end, where the river makes a right-angled turn to enter the gorge from the wide valley beyond, you arrive at a little bar (open weekends and holidays) perched above the bend in the river. Cross the river by a rail-less bridge below the bar, turning right on the far bank to follow a wide track directly to Canto Cochino car park.

If the intention however is to go either up the Majadilla valley or into Pedriza Anterior via the Barranca de los Huertos, stay on the right side of the river, following the path into the rocks above the bar, from where it leads to a wooden bridge across the Majadilla stream, just above its junction with the main river. For the Refugio Giner and the Collado de la Dehesilla, go straight on past the bridge. For the Barranca de los Huertos,

Yelmo or La Gran Cañada, take the path to the right rising into dense, tall cistus. For Canto Cochino, cross the bridge and head diagonally right across a small meadow to a footbridge across the River Manzanares, which leads into Canto Cochino lower car park.

ROUTES IN LA PEDRIZA ANTERIOR

56.* EL YELMO (1716m) Normal route.

Total ascent:　　　**c.74m**

El Yelmo, also known as La Peña del Diezmo is the magnificent smooth-sided dome which crowns the chaotic skyline of La Pedriza Anterior. Its 175m south face is a magnet for climbers and its situation in the middle of some of the most spectacular rock scenery in the range makes it the natural focus for the walks in this sector. These all pass through either the north or south meadows, level terraces of grass and mat juniper, which border the dome on either side.

There isn't a walkers' route to the top of the rock though experienced scramblers can take the 'normal' climbing route, described here, which doesn't require a rope. The climbing grade is based on a couple of moves in the long fissure which is the key to the upper part of the dome. However, the situation is claustrophobic rather than exposed. Continuously moving, it is possible to be up and down in less than 30mins, but at busy times you may have to queue at the top and bottom of the fissure, which has only one passing place.

In the northern meadows, at the northeast corner of El Yelmo, a satellite mass of rock is connected to the main dome by a small saddle. The quickest way to reach the latter is to climb the rock wall below it, on an obvious but narrow terrace which runs diagonally up from right to left. A longer but less steep approach starts in the small valley on the south side of the satellite. Cairns lead over a series of slabs and terraces to the col.

From there, a deep narrow cleft runs up into the dome at no great angle for about 15m. The two problems for a non-climber are squeezing into the very narrow entrance then, higher up, a metre or so of

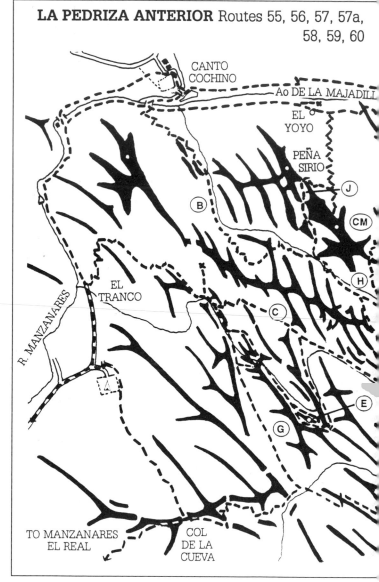

LA PEDRIZA ANTERIOR Routes 55, 56, 57, 57a, 58, 59, 60

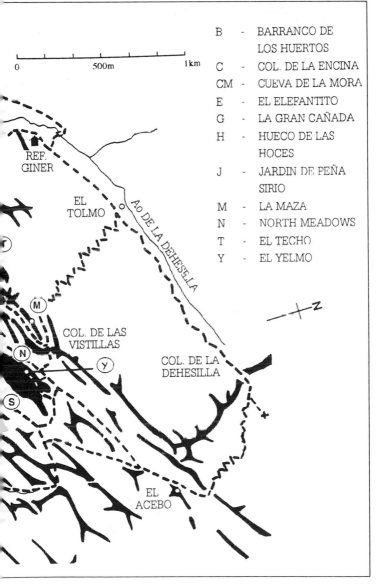

B   -   BARRANCO DE
            LOS HUERTOS

C   -   COL. DE LA ENCINA

CM   -   CUEVA DE LA MORA

E   -   EL ELEFANTITO

G   -   LA GRAN CAÑADA

H   -   HUECO DE LAS
            HOCES

J   -   JARDIN DE PEÑA
            SIRIO

M   -   LA MAZA

N   -   NORTH MEADOWS

T   -   EL TECHO

Y   -   EL YELMO

chimneying to get onto a large boulder. Coming out of the cleft on to deeply fissured slabs, work up and round to the right to reach the survey point on the summit.

57.* EL TRANCO - COLLADO DE LA CUEVA - SENDA MAESO - EL YELMO (SOUTHERN MEADOWS c.1580m) - LAS CERRADILLAS - LA GRAN CAÑADA - MIRADOR DEL TRANCO - EL TRANCO.

> **Time:** 5-5½hrs
> **Total ascent:** 620m

This approach to El Yelmo up the slopes above Manzanares el Real and the reservoir is magnificent. This is not only because of the views back to the south, but also because of the intricacies of the route which cuts across the grain of the many parallel ridges which make up Pedriza Anterior. Instead of taking the most direct route back to El Tranco it makes a detour, with some scrambling, by way of the Elefantito rock and the Cerradillas valley to include some more of the secret corners of this complicated landscape.

Park where the road ends at El Tranco (960m) and walk back along it for 5mins to a left branch signposted to a campsite. Follow this side road to the end of a row of cottages then leave it there for a dirt road a little to the left which heads towards the rocks between a few more villas. Bearing right it runs along the campsite boundary fence and up into a small boulder and cistus-filled valley which leads to the **Collado de la Cueva** (1130m, *35mins*) on the Alcornocal Ridge.

Here you pick up the yellow and white paint marks of C1 which will be followed almost to the base of El Yelmo. At first they climb the complicated structure of the ridge, following a succession of rocky staircases interspersed with small meadows (above one of which can be found the Ave Maria Cave) to arrive at the long grassy corridor known as the **Gran Cañada** (*35mins*). Cross the stream and pick up the stripes again on the rocks on the upper margin of the terrace. These continue to the right for about 50m before turning up into the rocks.

The next stretch is known as the Senda Maeso although the markings continue as yellow and white. The path rambles upwards searching out the easiest way through a succession of rock palisades with one short scramble where the stream runs over slabs. A little higher up at the end of a corridor, the path wriggles through a tiny notch in a ridge to drop a few metres into a transverse grass-floored passageway. Follow the markings left, at first through tall heathers and then up cistus-covered slopes towards the eastern profile of El Yelmo. Where C1 turns off to the right, continue straight on to the meadows below the south face of the dome (1580m, *1hr 5mins*).

At the far end and level with the main South Face, go left and slightly downhill on a well-trodden path with some cairns and red paint slashes. Soon dropping steeply, it crosses a slope towards the Collado de la Encina on the crest of a spur and this is the direct route back to the Gran Cañada. To make the detour to the Cerradillas valley, leave the path just before reaching the shoulder, heading for a single stone marker perched on an outcrop a few metres downslope. Beyond it a cairned path drops steeply into a narrow, left-trending valley. Scramble down it until the cairns move right, across a meadow then into a smaller one. To the right is a cairn and a wall made from a handful of rocks, beyond which a bouldery slope drops to a parallel grass-floored valley. Follow the track there to the right, rising immediately to a small col with the improbably sculpted rock **El Elefantito** (*35mins*) straight ahead below

You can pass to either side of the outcrop to continue on tracks along the left-hand slopes of the descending Cerradillas valley. When the valley narrows, the main track crosses to the right bank to enter a small grassy bowl. Leave either to the left at the top of the bowl or at the bottom end to the right of the stream. Both routes drop on to the **Gran Cañada** (*25mins*).

Turn right on the path which follows the stream until they both swing left to leave the Gran Cañada. The stream plunges into a narrow ravine but the path, after a few metres, moves to the right over a small shoulder. Marked with red stripes, badly eroded and with many alternative strands, it works down the southern slopes of the massif. After crossing the Mirador del Tranco, another wide grass terrace, it takes a final plunge into the steep rocks above **El Tranco** (*45mins*).

57a.* MANZANARES EL REAL - ALCORNOCAL RIDGE - LA GRAN CAÑADA - SENDA MAESO - EL YELMO (SOUTHERN MEADOWS, c.1580m) - LAS CERRADILLAS - LA GRAN CAÑADA - EL TRANCO - MANZANARES EL REAL.

Time:	6-6$\frac{1}{2}$hrs
Total ascent:	680m

This is an alternative start to Route 57 for those staying in the town without a car. The 3km road walk back from El Tranco can be avoided by retracing the route from the Gran Cañada down the Alcornocal Ridge.

In Manzanares el Real (910m), leave the main square from the corner to the right of the Town Hall, along the street called Calle Panaderos which ends at a mini roundabout. Beyond it, take the lane which makes a reversed S up to the right (Calle de Riscos), turning right at the top of it, then next left into a much longer street. In the bottom of a pronounced dip, just before a swimming pool, a short street to the right leads to a parallel road. Turn left into this and continue to a T-junction. Immediately opposite, a rough track starts in a gap between the houses and the yellow and white paint marks of C1 appear (*20mins*).

After leaving the villas behind, the path starts to climb the slopes of the Alcornocal Ridge although markings are scarce here. Head slightly to the right until the paint is picked up again leading to the crest of the ridge and in a couple of minutes more to the **Collado de la Cueva** (1130m, *30mins*) with El Tranco and a campsite visible below to the left. From there, follow Route 57 all the way back to El Tranco, then the surfaced road back to the town.

58.* EL TRANCO - LA GRAN CAÑADA - COLLADO DE LA ENCINA - EL YELMO (SOUTH MEADOWS, 1580m) - HUECO DE LAS HOCES - MANZANARES GORGE - EL TRANCO.

Time: 4¹/₂-5hrs
Total ascent: 620m

This route is good in either direction and can be extended in various ways. The climb to El Yelmo is a reversal of the descent in Route 57, missing out the Cerradillas diversion. The return route is down the spectacular, steep and enclosed valley of Hueco de las Hoces which involves a short passage of strenuous scrambling at one point where giant blocks choke the valley floor.

From El Tranco (960m), the track to the Gran Cañada starts at a flight of steps to the right of the restaurant called Casa Julian and at first works diagonally left behind it, before turning upslope into the outcrops. The track is tortuous, steep, often multi-stranded and badly eroded in sections, but is clearly marked with red stripes. From the wide terrace of the **Gran Cañada** (c.1300m, *55mins*) take a path rising steeply up the slopes behind, which works right into a rake culminating on a small shoulder at the Collado de la Encina. Beyond it, the track crosses the back of a hollow then rises more steeply, moving left into the **south meadows** (1580m, *1hr*)

Go left below the big South Face of the dome until the track seems to disappear among a jumble of huge blocks. A couple of lines of cairns worm their way down (one through a "tunnel", into a sloping meadow with scattered debris. At the lower end, the ground drops away more steeply and the path, at first hugging the base of the outcrop to the left, descends to join the main track down the Hueco de las Hoces (*20mins*).

Red paint stripes lead downvalley into a narrow section piled with enormous blocks, which calls for a steep scramble up to the right. The rock gives way to grass slopes followed by slabs which lead down to the stream. Crossing to the left bank, the track follows the stream which steepens for its last plunge to the Barranco de los Huertos hollow. There are various path strands through the chaotic terrain but don't cross the stream as our route eventually crosses the descending crest to the left, just before two prominent, vertical-sided outcrops with rounded blocks balanced on top (*25mins*).

On the far side of the spur, the track stays high in a traverse at first then drops sharply to a group of boulders forming two arches. The path passes through the second one and takes a curving route down into the grassy hollow of Barranco de los Huertos. Then, following the streambed beyond the lip a short way, it crosses the cistus-covered slopes diagonally left to arrive at a footbridge over the **Majadilla stream** (*30mins*). (There are many alternative tracks down the slope which finish at various points upstream from the bridge.) From the bridge, reverse Route 55 to **El Tranco** (*25mins*).

59.* CANTO COCHINO - COLLADO DE LA DEHESILLA - EL YELMO (NORTH MEADOWS, c.1650m) - HUECO DE LAS HOCES - BARRANCO DE LOS HUERTOS - CANTO COCHINO.

Time:	5-5½hrs
Total ascent:	630m

Good as the preceding routes are, if you have time to do only one walk in the area, this route would be a better choice as it starts in the heart of the park and covers the whole range of La Pedriza scenery: a gentle riverside approach to the col, passing through pine forest then cistus scrub with good views into the Cirque, followed by a stiff climb through sculpted rock formations to the high meadows surrounding El Yelmo. The dramatic descent down the Hueco de las Hoces has already been described in Route 58.

The path on the left of the Majadilla stream which connects Canto Cochino with the Refugio Giner is the most used route in the park and is nicknamed the Autopista. (Weekend crowds can be avoided by using the less popular track on the other side of the stream - see Route 60.) A little above the hut, in the middle of the open, cistus-filled slopes of the Dehesilla valley, the track passes an extraordinary isolated boulder, called El Tolmo, which is 18m high and 73m in circumference. Because of its overhanging sides, it is a popular practice spot for rock climbers.

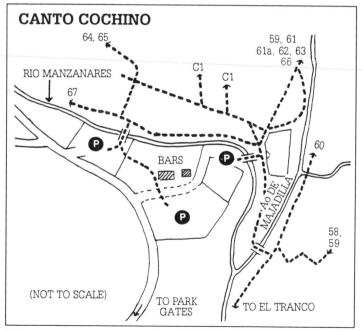

CANTO COCHINO

64, 65

RIO MANZANARES

67

59, 61
61a, 62, 63
66

C1

C1

BARS

60

58, 59

(NOT TO SCALE)

TO PARK GATES

TO EL TRANCO

Starting at the Canto Cochino car park, take the road to the right of the bars which leads down to more parking and the Manzanares River. Cross the wooden bridge and turn left, following the fence for a few metres to its corner. Here in open pine forest, paths lead off in several directions. Keep along the fence to its next major change of direction where the path forks. Take the left branch (straight on) which has faint white, red and yellow paint stripes on the trees. The path follows the left bank of the Majadilla stream and the markings improve (occasional P2/GR10 signs as well as the stripes). It is wide and well-beaten but keep to the markings to avoid detours on to the numerous alternative paths leading down to the stream.

A few metres after route P2 (yellow/white paint) leaves to the left, cross a wooden bridge (*35mins*) over the stream, still following the red and white GR10 markings. They cross a small meadow and climb a rock and scrub slope to meet a horizontal path at the P. Acuño fuente. The Giner Refuge is just to the right and the path from it to the fuente continues left up into the wide cistus-filled Dehesilla valley. After passing the El Tolmo boulder, set in a grassy clearing to the right of the stream, it makes for the deep saddle on the skyline, the **Collado de la Dehesilla** (1451m, *45mins*).

Cross the col and take the well-trodden path, gently rising diagonally right. The C1 and yellow and white stripes soon appear and the gradient increases sharply (ignore branch to left). Continue to the crest, bypassing some steep slabs to the left if they are wet or iced. When the angle eases among spines of rock, the track works round to the right for the first views of the Santillana Reservoir. Continuing to swing to the right, it rises gently to a small col with a conspicuous tower to the left of it called **El Acebo** (1610m, *40mins*).

Beyond the col is a wide scrub-covered terrace rising gently ahead. The track takes a long diagonal across it, heading for a large outcrop with a "window". Just beyond it at the top of the rise, leave C1 for a cairned track branching to the right which leads in a few minutes to the **north meadows** (1650m, *25mins*). (At this point it is worth taking a short detour to the Collado de las Vistillas (1668m) on the clear path up to it on the right. With a foreground of the spectacular shape of La Maza, there are views across the Western Basin to La Maliciosa, the Bola del Mundo and the Cabezas de Hierro.) If it is likely to be your only visit to the area, it would be worth walking round El Yelmo in a clockwise direction (clear paths down a gentle slope) to reach the south meadows and the much more impressive south face of the dome (*10mins*). From there

La Pedriza Anterior from the Santillan Wall

Route 58 can be followed into the Hueco de las Hoces.

The most direct route, however, is from the northern meadows which drop away directly into the steep, debris-filled defile of Hueco de las Hoces and the clear path is marked with red stripes and numerous cairns. The valley descends steeply for about 10mins then the gradient eases in a wider section with a grassy amphitheatre to the left and the steep corridor down from the southern meadows joining to the right. From there follow Route 58 as far as the footbridge over the Majadilla stream. Cross the bridge then go to the left of the stone forestry buildings to pick up the path to the bridge leading into Canto Cochino car park.

60. CANTO COCHINO - EAST BANK OF THE MAJADILLA STREAM - JARDIN DE PEÑA SIRIO - HUECO DE LAS HOCES - EL TECHO - CORRAL CIEGO - LA MAZA - COLLADO DE LAS VISTILLAS (1668m) - EL TOLMO - REFUGIO GINER - CANTO COCHINO.

Time: 6-6½hrs
Total ascent: 628m

This route is designed to explore the dense network of ridges and corridors just to the north of El Yelmo and involves a steep climb from the valley and several passages of scrambling through the

maze of little canyons and enclosed gardens which make up this fascinating area. The initial climb up the slopes above the Majadilla valley is steep and the paths are difficult to follow, but the impact of the Peña Sirio "garden" is much greater from this entrance than from the Hueco de las Hoces. From the Collado de las Vistillas, several longer or shorter ways back to Canto Cochino are possible. The direct descent to the Dehesilla stream described here is steep and rough, sometimes loose and there are some slab bands to cross, which in winter may be thickly iced.

From the lower car park at Canto Cochino (1040m), cross the footbridge over the River Manzanares. The path to the right leads across a small meadow to another bridge at the Majadilla stream. Take the track upstream on the opposite bank (this is the alternative route to the Giner Refuge), and where it rises into boulder-scattered ground at the end of a long narrow meadow, go right at a fork to a prominent rock called **El Yoyo** (*20mins*). (While it looks like a stubby finger as you approach it, it is in fact roughly disc-shaped with a concave face overlooking the path.)

A minute or so after passing the rock, the path crosses what looks like a dry streambed of small rock debris. Climb up it briefly to pick up a narrow cairned track leading through tall cistus mixed with other shrubs. Trending slightly left, it becomes easier to follow up a short rock band into thickets of less dense cistus, mixed with small evergreen oaks higher up.

While working up this steep ground, try to identify in the mass of large boulders scattered across the slope above the two which are nearest to the poorly marked turn-off to the Jardín de Peña Sirio: on the skyline is the big whale-backed dome of Cueva de la Mora towards which the path is heading. To the right and slightly in front of it is a subsidiary dome with the breach which leads into the Jardín to the right of that. A little below the main dome, pick out a pair of outcrops - a shark's fin and a larger pyramid to its right. Some 30m before the path reaches them, a faint horizontal track leaves to the right (cairn at the junction). This rises gently through dense oak wood to come out at the foot of the subsidiary dome. Continue to the right below the face and round into a canyon, choked with giant blocks. The path keeps to the left-hand wall and leads into the **Jardín de Peña Sirio** (c.1400m, *55mins*), a quiet space enclosed by spectacular rock formations.

At the far end, follow cairns through two successively higher gardens. In the last, El Yelmo comes into view and the markers drop into the Hueco de las Hoces to join the path up the valley at a slab slope just above the streambed. Follow the red stripes of the new path through a pile of huge boulders, which involves some scrambling, and into a wider section of valley below the western end of the dome. Just before the path passes under an arch formed by two blocks, move across the streambed to the left, into a grassy amphitheatre. At the back of it, a jumble of rocks leads up to slab bands below and to the right of a chunky outcrop on the skyline. The object is to reach the right-hand edge of the outcrop and, while the scramble straight up into the blocks requires a little route-finding, there are no special difficulties. Exit right from the slabs onto a wide grass terrace below and to the left of the chunky outcrop (*50mins*).

The descent starts in a steep cleft then on a huge sloping slab to the left of a giant block with a low roof. Continue down easier ground into a big corridor which curves up to the right and is enclosed downslope by a large vertical wall. The route now climbs this corridor and the thick deciduous oak scrub which fills it can be avoided by taking a high line on the right (odd cairn). Further up, the ravine divides on either side of an outcrop called El Techo (the Roof).

Fight your way through the oak scrub in the steep right branch to enter a narrow cleft, roofed in with a series of chock stones. At the back of this long cave, a small hole in the roof leads up into the last few metres of corridor below a small col (*30mins*). On the far side, there is a very short but steep drop into a grassy hollow, backed to the left by a vertical wall. At the far end of the latter, turn up into a collection of giant boulders at the start of another corridor and work through them to an open area floored with a sloping slab. At its right edge, ignore the line of cairns continuing up into more boulders. Instead, turn back from the lower right-hand corner, to climb into a gully in the wall on that side, where an unusually large deciduous oak tree is growing.

The top of the gully leads into an almost level narrow canyon. At a crossroads of similar passageways, go straight on over a small col and into another garden. An exit to the right over a small rock bar leads directly to the northern meadows and the ground falls away to the left with good views of the Cirque and Las Torres. However, this route continues straight ahead up a steep corridor with the strange rock formation of La Maza to the left of it, to reach the **Collado de las Vistillas** (1668m, *35mins*) at its head.

The far side of the col leads into the northern meadows, but this itinerary returns downslope for a few metres. It then leaves on a different path to the right, down a short slope of chunky scree which forms a gap in the rock spine. Coming out onto the scrub-covered, rocky slopes of the

Dehesilla valley, cairns zigzag steeply down to the **Tolmo** (c.1200m, *45mins*) boulder, on the stream bank. Reverse the start of Route 59 to **Canto Cochino** (*40mins*).

ROUTES IN THE CIRCO DE LA PEDRIZA POSTERIOR

I have divided the horseshoe into three sections (Routes 61, 62 and 63) to make comfortable circular day walks, but any combination of adjacent sections or the complete tour of the ridge (Route 66) are possible in a long day. The yellow and white marked C1 track takes you through the many complications of the ridge all the way from the Collado de la Dehesilla to Canto Cochino.

61.* CANTO COCHINO - COLLADO DE LA DEHESILLA - NAVAJUELOS - PARED DE SANTILLAN - COLLADO DE LA VENTANA - LA VENTANA STREAM - AUTOPISTA - CANTO COCHINO.

Highest point:	1800m - south of the Collado de Ventana
Time:	5¹/₂-6hrs
Total ascent:	760m

This walk includes the first 2km of the horseshoe to the north of the Collado de la Dehesilla. In fact there is no real sense here of being on a ridge until the meadows of Navajuelos are reached because the first section is a tightly packed series of parallel transverse spurs. The path takes a tortuous route through the highest part of these, searching out the easiest breaches and connecting up a series of enchanting gardens, almost entirely enclosed by spectacular walls and towers of rock. There are short passages of quite strenuous but unexposed scrambling both in the climb up from the Collado de la Dehesilla and to circumvent the big Santillán Wall beyond Navajuelos.

Take Route 59 as far as the **Collado de la Dehesilla** (*1hr 20mins*). To the left side of the flat meadow at the top of the saddle is a 6m boulder with Collado de la Dehesilla 1451m painted on it, as well as the first yellow and white stripes of route C1. At first, the track works up and across a transverse spur to the right of the ridge line, scrambling over, round and

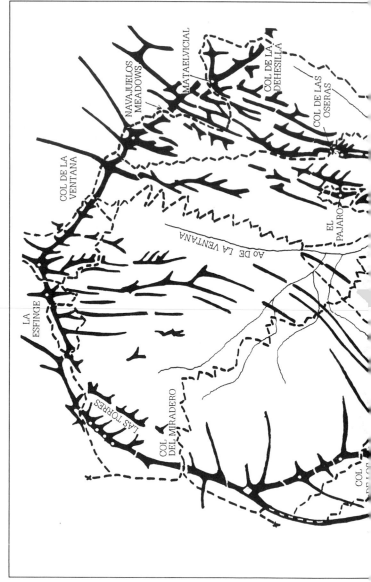

COL DE LA VENTANA

NAVAJUELOS MEADOWS

MATAELVICIAL

COL DE LA DEHESILLA

COL DE LAS OSERAS

EL PAJARO

Ao DE LA VENTANA

LA ESFINGE

LAS TORRES

COL DEL MIRADERO

COL

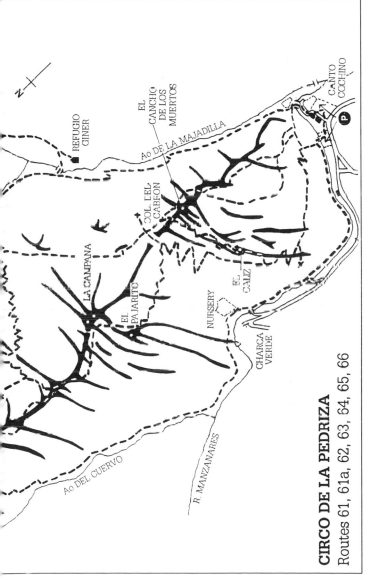

CIRCO DE LA PEDRIZA
Routes 61, 61a, 62, 63, 64, 65, 66

even under the debris fallen from the towers above. It then climbs a steep rocky staircase, with the cliffs of Mataelvicial to the left to reach a narrow col (*20mins*).

Beyond it is a sequence of rock-enclosed gardens linked by small cols. From the last of these, a treeless meadow encircled by improbably-shaped rock towers, an interesting tunnel exit connects it with a wide corridor running to the right. The track works along it, crossing the top of a couple of wide gullies which plunge to the left and give the first views across the Cirque. The corridor finishes in a rock enclosed meadow with a few pines, which is crossed diagonally left to arrive at the wide saddle of the **Navajuelos Meadows** (1670m, *35mins*). This once must have been a fine open balcony for views into the Cirque on one side and the Eastern Guadarrama mountains on the other, but plantation now blocks part of the panorama.

Go right at a T-junction in the middle of what remains of the open ground, then into plantation to arrive abruptly at the foot of an impressive rock barrier, the highest part of which is the Pared (Wall) de Santillán. Climb steeply through a cave formed by the conjunction of some giant blocks, then scramble to a gap to the right of the main rock faces.

Beyond it, the ground drops away to the right into the deep hollow of San Blas, but the path keeps high, just below the ridge towers, to cross another rocky spur before dropping to an open section of crest (from where alternative Route 61a leaves to the left). The next rock band is little more than a boulder-strewn rise, after which there is a gentle descent to the wide saddle of the **Collado de la Ventana** (1784m, *40mins*), with Cerro de los Hoyos, a great wall of twisted organ pipes, beyond.

At the lowest point on the saddle, just before a block of pines, a cairned track leaves to the left, into plantation at first, then emerges onto the open scrubby slopes of the steep valley of the Ventana stream. Follow the many zigzags down into the trees filling the Cirque below. The path eventually straightens out to follow the left bank of the stream before crossing it at a ford (*55mins*). Continue downstream, now following yellow and white stripes (P2), which lead past the wooden bridge below the Refugio Giner, to become the "autopista" to **Canto Cochino** (*40mins*).

61a.* CANTO COCHINO - COLLADO DE LA DEHESILLA - NAVAJUELOS - PARED DE SANTILLAN - 1782m COL - COLLADO DE LAS OSERAS - EL TOLMO - CANTO COCHINO.

Time: 6-6¹/₂hrs
Total ascent: 742m

Instead of returning from the ridge on the straightforward zigzags from the Collado de la Ventana, this is a strenuous alternative down the increasingly steep, enclosed, tree-choked channel which drops towards the junction of the Ventana and Dehesilla streams from the Navajuelos meadows. Although it is possible to follow it all the way down to the stream banks, the lower section is pathless, the vegetation dense and the scrambling more difficult than higher up. Instead, this route cuts across the enclosing left-hand ridge at the hidden Collado de las Oseras to plunge steeply down the northern slopes of the Dehesilla valley, arriving at the stream near the giant boulder, El Tolmo.

Follow Route 59 to the Collado de la Dehesilla then Route 61 as far as the open section of ridge after the Pared de Santillán (1782m saddle). Take the path starting at a large cairn and heading slightly back to the left-over mats of heather and following small stone markers. At first, it drops only slightly making for a gap in the descending spur of rock towers to the right. A short distance before reaching the col, go downslope following small cairns into the first scattered trees - there is no clear fork.

Dropping steadily in a wide hollow between the ridges of Dos Torres to the right and Cancho de la Herrada to the left, the path enters the main channel and joins the track coming down from Navajuelos (*35mins*). As the tree cover thickens and the ground steepens, the line works over to the impressive rock walls to the left of the narrowing gully, eventually running along the base of them with one tricky step where a couple of footholds have been cut.

From then on, follow the stone markers with care in the complicated terrain. The turn-off to the hidden Collado de las Oseras is just before the next obvious feature on the left-hand ridge - a sculpted turret, part of the Buitreras group: at a large boulder with fading white graffiti at the head of a steep rock gully, turn up to the left, following cairns for just the few metres to the col (*30mins*).

The well-marked path zigzags steeply down the far side of the ridge, passing on the right a spectacular wall with circular erosion holes and a cave beneath. The angle hardly eases until the pine trees along the bank of the Dehesilla streambed are reached (*25mins*). Various paths cross the bed to join the GR10 (red/white stripes) on the far side. Head downstream, passing El Tolmo and reversing the start of Route 59 to **Canto Cochino** (*40mins*).

62.* CANTO COCHINO - MAJADILLA STREAM - CIRCO DE LA PEDRIZA - COLLADO DE LA CARABINA (OR MIRADERO, BOTA OR POLLOS) - BASE OF LAS TORRES (c.2000m) - LA ESFINGE - LA VENTANA STREAM - MAJADILLA STREAM - CANTO COCHINO.

Time:	**6½-7hrs**
Total ascent:	**960m**

Las Torres are four chunky towers set so close together they have the appearance of a fissured wall. They are the highest point in La Pedriza and the most inaccessible from the roadhead, being positioned right at the back of the Cirque. In spite of their height, they seem to lack the dominating presence of El Yelmo, possibly because of their situation on the ridge between other impressive outcrops. Still, this is one of the best days out in La Pedriza, the remoteness enhancing the usual delights and surprises of the rock scenery, and there is the contrast between the equally spectacular views into the Cirque on one side and the Manzanares upper valley on the other.

To maintain the anti-clockwise traverse of the ridge, established in Route 61, this walk should be described in reverse, but the approach to the Collado de la Carabina, climbing right to the back of the Cirque through shelves of forest alternating with rock bands, is much more interesting than the many zigzags up to the Collado de la Ventana. Having said that, P2, as the Carabina route is called, isn't entirely clear: the paint marks are sometimes widely spaced and cairns have often been improvised but still leave a number of doubtful forks. All of these, except the one specified, are just variations on the main path and eventually lead back to it.

Follow Route 59 as far as the fork in the track before the wooden bridge across the stream (*35mins*). Go left on the broad path which swings up

Majadilla Valley, Circo and Las Torres

into the trees and is marked with yellow and white stripes (P2). It soon narrows, working round into the valley of the Pollos stream with occasional impressive views of the huge rock monolith of El Pajaro on the opposite slopes. Passing the ford where the track for the Collado de la Ventana branches off, P2 continues on the left bank in forest, until a sudden fork to the left after about 10mins signals the start of a zigzagging climb through the first band of rocks. Go right at any ambiguous forks to avoid straying onto a link path to the Senda ICONA.

Once beyond the rocks and on the next 'shelf' of forest, pass over a well cairned crossroads in the middle of a cistus thicket (*35mins*). A minute or so beyond it, the track crosses a stream onto a big horizontal rock slab. Drop off it to the left and follow the stream for a few metres before crossing it to the left. Soon crossing back, head slightly right across another slab. After that point, the paint or cairns become clearer and the general rule is that the main track sticks fairly closely to the course of the stream. After working up through much steep rock and forest, the path eventually comes out onto open broken ground just below the skyline. Follow the P2 sign diagonally right to the **Collado de la Carabina** (1879m, *1hr 20mins*).

Turn right, following cairns which initially move out onto the slopes

257

leading up to the back of the Torres. In a few minutes, the paint marks divide, with P2 going left to contour round the great empty bowl to the north below the Cuerda Larga. Continue instead on C1 which climbs the slopes towards the Torres, arriving at a col in the ridge beyond the easternmost tower and the highest point on the route (c.2000m, *20mins*). (An easy scramble to the top of the highest torre leaves to the right here.)

The track now drops back on to the Cirque side, crossing a bowl and descending to a wide terrace to the right and below the main ridge outcrops. From here the terrain to be crossed to reach the Ventana valley can be seen ahead - row after row of narrow, serrated ridges running down from the main crest into the Cirque. Although the route is complicated with the track sometimes descending and sometimes climbing the corridors between the ridges to search out the easiest crossing points, the markings are good for the whole of this section and at two points the marked path divides to take alternative routes on opposite sides of the main ridge.

After descending part of the wide, tree-filled corridor of the Callejón de Abeja (45 mins) the track then makes its way through the last major rock spine by way of a steep gully involving some interesting scrambling/ caving, to enter the wide, shallow Ventana valley. Once out of the outcrops, C1 drops over mixed ground towards the Ventana stream but soon turns sharply left to contour round towards the Collado de la Ventana. A couple of minutes after the turn, look for a cairned short cut to the right which heads down to the big zigzags of the path from the Collado (*1hr 10mins*). From there, follow Route 61 back to **Canto Cochino** (*30mins*).

63.* CANTO COCHINO - MAJADILLA VALLEY - CIRCO DE LA PEDRIZA - COLLADO DE LA CARABINA (1878m) - LAS MILANERAS - COLLADO DEL CABRON - CANCHO DE LOS MUERTOS - CANTO COCHINO.

> **Time:**   7-7½hrs
> **Total ascent:** 854m

This route covers the most southerly section of the ridge, wandering between the big towers of the crest on a long slow descent from the Collado de la Carabina to Canto Cochino. The walk is probably the most strenuous of the three with some scrambling sections,

although only the steep drop just beyond the Tres Cestos Pass could present any real difficulties, especially in wet or icy conditions.

Follow Route 62 as far as the **Collado de la Carabina** (1878m) and take the C1 ridge route left (yellow and white stripes) to move out from the wide col onto the slopes to the right of the crest. When the path starts descending the long rocky spur running down into the Manzanares valley, keep to the paint marks which on two occasions suddenly turn left to run horizontally through a band of trees (while inviting lines of cairns beckon down the ridge). After leaving the second band of trees, the track continues over more broken, steeper ground just below the outcrops which make up the main crest.

This section leads to the **Collado de los Tres Cestos** (1764m, *35mins*), a hidden col on the ridge, identified by the striking sculpted tower shaped like an Easter Island head, which overlooks the pass. Dropping slightly to round the tower then climbing to another small col, the markings plunge into a steep gully leading back down into the Cirque. If you wish to avoid the difficult moves in the upper section, ledges can be linked up on the right-hand wall of the gully. Although there are no more technical difficulties, the ground remains consistently steep until the forest is re-entered (*35mins*). After a short level traverse, a path joins from the left and C1 swings steeply uphill to rejoin the crest of the ridge (*10mins*). It then follows a long, garden-like section of ridge, dotted with rock outcrops among the cistus.

At the end, the path rises to the right to round the first outcrops of another upsurge in the ridge. On the far side, a climb down a 15m wall leads into a depression. Take the right fork at some cairns there, to head towards a tiny col between the main mass of rock and an isolated tower. Beyond the col, the path crosses a smaller tree-filled hollow to yet another cleft which is poised above a steep narrow gully, the exit from this last collection of towers. Issuing from the cleft but still on steep ground, it follows a big wall round to the right before dropping left into a mixture of rock, trees and cistus, to make more or less straight for the pretty, semi-wooded saddle of the **Collado del Cabrón** (1303m, *1hr 10mins*).

Turn left to cross the col then right at a crossroads, still following the yellow and white paint which leads below the interesting rock faces of Cancho de los Muertos and down the open cistus-covered slopes above the car park. Approaching the river, the path re-enters the pines and meets a wide path which to the left leads to the bridge into the car park at **Canto Cochino** (*50mins*).

64.* CANTO COCHINO SUBSIDIARY CAR PARK - COLLADO DEL CABRON - EL PAJARITO - LAS MILANERAS - CUERVO STREAM# - RIVER MANZANARES - CANTO COCHINO.

Time:	**6-6¹/₂hrs**
Highest point:	**c.1820m on the ridge running down to the Cuervo stream**
Total ascent:	**c.820m**

This walk reverses Route 63 from the Collado del Cabrón, but where C1 suddenly descends into the forests of the Cirque, this route continues along the crest until the chunky towers of Las Milaneras force a fascinating scramble, crossing the ridge a couple of times before rejoining C1 below the last steep pull up to the Tres Cestos Pass. Instead of continuing all the way to the Collado de la Carabina, a subsidiary ridge is followed down to the River Manzanares, giving a chance to enjoy some of the beautiful, remote country of its upper reaches. It is quite an athletic route and although the scrambling is not exposed, there is some reliance on the friction of the rock, which would make it difficult in wet or icy conditions.

Drive past the main Canto Cochino car park to another one a little further along on the right. The walk starts at the bridge across the River Manzanares below the parking area (1040m). Go upstream a few metres then right on a wide trace of path through the trees and to the right of some low rock outcrops. At a crossroads, reached in a couple of minutes, go straight on with the path now marked with solid white circles.

Ten minutes further on, just after passing a branch to the left, take a right fork which climbs the slope above in two big zigzags. The path then runs out onto an open shoulder, with good views of the upper Manzanares valley, before swinging right into the trees to follow the right-hand slopes of a valley to the **Collado del Cabrón** (1303m, *45mins*) at its head. The upper portion of this path makes big zigzags on the steeper ground just below the col, but has the usual short cuts.

The path to the ridge leaves to the left just as you arrive at the col, marked C1 with yellow and white stripes. Reverse Route 63 as far as the point where C1 leaves the crest down the right-hand slope (*55mins,*

Also shown on maps as Arroyo de los Hoyos de las Sierra or Arroyo del Chivato

painted arrow and large cairns). Continue instead along the crest, now following orange spots, which after about 10mins lead up into the first rocks of the Milaneras outcrops. There they disappear, but the path continues diagonally right and steeply up into a cave produced by the conjunction of some big blocks. Climb the short wall to the left of the cave on to a terrace above.

Cairns mark the way along the right side of the main ridge, linking up small grassy terraces with a few deciduous oaks among the rocks. The markers then head more steeply up a shallow depression to the crest where, in a grassy bowl, they turn right, over a col at the start of a subsidiary spur heading down to the Manzanares valley. After a short sharp drop from this gap, the path appears to head steeply down to the left following the spur. Instead, continue across a band of rock to a point just before a cairn at the entrance to a small cave. Then climb through a gap above it to arrive in a gully running back up to the main ridge and filled with huge blocks.

Climb the gully, following more cairns to recross the ridge and swing left on more grassy terraces with oak trees. At a small col between the main massif and a buttress, the cairns disappear but the way is obviously down the steep gully below, filled with oaks and enclosed to the right by the big walls of Las Milaneras. Just as the ground starts to rise again, C1 is rejoined coming up from the right (50mins)

Now reverse Route 63, recrossing to the western slopes and following C1 until it emerges from a band of trees on to the the crest of a broad, bare rocky spur running down to the left (1820m, 50mins). Leave the stripes, which turn upslope towards the Collado de la Carabina, and follow cairns down the spur. The ground is quite complicated and there are a number of interweaving routes (all cairned) - some along the crest and one line in the forest to the left. Whichever is taken, there is a feeling of a slight trend to the left as the ridge curves in that direction.

All the paths merge on the left side of the ridge somewhere above or around a magnificent, isolated Scots pine, with a massive trunk and spreading crown, the branches of which sweep down almost to the ground (35mins). The track continues below and to the left of the tree but almost immediately splits. Go left on the horizontal branch into the forest which then heads downslope for a while before moving left across a small rock spur. After following the left side of the rib a short way downhill on open ground, another sudden lurch to the left takes it back into the trees (follow cairns carefully).

The path now becomes much clearer and drops steeply through the forest to just above the banks of the **Cuervo stream** (*25mins*), which it now follows downstream high on the left-hand slopes, dropping to the water's edge only as the stream is about to enter the River Manzanares. The path then swings left at the lower edge of a plantation to follow the Manzanares downstream (*25mins*). There is a parallel path running nearer the river and either can be taken.

In about 20mins both tracks disappear on the steep slabby ground above the Charca Verde, a large pool in the river (and popular swimming spot in summer). The easiest way through this complicated terrain is to find and follow a pipeline which crosses the rocks some way above the water. On the far side of the difficulties, drop down to the river bank to pick up a clear track which heads away from the water and past a tree nursery. Returning to the river at a footbridge, continue following the left bank until the bridge to the car park is reached (*55mins*).

65.* CANTO COCHINO - CANCHO DE LOS MUERTOS WEST RIDGE - COLLADO DEL CABRON - SENDA DE ICONA - PUENTE DE LOS POLLOS (c.1500m) - VENTANA STREAM - EL PAJARO - EL TOLMO - REFUGIO GINER - CANTO COCHINO.

Time:	7-7¹/₂hrs
Total ascent:	670m

Here is a chance to wander at middle height through La Pedriza Posterior, linking climbers' paths to reach some of the spectacular rock formations little visited by walkers. Although the highest point is only 1500m, this is not a gentle stroll and involves some sustained and at times difficult scrambling around the rock features. However, by going directly to Cancho de los Muertos on C1 and missing out the diversions to Puente de los Pollos and El Pajaro, the route, all on good paths, would be about the gentlest possible circuit in La Pedriza.

El Cancho de los Muertos, the most southerly group of rock towers on the horseshoe, has already been visited at the end of Route 63. Although the most direct way to it is to reverse that route, the slightly longer approach by the west ridge well repays the extra effort with delightful rock scenery along the crest and views of the upper Manzanares valley to the north. Then, from the Collado del Cabrón, the Senda de ICONA provides a beautiful

Risco del Pajaro

balcony above the Dehesilla valley, and is lined with a huge variety of wild flowers in May and June. This good path is abandoned temporarily to plunge into the forest in search of the Puente de los Pollos, a natural arch of some size found in one of the bands of rock which cut across the Cirque.

Then, after returning to the path to contour across the Cirque, its eastern slopes are climbed to explore the lower end of a big rock spur which culminates in the impressive cone-shaped tower and popular climbing crag, the Risco del Pajaro (the Bird). Griffon vultures nest on a ledge on the north side of the spur and the path takes you close enough to hear the powerful hiss of their wings as they take off. The route then climbs onto the narrow crest behind the main face at a point where there is a spectacular circular erosion hole. The descent from there, down a very steep gully packed with enormous blocks and boulders, involves some tricky scrambling.

From Canto Cochino, take a footpath which starts to the left of the bars, keeping high above the river bank to reach the subsidiary car park. Then follow Route 64 as far as the open shoulder above the two big zigzags. Before re-entering the trees (*30mins*), strike up the slope to the right keeping to the right-hand edge of a block of plantation until the cistus-covered crest of the west ridge of Cancho de los Muertos is reached.

A number of small tracks head up the ridge, making for the distinctive rock formation known as El Calíz (The Chalice). The path passes to the left of it then takes a meandering and at times indistinct line between the outcrops on the crest. Both the path and occasional cairns are almost totally obscured in high summer by a sea of frothy dried grass, but the general formation of the ridge is a string of enclosed rock gardens with the rocky spine of the true crest to the left of them. The path follows a pattern of crossing to the left of the crest at the top of each garden, then quickly crossing back to enter the next one. Just before the ridge merges into the wider and steeper rock band which culminates in the towers of Cancho de los Muertos, trend left through a small stand of pines to cross a low point in the rock spine once more. After dropping to the right down a sloping slab, climb back up to the right towards a cairn marking a track which winds steeply into the rock band. Higher up the angle eases across a set of slabs to come out on a grassy col to the left of the main towers (1330m, *35mins*).

On the far side of the col, which looks into the Majadilla valley, the cairns head to the left, forcing a scramble over two small rock fins before working across a cistus thicket to enter the forest. A sharp descent here soon reaches C1 with the yellow and white markings. Follow it left to a crossroads at the **Collado del Cabrón** (1303m, *10mins*). The true top of the col lies to the left, but the path known as the Senda de ICONA starts straight ahead. It takes a slightly rising line round into the Cirque through alternate plantation and boulder-strewn clearings. Some 20mins from the Collado, the track swings left on an open shoulder with good views of Las Milaneras and Las Torres on the skyline. Before reaching the next area of trees, turn left at a fork up into rocks and boulders (orange spots and sign Malvis 1400m).

Leave the orange dots in a cistus-filled clearing in the forest (*40mins*) where they turn upslope, Continue instead on a path back into the trees

*El Calíz
(the Chalice),
La Pedriza*

which starts to descend gently through dense plantation. Almost immediately cairns lead into the trees on the left - the start of a vague path up to the Puente de los Pollos. Crossing a dry streambed they climb into one of the rock bands which bisect the cirque. Although cairns are plentiful, the route becomes very steep and complicated, involving a scramble up and sometimes under a tight jumble of giant blocks. **The Puente de los Pollos** (c.1500m, *15mins*) is directly above.

Return to the main path by the same route and continue to the left, going over a well-cairned crossroads and then crossing a couple of streams. Finally the more substantial Ventana stream is reached and the track on the far side merges with the one descending from the Collado de la Ventana to follow the left bank of the stream. Lower down, the great bulk of El Pajaro come into view to the left above slopes laid bare by fire a few years ago. Take a path leaving to the left marked by several cairns (c.1270m, *50mins*).

Various interwoven strands make their way up the slopes covered in a messy mixture of rock, small holm oaks, cistus, grasses and fallen trees, heading for the wide corridor to the left of the main crag. Passing below the griffon vultures in the cliffs to the right, continue up the narrowing channel, now scattered with deciduous oaks, to the point where the cairns finish at the foot of some sloping slabs. Scramble up towards the cleft in the crest to the right, which is roofed with a huge tilted slab. Climbing onto the crest, move to the right to look at the erosion holes and the spectacular rock formation known as the tail of El Pajaro (*40mins*).

Return to the top of the cleft and drop into the steep rock on the southern side using the ledges and fissures from which small oak trees are sprouting. Trend slightly left over easy blocks then follow more trees down to the right into a small sloping hollow. Circle below the giant boulder which fills its right side, to climb back up into a miniature canyon which is in fact the start of a long steep gully completely roofed in with blocks. Emerging at the bottom end, continue straight down into another hollow surrounded with more huge boulders. Climb over them diagonally right, then follow a narrow ledge back left to drop to the head of the wide but very steep corridor which runs down to the right, parallel to the ridge. Scramble down until a cairned path (*40mins*) can be picked up where the gully issues onto easier tree-covered slopes.

A few minutes below, the main path to the base of the crag is joined. Follow it left to cross the Dehesilla stream next to **El Tolmo** (*20mins*). From there reverse the start of Route 59 to **Canto Cochino car park** (*40mins*).

66. TOUR OF THE CIRCO DE LA PEDRIZA RIDGE (SENDA TERMES): CANTO COCHINO - COLLADO DE LA DEHESILLA - NAVAJUELOS - COLLADO DE LA VENTANA - LAS TORRES (base c.2000m) - COLLADO DE LA CARABINA - LAS MILANERAS - COLLADO DEL CABRON - CANCHO DE LOS MUERTOS - CANTO COCHINO.

Time:	9$^{1}/_{2}$-10hrs
Total ascent:	1027m
Time in reverse:	10-10$^{1}/_{2}$hrs
Total ascent:	1036m

This is clearly a long and energetic day out and the schedule hardly allows time to explore and savour the intricacies of the ridge but would suit fit walkers whose time in the area is limited. In summer, there is no reliable water supply anywhere along the crest.

From Canto Cochino car park follow Route 59 to the **Collado de la Dehesilla**, then Route 61 to the **Collado de la Ventana**. From there, continue on C1 to the left of the crest (reversing Route 62) to the **Collado de la Carabina** then follow Route 63 back to **Canto Cochino**.

ROUTES IN THE WESTERN BASIN

Although more typically Guadarrama-like in its structure and appearance, this side of the upper basin holds much interest for walkers, not least for the wonderful views it offers of La Pedriza. Two overlapping circular routes are described here, one following the valleys, the other the ridges, but Routes 51d and 64 also include sections in this area.

67.* CANTO COCHINO (SUBSIDIARY CAR PARK) - MANZANARES RIVER - COLLADO DE LOS PASTORES (1741m) - PICNIC SITE - CANTO COCHINO.

Time:	6-6$^{1}/_{2}$hrs
Total ascent:	701m

One of the classic Guadarrama routes starts at the Puerto de Navacerrada, crosses the Bola del Mundo then follows the course of the River Manzanares from its source to Manzanares el Real. It is possible to do this in a day from Madrid, using trains and buses, but is more problematical if you have to return to the start for a car. As an alternative, therefore, this route follows the river upstream from Canto Cochino to a point where a convenient circle back can be made.

Except for a short section at the beginning of the walk, the river always runs in a rocky channel with many pools and rapids but it is above the Charca Verde pool that the valley itself becomes more enclosed by the spurs running down from Las Milaneras on one side and the eastern ridge of Maliciosa Chica on the other. The return route is over the latter ridge to descend into a much more open tributary valley, following a forestry road which makes a fine belvedere for views of La Pedriza Anterior, Manzanares el Real and the Santillana Reservoir beyond. This is an interesting walk at any time of the year, but is probably the only one worth considering in La Pedriza in the hottest part of summer, when you could make a day of swimming in the shady pools then complete the more open upper section in the cool of the evening.

(When the streams are in spate in the spring, there may be difficulties in crossing the Cuervo stream.)

Park in the subsidiary car park (1040m), next turn on the right after Canto Cochino, then reverse the end of Route 64 to where the Cuervo stream meets the River Manzanares (*50mins*). This junction is not so obvious from the upper path and it is quite easy to continue into the Cuervo valley thinking that you are still following the Manzanares: leave the path at a cairn where it swings uphill to the right, just inside the lower edge of a plantation, and cross the stream to pick up a path a few metres above the Manzanares which leads to a forestry road with a bridge just to the left (*10mins*).

From here, there are paths on both sides of the river. The one on the left bank is better but when the river is in spate, it can be difficult to cross to the right bank where the two strands merge (*25mins*). From there, well-made zigzags work up steeper open ground then the track narrows and keeps more or less parallel to the river until it meets a dirt road just below a bridge (*1hr 50mins*). Crossing the bridge, the road turns back up the opposite slopes to the **Collado de los Pastores** (1741m, *15mins*). On the far side, after two hairpins, it continues in a long sweep on a gently descending line round the back of a bowl to gain the eastern slopes of the Cuerda de los Porrones.

THE WESTERN BASIN Routes 51d, 67, 68

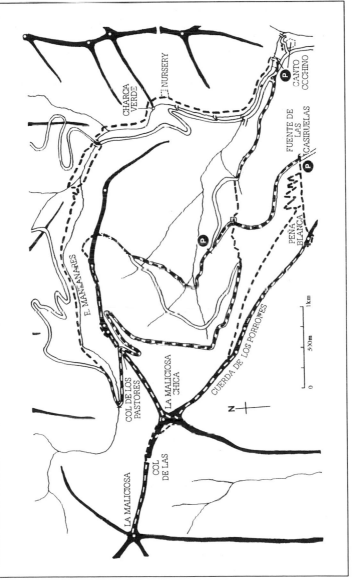

Coming to a sharp left-hand hairpin (*50mins*), head straight on at the outside of the bend onto a small man-made terrace. From its lip, a narrow cairned path heads diagonally right, meeting after a minute a track coming down from the ridge. Turn downhill on to this and follow its tortuous course through cistus and pine until it meets a horizontal path in sight of the metalled road below. Follow this new track to the right to join the road, opposite a car park and picnic spot. Make for the gap between the two large outcrops at the back of the car park and take a rough road round to the right, leaving it downhill on dirt road or firebreak (at the time of writing, forestry operations are altering this section) to meet again the returning loop of surfaced road. Follow it right and take the only right fork, which leads to the entrance of the car park (*35mins*).

68. FUENTE DE LAS CASIRUELAS - SIERRA DE LOS PORRONES - LA MALICIOSA CHICA (1938m) - EAST RIDGE - COLLADO DE LOS PASTORES - FORESTRY ROAD - FUENTE DE LAS CASIRUELAS.

Time: 5-5¹/₂hrs
Total ascent: 658m

The Sierra de los Porrones is the southeast end of the long handsome ridge thrown out from La Maliciosa which includes the subsidiary summit of La Maliciosa Chica and completely encloses the southwest side of the upper Manzanares basin. From the Fuente de las Casiruelas, the wide crest is reached at the first notable peak, Peña Blanca. It is then followed, around or over the succession of rocky tops which punctuate what is for 2km, a wide barely rising esplanade with extensive and contrasting views of the La Pedriza towers to the east and the overlapping smoother profiles of the ranges to the west. The crest outcrops are very fruitful places for scramblers to explore, although the path avoids most of them.

From the top of La Maliciosa Chica, the dominating view is of the majestic south face of La Maliciosa with the Cuerda Larga sweeping east beyond the deep cleft of the Manzanares valley. Although dwarfed by its big neighbour, La Maliciosa Chica throws out two substantial transverse ridges and it is the narrow rock-spiked eastern one which is followed here and it is involves some mild scrambling. A forestry road is then used to regain the slopes

of the Sierra de los Porrones. The walk could be extended to the summit of La Maliciosa from La Maliciosa Chica (see Route 51d).

Note: The road to the start of Routes 51d, 68 and 68a was closed to traffic in 1995 because of the poor state of the surface, but I have still included them as the road may be re-opened after repairs.

About a kilometre after the park gates take the left branch (i.e. straight on) at the road fork. The surface is badly potholed and therefore slow going but leads over the low continuation of the Cuerda de los Porrones into the upper Manzanares basin, with very striking views of the El Yelmo massif. The start of the walk is about 4km from the road fork but isn't particularly easy to spot: there is a layby for a few cars and a warning about lighting fires to the right, while on the left is the corner of a dense plantation of tall pines, with the stonework of the fuente visible a few metres inside (1260m).

The route begins opposite the layby in a firebreak running between the plantation and the remains of a stone wall. The wall improves higher up and a track follows it on its right side straight up towards the pointed profile of Peña Blanca on the skyline. As the summit is approached, the best track wanders back and forth across the wall, until the latter finishes and cairns are followed steeply up into the outcrops, arriving at a narrow col just to the left of the highest point of **Peña Blanca** (1608m, *45mins*).

Go straight down the far side for a few metres to find the next cairn. Once this is located a line of small stone markers can be followed to the right, contouring over the steep, bouldery cistus-covered slopes. The track is very faint until it approaches the flatter section of ridge between Peña Blanca and the next rocky summit. From here, follow the wide crest northwest, often with a choice of tracks which are generally well-cairned through the rock sections, to arrive at the foot of Maliciosa Chica (1668m, *1hr 10mins*).

The broad slope ahead bristles with outcrops and various interweaving tracks lead through them to the skyline, which is the crest of the southwest ridge of the mountain. From there, the angle eases and the track turns a little towards the right in the direction of the summit (1939m, *45mins*). Now head in the direction of La Pedriza, across the level pathless mixture of rock, juniper and broom, which is the start of the east ridge. As the ground starts to drop, keep as near as possible to the rocky crest with good views of the infant River Manzanares to the left. Discontinuous cairns and faint tracks appear in and around the outcrops from time to time. Arriving at the **Collado de los Pastores** (1741m,

35mins), follow Route 67 as far as the car park/picnic spot then continue to the right along the road to the **Fuente de las Casiruelas** (*35mins*).

68a. COLLADO DE LOS PASTORES - CERRO DE LA MALICIOSA (1774m) - CERRO DE LAS BARRERAS - FORESTRY ROAD - FUENTE DE LAS CASIRUELAS.

Time:	**3hrs**
	Total time for Route 68 + 68a: 6¹/₂-7hrs
	Ascent minimal - over rock outcrops

This is an optional extension to Route 68. Beyond the Collado de los Pastores, the narrower continuation of the east ridge of La Maliciosa Chica makes a fine scrambling route around the towers of Cerro de la Maliciosa then onto the interesting fractured dome of Cerro de las Barreras. There then follows a final spectacular section along the edge of a huge band of slabs plunging to the River Manzanares.

At the Collado de los Pastores (1741m), cross the road to continue along the ridge over two low outcrops before the first of major rock obstacle is reached. Keep more or less to the crest with the option in the descent of dropping into a parallel, juniper-filled corridor to the right. A clear path appears here to cross a grassy depression to the left of the low rocky crest. At the far side of the hollow are the first rocks of the second obstacle, known as the Cerro de la Maliciosa. It is possible to continue over it, again more or less on the crest, as far as two inclined towers. These can be turned only on the right by connecting up heavily vegetated terraces on a steep slope. As this last section is a bit of a struggle, it is perhaps a better idea to leave the crest to the left, back at the end of the path across the grassy depression. A narrow juniper-filled rake hugs the base of the steep slabs below the Cerro, and runs out onto grassy terraces which can be connected up to climb back to the ridge.

Both routes return to the much broader crest just beyond the inclined towers. A cairned path emerges descending to a wide, bare saddle beyond a narrow band of trees. Follow stone markers straight up into the complicated rock formations of the **Cerro de las Barreras** (1646m, *50mins*). The top is an interesting place to explore, but the cairns make a traverse on the left side of the chaotic blocks of the summit area before swinging up to the right, towards a broken dome with a roof (the true summit). It skirts this outcrop to the left in a corridor, where a scramble over large blocks leads into a downwards-sloping tunnel formed by a huge wedge of rock leaning against the main outcrop.

At the tunnel's exit, turn left immediately at a cairn to follow the right side of a giant block downslope. Pick up more markers at its lower end, leading down in a few more metres to a horizontal path. Follow it to the right then down to a lower terrace. From there, markers and path turn right and become clearer, making a gently descending traverse, parallel to the descending crest above. To reach the huge area of slabs above the River Manzanares, leave the main path on one of the lines of cairns running straight downslope - there are various options with one daring line running out onto the slabs themselves. All routes converge well above the river, to swing right into plantation. Crossing a shallow dry gully, ignore the cairns running down it to continue on the horizontal path to a ruined stone wall and the start of a disused forestry road (*45mins*).

Ten minutes down to the left is the last flourish of the ridge, Cerro Ortigoso, a pleasant mixture of meadow, rocks and trees, but the route continues along the gently descending terrace of the old road to join the main forestry road at a hairpin bend. Follow it down to the barrier where it meets the surfaced loop road (*30mins*) which circles the basin. The Fuente de las Casiruelas is 2km along the uphill section (*25mins*).

CHAPTER ELEVEN
Eastern Guadarrama

TOPOGRAPHY

This eastern sector doesn't form a physical entity but is composed of what is left of the two separate branches enclosing the Lozoya valley. On the north side, the chain, sometimes known as the Sierra de Carpetanos, or Somosierra, continues northeast from the Peñalara massif through the main tops of Flecha, Peñacabra, Nevero, Reajo Capón and Muela. All of these are over 2000m but are little more than undulations in the ridge, which falls gently thereafter to Puerto de Somosierra (1444m). In the 45km length of this section, there is only one road-carrying pass (Puerto de Navafría, 1773m), reflecting the isolated nature of both sides of the chain.

The southern branch is the continuation of the Cuerda Larga, east of the Puerto de la Morcuera (1796m). Here, there is a realignment of the range to SW-NE and a fairly sudden loss of height, with Perdiguera, the highest point, reaching only 1868m. Two projections to the south add interest to that side of the chain: the first is a long ridge from Perdiguera to Pico de la Pala (1542m) above Miraflores de la Sierra; the second is a wedge-shaped piece of high land south of Bustarviejo. They enclose between them the pretty, "hidden" valley of the Arroyo del Valle, with its extensive cover of deciduous oaks.

The main ridge is crossed by one road pass at the Puerto de Canencia (1490m), linking the villages of Miraflores de la Sierra and Canencia. The highest point on the remaining section of ridge to the east is Riofrío (1838m), after which there is a gradual tapering off to the Burgos-Madrid road. However, Mondalindo (1833m), just to the west of Riofrío, is the real focus of interest here, as it has a more mountain-like appearance with its long north ridge running down to Canencia and its short southern spur ending in spectacular crags above the Bustarviejo-Valdemanco road.

Between the villages of Valdemanco and La Cabrera, there is a final dramatic flourish of high ground, known as the Sierra de la Cabrera. Although its highest point, Cancho Largo, is only 1568m, the ridge's slightly isolated position and jagged profile exaggerates its scale, and the scenery is reminiscent of La Pedriza, in some ways. It lies on an east-west axis to the south of the main chain and is connected to it by the broad saddle of the Puerto del Medio Celemín (1310m).

El Paular Monastery

VILLAGE BASES

The Lozoya valley is an attractive base for walking in Eastern Guadarrama with its string of small villages, tiny stone-walled fields and wealth of deciduous trees. The main village and therefore the best place to find accommodation is **Rascafría**. Like so many other Sierra pueblos its economy is now mainly based on services for second-home owners and Sunday-lunchers, i.e. bars and restaurants, but there are also some hotels and pensions. Although much altered in the last few years the village has an attractive centre round a triangular plaza with a large old elm tree.

One and a half kilometres south of the village is the added attraction of the Monasterio de El Paular. Originally a 15th century Carthusian foundation, it controlled extensive land in the valley and therefore the local agricultural economy for about 300 years. Earthquakes and wars led to its eventual abandonment until it was restored in the 1950's and a small Benedictine house was established. History, setting and an interesting mixture of architectural styles and materials (including some local limestone) combine to give it a powerful atmosphere and make it an attractive alternative to staying in the village centre. The hospice part of the

275

monastery has been converted into a luxury hotel, while the monks provide simple cells for men only. There is also a campsite 3-4km along the Puerto de los Cotos road.

Nevertheless, the Lozoya valley only makes sense as a base if you intend to do the routes from the Puerto de Navafría, perhaps combined with some of those in the Puerto de los Cotos area. For the rest of the walks in this section, the villages of **Miraflores de la Sierra** and **Bustarviejo** on the southern slopes of the range are much more conveniently placed and are also within comfortable driving distance of La Pedriza. Both occupy sheltered positions on sunny southern slopes and have a great deal of charm, with something of a softer aspect than villages further west, perhaps because at times the grey granite architecture gives way to whitewash and red pantiles. Bustarviejo has one hotel, Miraflores two or three.

ROUTES

There is plenty of good, varied walking at this end of the range with fine ridges, a string of glacial hollows in the north and the rocky chaos of La Cabrera in the south. In addition, the high ground rises out of a slightly gentler landscape than that to the west - the pastures look richer and a variety of deciduous trees line the water courses and field systems. Higher up the slopes, remnants of the original deciduous oak woodland are found among the pine plantations.

However there are problems for the visitor with or without a car: no public transport to any of the road passes, no taxi service in the Lozoya valley, the destruction of many of the best approaches to the ridge by modern forestry methods and the difficulty of making good circular routes from the valleys. Walkers staying in Guadarrama for only a short period are unlikely to want to grapple with these difficulties, when there is a wealth of interesting and accessible walking in the rest of the range. Therefore I have included only the handful of walks which can be conveniently embarked on by visitors.

69. *SIERRA DE CARPETANOS.*

The one road pass over this northern branch of the range, the Puerto de Navafría, crosses it at roughly the halfway point and the ridge to each side of the pass has quite different characteristics. To the west and south the high ground suffered some glaciation like the neighbouring Peñalara

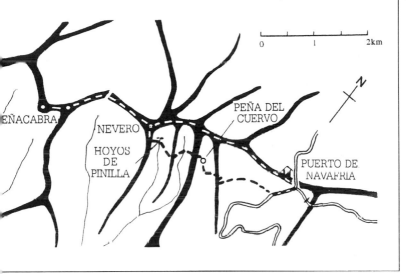

SIERRA DE CARPETANOS Routes 69a, b

massif. This has resulted in a continuous string of corries backed by steep crags above the Lozoya valley. Although not on the same scale as those of Gredos or even Peñalara, many of these hollows would provide interesting approaches to the ridge were it not for the lack of paths up the lower slopes through oak scrub, thorn thicket and tree terraces. It is also a great shame that the tracks over the Puertos de Reventón and Malagosta, two of the oldest and for centuries most frequented in the range, have similarly disappeared under plantation and undergrowth. While local walkers have forced ways through the difficulties, linking in with the modern forestry road system, on the whole it is more satisfactory to spend the time on the open ridge with its spectacular views down into the corries.

By contrast, the ridge to the northeast of the Puerto de Navafría is forested almost to the crest on both slopes and there are fewer rock passages to interrupt this cover. Nevertheless, there is interesting walking here, but it is best exploited by local walkers who can arrange to be dropped at the pass and picked up later in any of a number of quiet villages on either flank of the range. In view of these limitations on both sides of the road, the two best options for visitors, described here, are an out-and-back route along the glaciated section of crest and a variation which traverses from the pass into one of the corries.

69a. PUERTO DE NAVAFRIA - NEVERO (2209m) - PEÑACABRA - POINT 2159m - RETURN.

> Time: 4¹/₂-5hrs
> Total ascent: 774m

In spite of the indifferent quality of the routes between the valleys and the crest mentioned above, I would have preferred to have made this a line from the pass to the Puerto de Malagosto followed by a descent to Rascafría. However with no possibility of taking bus or taxi to the Puerto de Navafría, the route has to be retraced along the ridge back to the car. This return to the pass could be varied slightly by reversing Route 69b from Nevero.

After the initial steep start from the pass, the walking is very easy over the gentle undulations of the bare stony crest. Preferring to have a definite top to aim for, I chose point 2159m because of its dramatic position above two corries and before the crest starts a long gentle decline to the Puerto de Malagosto. Clearly, there is time in a day to continue much further along the ridge according to choice.

At the Puerto de Navafría on the Segovia side is the private and locked Navafría Refuge and a small stone enclosure round a number of pine trees. The latter is apparently a cemetery for some Italians killed on this part of the front during the Civil War, although the only evidence of this is a smashed memorial stone.

Arriving from the south side of the Puerto de Navafría (1773m), park on the right, at the start of a wide, horizontal forestry road. Cross the surfaced road and start up the wooded western slopes, to the left of a wire fence. Where strands have been tied up for the purpose, cross it and continue on its right, up a steep stony firebreak. When this rough pathway swings away to the right (*20mins*) cross a gap in the fence and continue uphill, now on a narrow track between a double row of fencing. At the end of the latter, the path starts to zigzag up a steep rock shoulder between the first of the glacial hollows to the left and a deeply cut valley

278

to the right, to arrive shortly at the crest of the ridge and some Civil War bunkers.

The way along the broad stony top, punctuated by steep crags on the left, needs no detailed description. It can be confusing in mist, however, as there are no cairns and the spurs running down the Segovia side could easily be mistaken for the main ridge. The trick is to join up the Civil War fortifications, which top most of the rises along the crest, by following the remains of a single coil of barbed wire running between them. Keep to the right of the wire as at times it runs along the lip of the crags.

69b. PUERTO DE NAVAFRIA - PEÑA DEL CUERVO - HOYOS DE PINILLA - NEVERO (2209m) - PUERTO DE NAVAFRIA.

Time:	**4-4½hrs**
Total ascent:	**439m**

This route uses an old forestry road starting below the south side of the pass to reach a couple of interesting features on this side of the ridge: first the Peña del Cuervo, a rock finger of some size which seems to have emerged at random from the upper slopes. Scrambles are possible up the front to the railed top. The second is the Hoyos de Pinilla corrie below Nevero, which holds two small tarns and has a steep backwall possibly offering more scrambling lines, although the rock appears to be quite loose. The ridge crest is reached at Nevero, the highest point in the northern chain outside the Peñalara group. To make a circle, the route heads straight back to the pass along the crest, but it could be easily extended by walking the ridge to Peñacabra and back.

Park as for Route 69a then walk down the surfaced road to the south as far as a car park/picnic spot in a clearing on the right *(5mins)*. Follow a dirt road which heads left from the entrance and leave it beyond a metal rain gauge, continuing straight up a small slope into the trees. This initially vague path soon merges with an old forestry road, now overgrown with broom, but with a cleared line wide enough for single-file walking. Ignore an immediate branch up to the right but take the second one *(20mins)* which makes large zigzags uphill to come out of the pines onto broom-covered slopes.

The path contours round the head of a small valley but it is left to climb the scrub-covered slopes above, heading for the large isolated rock tower called **Peña del Cuervo** (*30mins*) when it comes into view up to the left. Higher up the slope behind the crag is a horizontal track which rounds a spur then contours in and out of a small valley. Cross a stone wall running down the next shoulder and head uphill and slightly to the left over easy ground to the lip of the corrie of **Hoyos de Pinilla** (2085m, *40mins*).

Climb the loose scree slopes to the left of the hollow on any of the rough tracks to find a line of cairns along the broom-covered crest of a shoulder which then lead through a series of rocky terraces to the survey point on the summit of **Nevero** (2209m, *20mins*). Reverse Route 69a to the **Puerto de Navafría** (*1hr*).

70. *MONDALINDO.*

As mentioned already in the Topography section, Mondalindo is 5m shorter than the highest top on the section of ridge to the east of the Puerto de Canencia but is nevertheless the natural objective for a day out in the area, being a more substantial and interesting mountain than the mere rocky punctuation which is Riofrío. The geology here appears to be slightly different from the rest of Guadarrama, resembling that of parts of the Sierra Pobre to the east. The differences are visible in the patches of slaty, mica-rich rocks which have a soft golden sheen and at times large shiny flakes. This was also the one place in the range where silver and gold was mined (see Route 70a) and quartz appears to have been quarried from a big seam on Mondalindo itself (see Route 70b).

70a. PUERTO DE CANENCIA - COLLADO CERRADO - CUESTA LA PLATA - CABEZA DE LA BRAÑA - ALBARDILLA - MONDALINDO (1833m) - RETURN.

> **Time:**   **4hrs 25mins**
> **Total ascent:**   **769m**

This is an easy and straightforward walk along the crest from the Miraflores-Canencia road. The alternation of woodland, meadow and rock scenery in the first part of the walk as far as Cabeza de la Braña contrasts with the open moorland scenery of the rest of the route. Walkers interested in industrial archaeology may like to

MONDALINDO Routes 70a, b

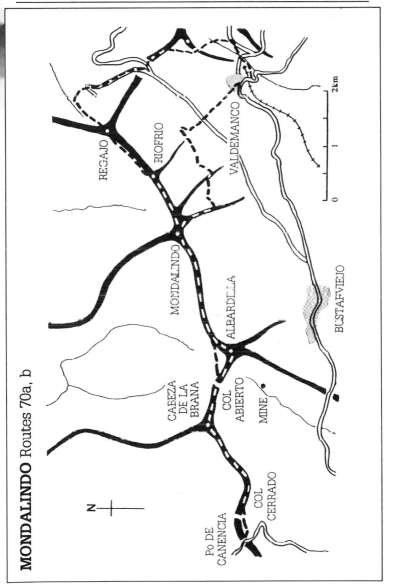

make a detour down to the old mines and foundry remains on the slopes to the south of the Collado Abierto. These are reached by following the course of the Mina stream. The mines were in production from the 17th century until about 15 years ago and extracted silver, then gold and finally arsenic. The ruined tower was a windmill for ventilating the mines.

Arriving at the Puerto de Canencia (1490m) from Miraflores, turn right onto a dirt road just after passing an elaborate fuente to the left. The road crosses a picnic area but is closed to traffic beyond the far edge of the clearing. From the chain barrier there, the walk starts by following the red and white stripes of GR10.1 which leave to the right. Rising through the scattered trees, the markings then shadow walls and fences round a low hill and down to the wide grassy saddle of Collado Cerrado.

GR10.1 keeps to the southern edge of saddle with a stone wall to the left, before heading down the slopes in the direction of Bustarviejo but leave this path just before it starts to descend, and move left up to the wall behind a red and white cross (*20mins*). The wall leads towards an open strip of ground between belts of trees on a steep slope below the rocks of Cuesta la Plata. Once above these outcrops, follow the edge of a plantation at an easier angle to the summit of **Cabeza de la Braña** (1776m, *45mins*).

From the well-made cairn on its summit, Mondalindo can be seen rising beyond a wide meandering open section of ridge. Follow the fence which runs along it across the Collado Abierto to the rounded top of **Albardilla** (*25mins*), then eventually up broad slopes leading to the summit of **Mondalindo** (1833m, *50mins*). The return to the Puerto de Canencia is by the same route, although Albardilla can be avoided by cutting straight across its sometimes boggy northern slopes directly to the Collado Abierto.

70b. VALDEMANCO - PEÑA DEL TEJO - COLLADO DEL MEDIO CELEMIN - REGAJO - RIOFRIO (1838m) - MONDALINDO - SOUTHERN RIDGE - VALDEMANCO.

Time:	5-5¹/₂hrs
Total ascent:	718m

This is a walk of enormous interest and variety with constant

changes of views and terrain. From the pretty village of Valdemanco, it starts with a taste of the dramatic shattered rock scenery of La Cabrera, then crosses the wide saddle above the village to join one of the medieval drove roads, the Cañada Real Segoviana. Leaving it to climb a small trackless valley, the ridge is gained near Regajo, then followed as far as Mondalindo, with good views across the Lozoya valley to Peñalara. The continuation of the route down the south ridge of Mondalindo brings you to the huge seam of quartz and just beyond it, a wall of crags plunging to the valley. A scramble down looks possible but this route takes a less steep although still interesting line down the slopes back to the village.

Driving from the Miraflores direction, the main road passes through the lower part of Valdemanco then crosses a bridge over a railway. Park on waste ground just beyond on the left, opposite a restaurant (1127m). A small footpath starts by the bridge following the railway cutting up towards the Sierra de la Cabrera. Crossing a small picnic site and dirt road, continue uphill until a gravel road is joined. Follow it a few metres until it starts to curve up to the right, then take the right hand of two wide tracks which continue up the valley. Go left at a fork (Route 71a goes right) to reach, with little gain of height, a breach in the left-hand enclosing ridge (1270m, *25mins*), below and to the left of the Peña del Tejo.

On the far side of this col, where the track starts to descend, work right and slightly uphill over big slabs and broken ground with no path, crossing on the way two wide tracks which lead down into the valley to the left. Just below the skyline, a third track, coming from the north side of the Sierra de la Cabrera, is joined. Follow it left to a wide saddle with a few blocks of plantation, the **Puerto del Medio Celemín** (1310m, *20mins*).

Slightly beyond the lowest point, cross a wide dirt road to join the Cañada Real Segoviana which heads up the right side of a partly pine-covered rocky ridge coming down from Regajo to the pass. The track soon turns away from the ridge, taking a gently rising line to the right across the slopes as far as a hairpin bend (contrary to what is shown on the IGN map). On the outside of the corner, cross the barbed wire fence then the boggy slope beyond it, working slightly uphill to the crest of a small rib which runs downslope, parallel to a streambed. Follow the rib up, using the odd cattle track, until a terrace with old stone enclosures is reached in the upper valley (*45mins*).

Of the three aerials which can be seen on the enclosing skyline from this point, the left-hand one is sited on the top of **Regajo** (1761m, *15mins*), which is reached by climbing the rough, trackless ground at the valley head. Just beyond the summit, a dirt road is joined and followed up the crest to the rocky summit of **Riofrío** (1838m, *20mins*) which also has a set of aerials. From there, continue through the mixed rock and grass of the ridge to the survey point on the summit of **Mondalindo** (1833m, *25mins*).

There is no clear path from the summit on to the south ridge until some motorbike tracks are picked up lower down. These lead to the quartz seam just behind the lip of the crags (*25mins*). From this small saddle, descend on motorbike tracks to the left, following them across a streambed, past a small spring and out onto the crest of another shoulder. Leave them there to descend the slopes through tussocky grass and loose stone (no path) to a grassy col with a stone animal pen (*25mins*). Follow more tracks left down into a deeper streambed at the foot of the crags of Peñas de las Cabras.

Crossing the stream, an improving path rounds the outcrops then runs horizontally through a pine plantation. At a three-way junction with a dirt road, head back down to the right for 50m until you find a clear track heading straight down the slope. This recrosses the meandering dirt road to arrive at the **Cañada Real Segoviana** (*25mins*) above Valdemanco. Cross the Cañada and continue straight down into trackless rock and cistus until a knot of dirt roads, serving outlying villas, is reached. The one heading straight down towards the village is the GR10 (faded red and white stripes and a Via Pecuaria sign). Where the drystone wall on its right turns away from the road, follow the wall and the markings down to another lane which leads into the village (*20mins*).

71. *LA SIERRA DE LA CABRERA.*

Lying between Valdemanco and the N1 Burgos road, this spiky little ridge is less than 5km long and has a highest point of only 1568m. Nevertheless, it is attractive walking country with dramatic rock scenery and a position slightly isolated from the main range which makes it a better vantage point than its height would suggest. To the south, the ridge presents an almost unbroken face of cliffs and towers, which protect a couple of pretty, secluded valleys. The northern slopes are typically less steep. Apart from rock climbers on the Pico de la Miel, this is a surprisingly little-visited area, considering its accessibility and good weather record. Like Las Machotas at the other end of the Guadarrama, the Cabrera Ridge can usually be relied on to be clear when the main range is in cloud.

The main paths in the area make two circuits, starting in the villages at opposite ends of the ridge and meeting at the Collado de Alfrecho. These are on the short side and could easily be combined. I have kept them separate because the single circuit would miss out the path on the south side of the Collado de Alfrecho, where there are close-up views of the vultures nesting on the cliffs to the east of the pass.

Indeed, the whole area is so small and the structure so simple, these route descriptions could just be used as reference points for detours up into the interesting territory along the ridge. The challenge for scramblers would be to follow the whole length of the crest, which the main paths touch only occasionally.

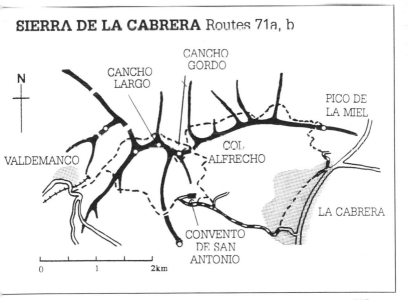

71a. VALDEMANCO - PEÑA DEL TEJO - COLLADO DE ALFRECHO - CANCHO GORDO (1560m) - CONVENTO DE SAN ANTONIO - VALDEMANCO.

Time: 4-4¹/₂hrs
Total ascent: 567m

To the west of the Collado de Alfrecho, the simple linear structure of the ridge is complicated by three prominent spurs thrown out to the south with the main crest turning northwest to run down to the Puerto del Medio Celemín, which connects it with the main massif. This circuit from Valdemanco crosses all the spurs as well as the main ridge and includes the ascent of Cancho Gordo, the prominent peak to the west of the Collado de Alfrecho and the second highest point in the area.

The Convento de San Antonio is an attractive building in a very pretty sheltered setting. It was originally a 12th century Cluniac foundation, but has had a varied history and at one time belonged to the family of Goya. It has been restored recently by the Local Authority.

Park as for Route 70b and follow it as far as the left fork to the Peña del Tejo. Instead, take the right one which leads to a fuente. Behind it, a path leaves diagonally right to join a dirt road, which makes a curve to the left before heading for the wide saddle on the skyline. Just before reaching the latter, take a track marked with cairns, leaving to the right and climbing to the crest of the shoulder running down to the saddle (*25mins*).

On the far side is a large elongated bowl-shaped meadow, which slopes up to the right on to a spur descending north from the main ridge. The point to aim for is the lower limit of the outcrops and debris on the crest of that spur, and it can be reached by joining up various tracks which cross the hollow. On the crest of the spur, the wide track narrows to a footpath and continues across the northern slopes to a rock terrace just above the **Collado de Alfrecho** (1420m, *25mins*).

The climb to Cancho Gordo starts here: small cairns lead up the steep grass and rock slopes behind the terrace, moving slightly to the left. As the base of the outcrops are approached, they work back diagonally right to a terrace below the main buttress. Go left up the terrace to a col. Ignore the descending line of cairns in the corridor beyond but follow another set which rise on the right to cross a small rock spine into a meadow. Go to the top of it, where a single cairn on the right indicates the start of a sloping rock ledge which cuts across the summit rocks to the foot of a 4m chimney directly below the summit of **Cancho Gordo** (1560m, *20mins*). Return by the same route to the **Collado de Alfrecho** (*10mins*).

A steep, cairned and often eroded track leaves down the south side of the col. Lower down it crosses to the right of the streambed and levels off to work right, round a broad cistus-covered spur coming down from Cancho Gordo. It then drops gently to a dirt road which joins a wider one a few metres further on. Go right on this to the Convento de San Antonio (*40mins*). (This road carries the GR10 markings, which are now followed all the way back to Valdemanco.)

Beyond the monastery, the road gives way to a track which curves round the head of a little valley and crosses a broad saddle to cut across the upper part of the Ronquillos valley, just above the field system. As the track rises up the slopes of the next spur, the red and white markings become confused, as there appears to have been some rerouting. The freshest marks climb left to cross a small shoulder, then move up to join a dirt road leading to the crest of the ridge above Valdemanco (*40mins*). It continues down to the picnic site above the railway cutting. Retrace the beginning of the route downhill to the restaurant (*20mins*).

71b.* LA CABRERA - PICO DE LA MIEL - COLLADO DE ALFRECHO (1420m) - LA CABRERA.

> Time: 4-4½hrs
> Total ascent: 320m

The eastern end of the ridge from the village of La Cabrera to the Collado de Alfrecho has a simple linear structure with steep cliffs and slopes to the south and wide gentle spurs running down to the north. This route crosses the crest at a col to the left of the Pico de la Miel, the big rock buttress which marks the eastern extremity of the ridge. The scramble to the summit is included in the time. The walk then continues along the upper northern slopes, occasionally getting among the rocks of the crest, as far as the Collado de Alfrecho.

La Cabrera village is strung out along what was the N1 Madrid-Burgos road until a bypass was opened. Drive up this main street to the northern end of the village and turn into a road on the left, just after a modern red brick school. Park anywhere on that road.

The walk starts on a dirt road which leaves uphill just after the turn-off from the main road. It soon takes a rising line left across the slope (keep to the uphill branch at a fork). Then, where it makes a hairpin bend to the right, leave to the left at the top of the bend, on to an agricultural terrace, but immediately fork right on to a higher one. At the far end, cairns lead straight uphill through a mixture of boulders and cistus to meet a horizontal path. Go left momentarily, looking for the continuation of the cairns up the steep slopes. These take as straight a line as possible given the bouldery terrain, to the base of the crest outcrops, where they move right into a gully leading up to a narrow col (*40mins*).

The climb to the damaged survey point on the **Pico de la Miel** (1384m, *10mins*) is a pathless scramble to the right of the col, picking the easiest line up the broken and overlapping slabs of the dome. Return to the col and continue west along the ridge, avoiding the first steep rocks above the col to the right. Above them, a clear path emerges in a rising meadow to the right of the crest. As the next high point is approached, the cairns avoid it, again on the slopes to the right, crossing a spur just below the outcrops and bringing the main range with Mondalindo into view for the first time.

In turning the next summit, again to the right, the path loses some height and joins tyre tracks coming up from the right. Follow them to the left, continuing towards the crest at a fork soon after. Turn right in a meadow before the skyline is reached. At the far end the path becomes clearer as it starts to wander among the rocks along the crest. Finally it plunges down the northern slopes again, but at a fork, follow the left branch, at first level, then steeply upwards to cross another shoulder. Beyond and to the left is the **Collado de Alfrecho** (1420m, *1hr 15mins*). Follow Route 71a down the southern side of the col to the dirt road (*35mins*). Turn left on it to reach the village (*35mins*).

PART FOUR

Long Distance Walks

THE GR10 IN THE SIERRA DE GUADARRAMA

There exists in Spain, as in France, a system of long-distance footpaths, called here Senderos de Gran Recorrido. The network, however, is very patchy compared to the French one, as it depends on the not always well-supported local mountaineering associations to waymark and maintain individual sections. The GR10, which theoretically links Lisbon with Valencia and traverses the whole length of the Systema Central, is only very partially marked out. In this central region, the Federación Madrileña de Montañismo have waymarked their section through the Sierra Pobre and Sierra de Guadarrama.

There is a main route and a northern loop into the Lozoya valley (GR10.1). Either of these makes an interesting 10-14 day tour, if some of the suggestions below for stopovers and extra day walks are incorporated. Indeed it is arguably the most satisfactory way to explore this range if you don't want to bring a car. But even if there isn't the time or inclination to complete the whole route, it passes through all the village bases suggested in the Guadarrama section, so in a two-centre holiday, say Manzanares el Real and Cercedilla, it would make more sense to walk the GR10 between the two towns than to take public transport into Madrid and out again.

There is space only for a list of the stages with possible adaptations and additions and some idea of accommodation and services. Generally the markings are good, even through the villages, although there are a few places where they are faded. The Alpina La Pedriza sheet marks the route and the 10.1 variation in that sector. Much of it is covered piecemeal in the Guadarrama walks section of this guide, so the appropriate cross-references are included.

A very useful guide has been produced for this part of the GR10: *Excursiones a pie por la Provincia de Madrid - GR10* (Domingo Pliego, Desnivel, 1988). Although in Spanish, it has many invaluable sketch maps of the route where it passes through villages and other problem spots. Like that guide, I describe the walk from east to west, mainly because it is a much more dramatic and appropriate finish to come down into the

THE GR10 AND GR10.1 IN THE SIERRA DE GUADARRAMA

N

GR10.1

(CO)

(F) (N)

(MA)

ALTO DE
LOS LEONES

CERCEDILLA

NAVACERRADA

B	-	BUSTARVIEJO
V	-	VALDEMANCO
MA	-	MATAELPINO
F	-	PUERTO DE LA FUENFRIA
N	-	PUERTO DE NAVACERRADA
CO	-	PUERTO DE LOS COTOS
M	-	PUERTO DE LA MORCUERA
C	-	PUERTO DE CANENCIA

EL
ESCORIAL

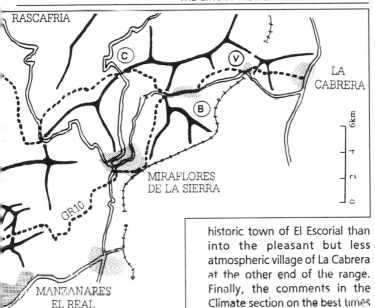

historic town of El Escorial than into the pleasant but less atmospheric village of La Cabrera at the other end of the range. Finally, the comments in the Climate section on the best times to visit the range apply with double force when backpacking. When not following the crests, much of the main route here crosses the southern slopes of the range, and would be gruelling in July and August.

Key to village services

H	-	Hotels and/or pensions	P	-	Post Office
C	-	Campsite	B	-	Bank/Bureau de Change
F	-	Food shops	Ch	-	Chemist
R	-	Bars and restaurants	D	-	Doctor
W	-	Drinking water	S	-	Railway station
T	-	Telephone	Bu	-	Buses

The GR10 markings actually start at the Guadalajara-Madrid border at the old reservoir of Pontón de la Oliva, east of the Madrid-Burgos road. It passes through low but interesting limestone hills and the picturesque villages of Patones and Torrelaguna. This covers two day-long stages: Ponton de la Oliva - Patones - Torrelaguna (16km) and Torrelaguna - La Cabrera (11.5km). However, there is no public transport to Ponton de la

Oliva or Patones and, although Torrelaguna has a bus service to Madrid, it makes sense to start the route description at La Cabrera, within the area covered by the guide and at the start of higher mountain country.

Stage One: LA CABRERA - VALDEMANCO - BUSTARVIEJO - MIRAFLORES DE LA SIERRA - 20km.

La Cabrera (H C F R W T P B Ch D Bu) is a large linear village on the old Madrid-Burgos road (now bypassed). Reverse Route 71b to the Convento de San Antonio then follow Route 71a to Valdemanco (F R W T).

Extension: Stay two nights in La Cabrera to do a warm-up day walk - Route 71b plus the ascent of Cancho Gordo (described in Route 71a).

The markings out of Valdemanco are faded. They follow a narrow lane between stone walls, which leaves uphill from the western end of the Calle Real to reach an old drove road (Cañada Real Segoviana) running along the southern slopes of Mondalindo into Bustarviejo (H C F R W T B P Ch D Bu - the campsite is 2-3km west of the village on the Miraflores road).

Follow the main road through the village and beyond to a saddle. The Cañada Real Segoviana leaves to the left along the eastern slopes of a wide valley down to the railway station below the town of Miraflores de la Sierra (H F R W T B P Ch D S Bu).

Stage Two: MIRAFLORES DE LA SIERRA - LA PEDRIZA - MANZANARES EL REAL - 23.5km.

From the railway station, continue on the Cañada, south of the town, crossing the Miraflores stream and the Soto del Real road to head southwest towards the Cerro de la Berrocosa. Rounding the hill, then the Soto del Real Reservoir to the south, the route makes a loop to the south (because of access problems) to the El Berrueco quarry, then heads back north into the Coberteros valley. (At the time of writing, there are problems with the section from El Berrueco into the valley, as a local (weekend) finca owner has painted out the markings and fenced across the path. There are plans to alter this part of the route.)

At the head of the valley is the Collado de la Dehesilla and from there Route 59 is reversed to the Refugio Giner (open holidays and weekends - dormitories and simple meals, but no guarantee of places). Continue downstream on the left bank of the Majadilla stream as far as a wooden bridge, then reverse Route 55 to El Tranco. There are rooms at two of the restaurants there, or it is a further 3km along the road into Manzanares el Real (H C F R W T P B Ch D Bu). The campsite is at El Tranco and there is also a basic one inside the park itself.

Extension: As the preceding walk from the Collado de la Dehesilla is the only section of the GR10 in La Pedriza, it is worth stopping for two or three nights at El Tranco or Manzanares el Real to explore the park further.

Stage Three: MANZANARES EL REAL - MATAELPINO (MATALPINO) - NAVACERRADA - 13.3km.

This is a short, easy stage, avoiding all high ground and includes some road walking. The route follows the street running west from the church until just after crossing the Manzanares River, where it goes to the right of the remains of a castle to join the lane leading to the park gates. Just before the latter, take a dirt road to the left, which crosses the Collado de la Jarosa then works northwest below the Torreta de los Porrones into Mataelpino (F R W T B). The route passes straight through the main plaza and out along the Cerceda road, soon turning right to follow the road to Navacerrada which runs along the end of the Ladera de Matas spur coming down from La Maliciosa. Leaving the road to reach the low Angostura Pass, the C607 is crossed to descend over fields to Navacerrada village (H F R W T P B Ch D Bu).

Alternative: In order to keep to higher ground and avoid road walking, take Route 67 up the Manzanares valley as far as the bridge below the Collado de los Pastores then continue up the valley and up the left-hand slopes to the Bola del Mundo. From there reverse Route 51a to the Puerto de Navacerrada (H S). Staying at this high pass, you are well-placed for several of the best day walks in the range e.g. Peñalara or Las Cabezas (train to Puerto de los Cotos then Routes 54a or b and 53b or c respectively). The GR10 can be rejoined at Cercedilla by following Route 49c over Siete Picos or Route 49d down the Navalmedio valley.

Extension: If you have taken the direct route to Navacerrada village, stay two nights in order to do one of the routes to La Maliciosa (51b or c) from the Barranca valley.

Stage Four: NAVACERRADA VILLAGE - CERCEDILLA - 6km.

A very short and uninteresting section which could be joined onto Stage Three. There is an unpleasant start from the village via the Hotel Arcipreste then across the cloverleaf road junction to the Fonda Real restaurant. After that, back roads are linked up into Cercedilla (H F R W T P B Ch D S Bu).

Alternatives:
1. Leave the GR10 where it turns off the reservoir road after the Fonda Real and reverse Route 49d to Puerto de Navacerrada (H S). This could be a base for a couple of days for a choice of day walks directly from there or from the Puerto de los Cotos - see Stage Three alternative above.
2. Take the bus or walk (as for 1.) to the Puerto de Navacerrada but continue on Route 49c over Siete Picos then down into Cercedilla the same day.

Stage Five: CERCEDILLA (CAMORRITOS) - PUERTO DE LA FUENFRIA - LA PEÑOTA - CERCEDILLA - 16km.

As there is obviously no accommodation on the top of La Peñota and camping is not allowed, I have made this section into an almost circular day walk. Take the mountain railway to Camorritos and follow Route 49d to the Navarrulaque Meadows. From there continue north on a forestry road which takes an almost horizontal line to the head of the valley at the Puerto de la Fuenfría, then continues across the southeast slopes of Cerro Minguete and Peña Bercial to the Collado de Marichiva. From there, follow Route 46 to La Peñota then return to Cercedilla on Route 43a.

Alternative: For a much harder walk, Route 48 circles the valley to La Peñota but keeps to the crest all the way.

Stage Six: CERCEDILLA - LA PEÑOTA - COLLADO DE LA SEVILLANA - (CASA TERE) - 11km.

This is a very pleasant day, following the main crest, although the initial climb to La Peñota is hard with a pack. The logical end to this stage is the Alto de los Leones road pass, but the restaurants there have no accommodation. The only practical alternative is to reverse Route 43a from Cercedilla all the way to the approach road to La Tablada railway station. Go right on it to the NV1 road and follow it downhill for a few minutes to the Hostal Casa Tere, which also has a restaurant and bar and is the only accommodation in the area. Therefore it would be wise to reserve rooms before setting out from Cercedilla - telephone: 854 1462.

Camping possibilities are limited by the lack of springs in the area. There is one in the firebreak below the Collado de la Sevillana but it is dry in late summer and autumn.

Stage Seven: CASA TERE - COLLADO DE LA SEVILLANA - ALTO DE LOS LEONES - EL ESCORIAL - 22km.

From the Casa Tere, return to the Collado de la Sevillana and follow the main crest west, over the Cerro de la Sevillana to the Alto de los Leones. Then follow the Cuelgamuros Ridge to Abantos on Route 40c, finally descending forested slopes on Route 40d to San Lorenzo de El Escorial (H C F R W T P B Ch D S Bu - the campsite is 6km outside the town on the Guadarrama road).

GR10.1 VARIANT

This alternative route makes a loop to the north, leaving the GR10 at Bustarviejo and rejoining it at the Puerto de la Fuenfría.

Stage One: BUSTARVIEJO - PUERTO DE CANENCIA - PUERTO DE LA MORCUERA - 17.2km.

This section is uphill most of the way although the gradients are reasonable. Leave the main road to the right at the saddle west of Bustarviejo, picking up the path to the west of a football pitch there. It works across the valley of the Mina stream and then climbs gently across the southern slopes of Cabeza de la Braña to reach the broad crest at the Collado Cerrado. The route then rounds a low hill, mostly through trees, to reach the Puerto de Canencia. On the far side of the metalled road, a forestry road winds up behind an elaborate fuente. This takes a line well to the north side of the main crest, reaching the Rascafría-Miraflores road about 1½km to the north of the Puerto de la Morcuera, but not far from the Morcuera Refuge (dormitories and simple meals, open all the year round), the only accommodation, or indeed inhabited building, in the area. Wild camping possibilities are limited as the only fuente (near the pass) is dry for part of the year.

Stage Two: PUERTO DE LA MORCUERA - EL PAULAR MONASTERY - 10.6km.

It is downhill all the way from the pass to the monastery which is described along with the nearby village of Rascafría in the East Guadarrama chapter. A wide path leaves the road below the north side of the Puerto de la Morcuera and descends the Aguilón valley, passing on the way the waterfall called El Purgatorio. The main valley road is joined exactly opposite the monastery (H R W T). Rascafría (H F R W T P B Ch D Bu) is 1.5km to the north. There is a campsite 3-4km in the other direction towards the Puerto de los Cotos.

Alternative: You could miss out Stages Two and Three by walking the Cuerda Larga (Route 52) from the Puerto de la Morcuera to the Puerto de Navacerrada (H S T).

Stage Three: EL PAULAR MONASTERY - PUERTO DE LOS COTOS - 11.9km.

This is another uphill stage mostly on disused forestry roads through pinewoods to the valley head. The route leaves the main road to the right, less than 1km south of the monastery, to climb to the Collado de Garci-Sancho, which separates the hill called Cabeza Mediana from the main Peñalara massif. The path is less clear after that but heads southwest through pinewoods to arrive at an elevated meadow next to the main road about half a kilometre below the Puerto de los Cotos.

There is a big refuge at the Puerto de los Cotos belonging to the Club Alpino Español, but open to the public (dormitories, meals, open all the year round). There are also two bar/restaurants. The nearest hotels are at Puerto de Navacerrada, a short train ride away, although the last train leaves in the late afternoon.

Extension: Two nights at Puerto de los Cotos or Puerto de Navacerrada for a day walk to Peñalara (Route 54a or b).

Stage Four: PUERTO DE LOS COTOS - PUERTO DE LA FUENFRIA - 23.6km.

This last section is almost totally in forest, as it crosses the wide Valsaín bowl, to the north of the main crest, losing then gaining 500m of height on the way. There is no accommodation at the Puerto de la Fuenfría and camping is forbidden. It is a further 6km walk down the Fuenfría valley to Cercedilla.

The route starts to the north of the railway at the Puerto de los Cotos and drops through the forest to the Madrid-Segovia road at the Puente La Cantina. From there a forestry road leads past the Casa de la Pesca, and crosses the Minguete stream. The road is finally abandoned for a steep narrow track which joins a wider one at a fuente just below the Puerto de la Fuenfría.

Alternatives:
1. Take the train from Puerto de los Cotos to Puerto de Navacerrada then walk to Cercedilla via Siete Picos (Route 49c).
2. Walk from Cotos via Peña del Aguila to Bola del Mundo (Route 53c) then reverse Route 51a to the Puerto de Navacerrada. Drop to the station and take Route 49d down the Navalmedio valley to Cercedilla.

TRAVERSE OF CENTRAL AND WEST GREDOS

The GR10 also passes through the Sierra de Gredos in theory, but it hasn't yet been waymarked except between La Mira and the Gredos Cirque. So, given the difficulties of moving around in the range without a car and the limitations of having to return to the same roadhead if you have one, this is a suggestion for a 6-7 day traverse which visits villages on both sides of the range as well as passing through the most spectacular parts of the Central and Western sectors. It should be said that it is a much more demanding tour than the one in Guadarrama, not only because of terrain and distances but also because it makes use of the wardened huts and therefore can only be undertaken in the heat of summer unless you are prepared to carry a couple of days' food supplies.

A tent is essential only for the last two nights, in the Covacha area, although camping is possible every night if preferred. If time is limited, stages 2, 3 and 4 would make an excellent shorter tour. More details of the villages, refuges and routes outlined below can be found in chapters Four and Five.

Arriving at the start: From Madrid, take a bus (Doaldi) from the Estación de Autobuses del Sur, near Atocha Station, to Arenas de San Pedro. At the time of writing, it is the 19.00 from Madrid which connects with an onward bus to Mombeltran. The village has two hotels and several food shops. If camping, ask the bus driver to stop before the village at the Prados Abiertos campsite.

Day one: Take a 15min taxi journey to the Puerto del Pico. Follow Route 21 to the Puerto de Arenal and Route 33 via the Puerto de la Cabrilla to El Arenal (7½-8½hrs). The village has a guesthouse and some fondas, but for the necessary early start the next day, it would be better to go on by taxi to Guisando (2 guesthouses and a campsite). It is also possible in season to stay at the basic ICONA refuge at El Nogal del Barranco, the start of the next day's walk. If coming from Madrid to Guisando for a shorter version of the tour, it will be necessary to take a taxi from Arenas de San Pedro up to the village. If you intend to stay at the Elola hut on day three, phone to reserve places from one of these villages (348158).

Day two: Follow Route 28 to La Mira and Route 18 into the Prao Puerto valley, leaving it above La Plataforma for the Prado de las Pozas Refuge (7-8hrs).

Day three: Move over to the Elola Refuge in the Circo de Gredos (Route 11 and 12, 2½-3hrs) and do a lightweight walk in the area. The possibilities include Portilla del Rey or Cabeza Nevada (Routes 13a and b), Venteadero and the Gutre Ridge (Route 14), Almanzor (Route 15), and Tres Hermanitos-Morazón (Route 16).

Day Four: If finishing the tour here, you could take Route 11 down the Garganta de Gredos to Navalperal (5-6hrs) for the afternoon bus to Madrid. To continue on the tour, follow Route 14 to the Gutre Ridge and descend into the Hoya del Belesar to reverse Route 9 to the village of Bohoyo (9¹/₂-10¹/₂hrs). The village has food shops and just one fonda, but at the time of writing there are buses to El Barco de Avila, the next nearest accommodation, at around 13.00, 19.00 and 20.30. The bus stop is 2km beyond the village at the junction with the C500. The same buses will drop you at the turning to Los Llanos for the Hermosillo campsite.

Day five: If staying in Bohoyo it wouldn't be unpleasant to walk the 14km of narrow lanes connecting Bohoyo with Navalguijo, through crumbling hamlets and a patchwork of orchards, as long as you started early in hot weather. Navalguijo has no services beyond two bars. Farmers there do appear to allow camping on their land - there is a popular and attractive spot where the road crosses the river below the village and another in a small oak wood a few minutes along the Caballeros valley path. Ask about them in the bars.

Day six: If staying in El Barco de Avila, the best option is to take a taxi to Navalguijo. Hitching may be possible but slow as there is little traffic. Follow Route 7 to the Laguna de los Caballeros (5-5¹/₂hrs).

Day seven: Continue on Route 7 to Covacha then reverse Route 8 to Guijo de Santa Barbara (approx. 6-7hrs. This route may involve some exposed scrambling.) Walk 3km down the road to Jarandilla de la Vera which has two hotels and a Parador. To return to Madrid, there is one bus a day via Arenas de San Pedro and one to Talavera de la Reina for a train to Atocha Station.

GLOSSARY ONE
NAMES OF COMMON FEATURES FOUND ON MAPS AND IN THE TEXT

aguja	needle-like rock tower
alto	summit
arista	arête, knife-edge ridge
arroyo	stream
barranca/o	gully, steep-sided river bed
barrera	ridge (lit. barrier)
cabeza	bulky, rounded summit
callejón	corridor between spines of vertical rock
camino	main footpath
cañada	main drove road
canal	narrow valley, gully
canchal	zone of outcrops
cancho	crag, outcrop
canto	rock formation, boulder
cerro	hill
charca/o	pond, or pool in river
chozo	shepherd's shelter at the summer pastures (Gredos)
collado	col, saddle
coto	hunting reserve or enclosed pasture
cuchillar	knife-edge ridge
cuenca	river basin
cuerda	ridge
cuesta	slope
cueva	cave
dehesa	meadow
embalse	reservoir
estación	train or ski-lift station
finca	small farm
fuente	spring, drinking fountain
garganta	gorge, ravine, stream (Gredos)
hoyo/a	bowl, depression
jardín.	garden (level space surrounded by rock outcrops)
ladera	slope
laguna	lake, tarn
lomo/a	hillside, slope
majada	high, mountain summer pasture, often with shepherds' huts
Meseta	the high tableland which makes up the centre of Spain
mirador	viewpoint
nava	isolated piece of level meadow surrounded by mountains
pantano	reservoir
parador	state-run hotel

peña/ón	crag
pico	peak
piedras	rocks
pinar/es	pinewood/s
pista	ski slope or various kinds of dirt road
portacho	col
portachuelo	col, small pass
portillo/a	col, small pass
pozo	well
pradera	meadow
prado	meadow
presa	reservoir dam
puente	bridge
puerto	pass (usually with a road)
punta	point, headland
refugio	mountain hut or shelter
regajo	stream
río	river
risco	cliff
roca	rock
senda	narrow cattle track
sendero	mountain footpath
solano/a	sunny (i.e. south-facing slope) or east wind
tapia	wall
trocha	temporary track e.g. those created by logging machines
umbria	shady, i.e. north-facing slope
vadera	wide ford
vado	ford
valle	valley
vega	upland pasture or meadow
venta	country inn
illo/a or *ito/a*	added to the stem of a word produces he diminutive form e.g. *prado* - meadow, *pradillo* - little meadow; *collado-colladito*

GLOSSARY TWO
THE MEANINGS OF NAMES MENTIONED IN THE TEXT

abeja	bee	cabrilla	little goat
abierto	open	cabrón	cuckold (insult)
acebeda	holly grove	calíz	chalice
acebo	holly tree	calvitero	place with little vegetation
águila	eagle	camorritos	line of low hills
aguilón	large eagle	campana	bell
alacrán	scorpion	campanarios	bell towers
albardilla	small saddle or cushion	cantina	bar, saloon
alcornocal	cork oak wood or copse	capón	castrated animal
aldea	hamlet	carabina	rifle
alevines	young fish	carpetanos	belonging to the ancient kingdom of
almorcho-			Carpetania
nes	series of crags on a spur	carrasqueta	small kermes oak
ameal(ito)	high isolated cliff	casa	house
angostura	narrow defile	castillejos	derived from castle; frame or parts
apretura	squeeze		of a handloom
arcipreste	archpriest	cebo	food, bait
arenal	sandy ground	ceja	brow, crown
arriba	above, high, upper	centenera	place where rye grows
atómete	from the verb to lean or look out, so	cerradillas/	
	a viewpoint	cerraillos	from enclosing or encircling
asperones	grindstones	cerrado/a	(en)closed
avellanares	hazel groves	cervunal	place where a species of cistus grows
azagayas	assegais, javelins	cesto	basket
bailanderos	dancers	chica	little
ballesteros	crossbowmen	chilla	decoy, hunting call
barco	boat	chivato	goat kid
barquillo	little boat	chorreo	gushing, spouting, dripping
becerríl	bullock from yearling calf	chorrera	spout, channel
bercial	place where an esparto-like grass	chorro	stream, trickle, dribble
	grows	ciego	blind
bermeja	bright red	cierva	hind
berrecosa/		cimera	uppermost, topmost
herroquera	boulder field	cinco	five
berrueco	granite boulder, isolated rock	claveles	carnations
blanco/a	white	cobardes	cowards
bola del		coberteros	coverers
mundo	globe	cochino	filthy or pig
boquerón	anchovy	cojo	crippled, limping, wobbly
borreguero	a good place for lambs	concha	shell
bota	boot	convento	monastery
braña	high summer pastures or group of	cospe	shaping a piece of wood with an axe
	shepherds' huts	covacha	little cave
buitrera	vulture nesting site	cruz	a cross
caballeros	gentlemen	cuba	cask, barrel
cabra	goat	cuelgamuros	steep or vertical walls
cabrera	goat girl	cuerpo	body

cuervo	crow	joyuelo	from jewel; valuable
culebrilla	little snake	lagarejo	from wine press
dos	two	largo/a	long
duque	duke	leones	lions
elefantito	little elephant	lijar	sand
enano	dwarf	lobo	wolf
encina	holm oak	llano/illos	plains, level areas
enebral	juniper patch	machos	males
entre	between	machota	hammer
ermitaños	hermits	madrigal	form of poetry set to music
escorial	gridiron (on which St. Lorenzo was martyred)	malejo	pretty bad
		maliciosa	
esfinge	sphinx	(la)	the spiteful woman
espaldar	back	malillo	diminutive of bad
espinar	thorn thicket	malo/a	bad
espino	hawthorn	mata	bush
flecha	arrow	mayor	bigger
flores	flowers	maza	club, bat, mallet, drumstick
fraile	friar	mediano/a	middle-sized, medium
frío/a	cold	medio	half
fuente	spring, drinking fountain	mediodía	midday
galana	exposed and well-proportioned	menor	smaller
gallo	cockerel	miel	honey
gamonoso	a place with abundant asphodels	mijares	place where millet grows
gancha	tree branch	mina	mine
gavilanes	sparrow hawks	mira	watch tower, look-out post
gordo	fat	miradero	look-out, vantage point
goterita	little trickle	mojón	landmark, boundary stone, cairn
gran/de	big	montón	pile, heap
granja	farm	mora	moorish girl, mulberry, blackberry
guijo	gravel	morcuera/o	cairn of loose stones
helechar	bracken bed	moreno	brown
hermana	sister	moro	moor, arab
hermano/itos	brother/little brothers	muela	tooth
herradura	horseshoe	muertos	dead
herreda	to do with shoeing or branding	naranjera	to do with oranges; machine gun
herrería	smithy	navajas	clasp knives
herrero	blacksmith	negro	black
hierro	iron	nevada	snow-covered or capped
hilo	thread, yarn	nevero	snow or ice-filled, place of perpetual
hombre	man		snow
hondo/a	deep	nieves	snows
horcajo	yoke	niños	sons, children
horcos	pitchforks	nogal	walnut tree
hornillo	little oven, furnace or kiln	Noruega	Norway
hoyuela	little hollow	novillera	someone looking after heifers, part
hoz (pl.			of a pasture for heifers
hoces)	defile, narrow pass, gorge	nuevo/a	new
hueco	hollow	oliva	olive tree
huerto/a	kitchen/market garden, orchard	ortigoso	from nettles
jaroso	cistus-covered	oscuro/a	dark

oseras	where bears live
oso	bear
pajaro/ito	bird
pajoso	full of chaff, straw-coloured, straw-like
pala	shovel, spade, bat, blade
paradilla	diminutive of stopping place
pastores	shepherds
pelado	(terrain of) bare rock
peluca	wig
peon(es)	labourer(s)
Pepeillo	Little Joe
peral	pear orchard
perdiguera	animal which hunts partridges
perro que fuma	the dog that smokes
pesca	fishing
pez	fish
pinar(ejo)	pinewood
pinillo/a	little pine
pintada	guinea fowl, painted, mottled, many-coloured
piñonero	pine cone-bearing
piornal	broom thicket
placero	stallholder, market trader
plata	silver
pobre	poor
pollos	chickens
pontón	wooden pontoon bridge
porrones	wine jars with long spout
poyos	stone benches
pozas	pools
pulpito	pulpit
purtgatorio	purgatory
quebranta	break
quinto	fifth
raso	level, clear, bare
real	royal
redondo/a	rounded
reguero	irrigation ditch, track
reina	queen
reventón	burst, explosion
rey	king
romeral	rosemary patch
ronquillos	noises or harsh sounds
salamanca	dark place, cave, sorcery
saltadero	jumping over point; waterfall
sarnosa	someone with scabies
sauce	willow tree
seco/a	dry
segundo	second
séptimo	seventh
serradilla	diminutive of jagged
serrano/illos	highlands
sevillana	from Seville
sexto	sixth
siete	seven
sordo	deaf (person)
soto	thicket, grove, copse
tablada	slaughterhouse
techo	roof, ceiling
tejo	yew tree
terradillo	little terrace
testero	bedhead, wall
tío	uncle, chap, character
tirobarra	lit, throw the stick - an old game
torre	tower
torreón	tower, turret
torreta	turret
tortuga	tortoise
tranco	threshold
travieso	naughty child, restless person
tres	three
trigo	corn, wheat
vaca	cow
valdeiglesias	valley of churches
Valdesquí	Ski Valley
valiente	fine, wonderful
vaquero	cowman
ventana	window
ventorrillo	small inn, road house
ventoso	windy
ventura	happiness
verde	green
viejo/a	old
vistillas	viewpoint, high place
yeguas	mares
yelmo	helmet
zapato	shoe
zorro/a	fox/vixen

Printed by CARNMOR PRINT & DESIGN
95-97 LONDON ROAD, PRESTON, LANCASHIRE, UK.